Bitter pills

**Population policies and their implementation in
eight developing countries**

Bitter pills

Population policies and their implementation in eight developing countries

DONALD P. WARWICK

Harvard Institute for International Development

Cambridge University Press

Cambridge
London   New York   New Rochelle
Melbourne   Sydney

Published by the Press Syndicate of the University of Cambridge
The Pitt Building, Trumpington Street, Cambridge CB2 1RP
32 East 57th Street, New York, NY 10022, USA
296 Beaconsfield Parade, Middle Park, Melbourne 3206, Australia

First published 1982

Printed in the United States of America

Library of Congress Cataloging in Publication Data
Warwick, Donald P.

Bitter pills.

1. Underdeveloped areas – Population policy.
2. Underdeveloped areas – Birth control.
I. Title.
HB884.W37   363.9′6′091724   81–21758
ISBN 0 521 24347 5   AACR2

For Ellen

Written in collaboration with Saad Gadalla,
Luis Leñero, Maria Elena Lopez, and Kivuto Ndeti;
and with the assistance of Rosalinda Garcia-Yangas,
Samir Khalaf, Frank Marino Hernandez, Soheir Mehanna,
Cecilia Ndeti, Ana Maria Nemenzo, June Prill-Brett,
K. Raghavendra Rao, J. B. Romain, and Christine Tennant

Contents

Preface

This is a study of what happens when national governments and international donors try to promote birth control in developing countries. My basic argument is that the possibility, shape, vigor, and results of population programs are organically related to a country's social and political environment. Far from being mechanical interventions whose course is set by programmed rationality, family planning programs gain and lose energy through interchanges with the surrounding society. Programs that ignore their social settings either become isolated from the lines of action or are ejected as foreign bodies. Those that are forced on a recalcitrant environment run the risk not only of practical calamity but of damage to human rights.

The research this book describes began with three core questions: How do governments come to adopt explicit population policies? How are such policies actually carried out? What explains the difference between programs that are implemented and those that are not? The research project's organizers were also concerned with the ethics of population control, particularly with the moral issues raised by the implementation of family planning programs.

To pursue these questions, the Hastings Center mounted a cross-national study of the formulation and implementation of population policies in the developing countries. With financial support from the United Nations Fund for Population Activities (UNFPA), the center sponsored major studies in Egypt, Kenya, Mexico, and the Philippines as well as smaller studies in the Dominican Republic, Haiti, India, and Lebanon. The research began in 1973, reached its peak in 1977, and continued on a declining scale until 1981. Although the UNFPA was the main source of funding, the Hastings Center contributed some of its own resources, and most of the time I spent in writing this book was my own. I was project manager throughout, working closely with staff at the Hastings Center and collaborators from the eight participating countries.

Each of the country studies was conducted by one or more scholars from that country under the general coordination of the Hastings Center. The center also received UNFPA support for research and conferences on various cross-cutting issues in population policy, particularly the role of donor agencies and the ethics of population control. To promote consistency across the country studies as well as between those studies and the work at the Hastings Center, the project set up an executive committee. This included the director of the Hastings Center, the project manager, and the country directors for Egypt,

Kenya, Mexico, and the Philippines. The committee, supplemented by UNFPA staff and other invitees, met in New York in 1974, in Cairo in 1975, in New York in 1976, and in Nairobi in 1977. That arrangement worked well for keeping the main participants in touch with each other and for handling such questions as clearances, funding delays, and publication rights. To be close to the major studies I also made several visits to the teams in Cairo, Manila, Mexico City, and Nairobi and lived in Mexico during the academic year of 1974-5.

Relations between the Hastings Center and the country collaborators were cordial and productive throughout the project. There were debates at the executive committee meetings, but matters were always resolved amicably. Relations between the Hastings Center and the UNFPA were a different story. Disagreements were evident early in the project but either were left unresolved or were apparently resolved at one meeting only to reappear at the next. The core of the problem was that the researchers wanted to pursue the subject wherever it led them and to publish the results without restraints, whereas the UNFPA wanted both inquiry and publication to stop at the point where they made waves. This is of course the classic tension between sponsors and researchers, but we mistakenly thought that it would not materialize in ways that would obstruct this study.

Why did the UNFPA take on this project? Institutional motivation is always difficult to fathom and is usually intertwined with personal predilections and bureaucratic politics. This study was no exception. That the project would be controversial was evident from the outset. In 1973, when the UNFPA gave the Hastings Center a preliminary grant to design this study, the family planning bandwagon was rolling along at full speed. Donors were still optimistic that latent demand for voluntary family planning services was high, that the delivery of such services was mainly a technical matter, and that such factors as culture and politics were of relatively minor importance in bringing down birth rates. This project plainly challenged each of those assumptions. Its critics, inside and outside the UNFPA, were quick to point out the disruptive potential of this research for the established paradigm of population control. Still, although it stirred sharp debate within the organization, the UNFPA leadership decided to recommend the project to its governing council. Why?

One reason was that the study had a strong advocate within the UNFPA. This person was convinced that the conventional approach to family planning was seriously flawed and that one of its greatest limitations was inattention to the cultural contexts of fertility decisions. He lobbied intensively for the project, even in the face of hostility from a superior. Second, with the World Population Conference almost at hand and with family planning orthodoxy almost certain to come under attack, the UNFPA wanted to demonstrate its breadth of approach and, more specifically, its sensitivity to cultural values and ethics. Third, the project seemed to mesh well with the managerial philosophy of the UNFPA's executive director, Rafael Salas. According to his associates, the Salas approach was to "let a thousand flowers bloom" with UNFPA funding. He was reportedly anxious to show that the UNFPA was not just another family planning organization in UN clothing and that it was indeed responsive to cultural differences. In a meeting with us, he emphasized that in his work with the green revolution in the Philippines he had taken pains to adapt agricultural programs to local values and felt that the same should be done with population programs. Hence, when an internal dispute over this project was sent to his office for resolution, he came down in the project's favor.

The main bone of contention between the Hastings Center and the UNFPA was publication rights. We debated that issue on and off from 1974 until 1976, but since there was nothing to publish the discussion remained academic. The Hastings Center and the country directors consistently pressed for open publication. The main UNFPA representative usually seemed to agree, but he emphasized the difficulties with academic freedom in the UN system. As the contract was silent on that question, the matter was up for negotiation. In 1977, the executive committee came up with a proposal that seemed acceptable to all concerned: The country directors would be free to publish their results under their own names within their own countries, whereas the Hastings Center would use their reports and any other project materials for a report to be issued under its name. The UNFPA representative agreed with this idea, and everything seemed to be settled. But the agreement fell apart soon afterward, when UNFPA officials in New York read some of the preliminary reports and found them too controversial. Most troublesome were essays on the values and behavior of international donor agencies and materials judged to be at least implicitly critical of the governments under study.

In May 1977, the UNFPA summoned the key Hastings participants to its offices in New York. Early in the meeting, Salas held up several project documents and stated emphatically that the UNFPA could not have its name associated with reports of that kind. He was particularly exercised about the draft reports on donor agencies, and he ruled that no more UNFPA funds could be spent on donor studies. Salas did offer to let us study the UNFPA itself, but subsequent events made that an improbable option. When informed that neither the Hastings Center nor the country directors could accept prior restraints on publication, he made a counterproposal. To protect the interests of the researchers, the studies could be published, but to protect itself the UNFPA would not be identified as the sponsor. When this offer was declined, the project's stock within the UNFPA plummeted. Finally an agreement was reached that project publications would list the UNFPA as the funding source but include a statement that the views expressed were those of the authors rather than those of the UNFPA.

A further dispute arose when the UNFPA reviewed the first draft of this book. After providing detailed comments on the manuscript, an anonymous internal reviewer concluded that the study was much too controversial to be issued by the UNFPA itself. Further discussions led to an agreement that I would publish the book under my own name with the disclaimer noted earlier. A similar fate awaited a popular summary of the research findings. The UNFPA originally agreed to review the summary and to issue it under its own name if the material was acceptable. In May 1981, UNFPA officials met with us to discuss the report and expressed dissatisfaction with its conclusions. Shortly afterward, a senior official wrote the Hastings Center to state formally that the UNFPA did not wish to publish the popular summary. With that the project came to an end.

The politics of research were not confined to dealings between the Hastings Center and the UNFPA. The original proposal had requested a block of funds that would be channeled through the center to those responsible for the country studies. We thought that this was the most direct way of handling the country research. But when the proposal was sent out for review, the funding arrangement was criticized, especially by Canada's International Development Research Centre. The main objection was that if the Hastings Center handled the country studies, too much of the project's budget would go to an American organization. Because the UNFPA had originally been established to help the developing countries, and because funds were contributed by its own donors mainly for that purpose, this objection could not be taken lightly. As a result, the final proposal stated that the UNFPA would support the Hastings Center as the coordinating body for the project and that funds for the country studies would go directly from the UNFPA to the researchers involved.

This expedient solved one problem and created a dozen others. For example, because the money was now going to member nations in the UN system, the UNFPA decided that the country directors would have to obtain permission from their own governments before the grants could be disbursed locally. Thanks to an astute UNFPA coordinator, this permission was obtained almost immediately in country A. In country B, the national population body also issued the clearance, but the foreign ministry decided that the project required the concurrence of another government agency. Because relations between the head of that agency and the proposed director of the country research were less than amicable, permission was neither granted nor denied. After a year in limbo, the team sought and received the support of yet another government department.

Permission was quickly granted in country C but then withdrawn after a dispute between the country director and a rival over the intended destination of the funds. The rival claimed that in the original negotiations it had been agreed that the project would go to his institution rather than to the country director. As the project representative in those negotiations, I can certify that this claim was preposterous, but that did not prevent it from being made and from holding up the research for a year. Country D also lost a year as a direct result of internal clearance procedures. There a subcommittee of the national population body sought assurances that the research would not duplicate studies already underway and would meet high standards of methodology. Although these demands did have substantive justification, they also represented an attempt by one social scientist to assert personal control over population research undertaken by others. As often happens, "coordination" became a euphemism for power. The net effect of these bureaucratic roadblocks was that in three of the four countries chosen for major studies, fieldwork could not begin until late 1975 or early 1976. Similar difficulties arose in obtaining permission for the smaller studies, one of which was directly vetoed by the UN resident representative in Brazil on the grounds that it was too controversial.

Despite the commotion and delays, the project was completed. Once the jurisdictional squabbles were settled within countries B, C, and D, the research teams were able to move ahead without further ado, whereas country A had no significant problems at any point. Even the UNFPA's embargo on donor research came only after most of the basic work had been done. The final coverage of donor agencies was less than I had hoped, but by means of research done on my own time and complementary information from the country studies, I was able to put together a reasonable picture of donor behavior (see Chapter 4). And whatever its objections to some parts of the project, the UNFPA made its payments on time, and its coordinators in the participating countries helped the project in many ways. Even after the project fell from grace in 1977, the UNFPA did little more than lop off pieces of the budget increase that had been requested for bringing the work to a conclusion. By 1978 the last of the country studies was complete, and I could begin to integrate the voluminous materials generated by the project.

Given the large number of contributors to this study and the debates that it occasioned, I should comment on how I handled the material available. I saw my task as that of preparing an interpretation rather than merely a synthesis of the findings. Hence this volume both goes beyond the country reports and omits much of their empirical detail. My main source of information about each country is the research report prepared for this project (see Appendix). I have tried to render a fair summary of that material, and I gave each country team a chance to correct my first draft. In the case of Mexico I added information based on my own observations and research during the year that I lived there. The material on donor agencies comes primarily from my own research and secondarily from the country studies. The framework of implementation analysis developed throughout and summarized in Chapter 12 is basically my own construction. The concluding chapter on ethics, though stimulated in part by discussions at the Hastings Center, also represents my own analysis and conclusions.

In short, the interpretations presented here should be regarded as those of the author rather than of the United Nations Fund for Population Activities, the Hastings Center, or any of the collaborators. Readers should specifically not attribute findings, conclusions, or policy recommendations to the UNFPA or members of its staff. The sole responsibility of that agency was for funding the research and for allied administrative assistance. Express or implied criticisms of any country, donor agency, program, or individual should likewise not be attributed to the UNFPA. Contributors to the project are responsible only for the materials submitted in their reports and for suggestions or corrections related to those reports.

I should also warn fellow participants in the population-versus-development debate that the present study does not fit neatly within that paradigm. Polemics about whether broadly oriented development programs or family planning should come first were necessary at the World Population Conference and helpful later, but they may have outlived their usefulness. I have long felt that governments and international donors would do best to promote basic health care, increase income, and expand opportunities for education before launching drives for family planning. But the more I pondered the terms of the debate the less happy I became with the narrowness of its compass. Too often, both sides disregarded the larger context of planned change, especially the realities of implementation. Even if one grants the need for improved living conditions as a prerequisite for successful family planning programs, the question remains as to how those programs should be organized once welfare has improved. Should pills be distributed with or without prior medical examination? How much medical backup should be available for the treatment of complications and side effects? How should programs deal with local religious leaders or traditional midwives who consider birth control harmful to morality or their own economic interests? In the end I concluded that the population-versus-development debate had become a procrustean bed that now inhibited rather than stimulated new thought on population policy. Many of the findings and questions in this book simply do not fit within its confines.

This project was made possible by the efforts of dozens of individuals, all of whose contributions are deeply appreciated. First thanks must go to Daniel Callahan, director of the Hastings Center, for helping to create the project and for bearing the brunt of its administrative headaches. No less vital was the work of the country directors for the major studies: Saad Gadalla of Egypt, Luis Leñero of Mexico, Maria Elena Lopez of the Philippines, and Kivuto Ndeti of Kenya. They were not only managers of their own studies and active members of the project's executive committee but also delightful colleagues. Their spirit of cooperation and our collective ability to work together speaks well for future possibilities of genuinely collaborative cross-national research in the social sciences. For me as project manager, it was both a privilege and a pleasure to work with them. I am particularly indebted to Luis Leñero for his kind hospitality and cordial colleagueship during my year in Mexico.

The collaborators on the smaller country studies, some of whom I was not able to meet personally, also deserve great thanks for their contributions. With small budgets and sometimes great obstacles to honest research, they were able to enlarge the empirical scope of this study without compounding its administrative complexity. My greatest personal regret in writing this book is that, in the interests of brevity, I had to omit much of the detail in their reports, particularly the anthropological study in the Philippines and the research on India.

Two other staff members at the Hastings Center played a critical role in the project. Michael Henry, my main counterpart at the center from 1975 to 1977, was not only an effective administrator but a constant source of intellectual challenge and good humor. His successor, Philip Clark, was also a congenial colleague and a helpful contributor to seminars on population ethics. Robert Veatch and Ruth Macklin of the center likewise made significant intellectual contributions to the project.

From 1974 through 1978 the Hastings Center was able to invite many scholars, practitioners, and agency officials to a set of conferences on the ethical dimensions of population policy. Those deserving special mention are Peter Brown, Michael Conroy, Davidson Gwatkin, Carl Hemmer, Peter Henriot, Thomas Merrick, John Ratcliffe, Susan Scrimshaw, Joep Van Arendonk, Stephen Viederman, and Charles Wilber. Alan Simmons greatly assisted the project with advice and insights at several of the executive committee meetings. Other participants included Sam Awudetsy, Michael Bayles, Peter Berger, Nazli Choucri, Leon Clark, John Cohen, Richard Dickenson, Laila El Hamamsy, Jason Finkle, Martin Golding, Gerardo Gonzales, Denis Goulet, Philip Gulliver, Mary Hollnsteiner, Samir Khalaf, Reza Khaleghi-Rod, James Kocher, Robert Lapham, Carol Levine, Mahmood Mamdani, Soheir Mehanna, Ifeanyi Menkiti, James Muinde, David Mutchler, Ralph Potter, K. Raghavendra Rao, Robert Repetto, G. Sabir Shakeel, Ozzie Simmons, Soelaeman Soemardi, Margaret O'Brien Steinfels, Peter Steinfels, J. Mayone Stycos, John Sullivan, and Gustav Thaiss. All contributed to the project, but none should be held responsible for its failings.

I owe special gratitude and appreciation to my wife, Ellen Donohue Warwick. She not only provided constant encouragement and support throughout the project but also participated directly as a paid research assistant and an unpaid critic. Her research on donor agencies, and particularly her explorations into public documents, greatly helped the analysis of donor behavior. G. Sabir Shakeel also provided valuable research assistance at the beginning of the study.

The project as a whole would not have been possible without the financial and administrative support of the UNFPA. In an area as delicate as population policy, the international legitimacy afforded by the United Nations was critical in recruiting collaborators and gaining cooperation once the studies were underway. Whatever the disagreements that cropped up later, the UNFPA deserves grateful recognition for sponsoring the world's first cross-national field study on the formulation and implementation of population policies.

Finally, I want to express my personal appreciation to Barbara Hanson, Emily Palmer, and Betsy Hayes for typing various drafts of the manuscript. Their professional work and their good humor were a great help in keeping up the momentum of writing. I am also grateful to the Harvard Institute for International Development for its financial assistance and moral support in this effort. To the many others who contributed to the project but who are not named here, especially the interviewers and analysts in the participating countries, I extend my sincere thanks for a job well done.

DONALD P. WARWICK

Cambridge, Mass.
May 1982

A note on sources and citations

Because this book draws on thousands of pages of reports prepared by many authors, including the writer, the task of documenting sources was not easy. For readability, the number and length of footnotes must be kept to a minimum. But readers also should know where given information originated. To strike a balance between these objectives, the following rules were observed:

1. Unless otherwise indicated, information about any specific country is drawn from the research report on that country. In the Philippines, where there were two separate reports, the source is usually the overall study completed by Maria Elena Lopez and her associates. In some sections dealing with Mexico, I introduced observations based on my residence there during 1974 and 1975, but that source is specified as well.

2. References to the country reports list only the last names of the authors, such as Leñero or Ndeti and Ndeti. Full details on authorship and publication are provided in the Appendix. Page numbers for the country reports are listed only for quotations or when otherwise necessary for clarity. Where the original of a report was in Spanish or French the pages cited are those of the English translation.

3. References in the country reports to other works are repeated in the footnotes as they appear in those reports, but with the names of the country authors in parentheses at the end. References presented in the usual form are those introduced by me.

Part I

Overview

1   The study

Beginning in the 1950s and increasing over the next decade, dozens of developing countries set out to control the size of their populations. From such giants as China and India to the diminutive islands of Hong Kong and Singapore, governments took steps to bring down the birth rate.[1] The mood at the outset was mixed. Fearing reprisals from religious leaders and assaults from political opponents, many national leaders were wary about fast action on birth control. But international donors teamed up with local promoters to urge them on. Survey after survey, they argued, showed that people were eager for family planning services. If governments would only have the courage to act, the clients would come. Heeding this advice and helped by generous international funding, countries began to set up voluntary family planning programs.

By 1970 it was clear that family planning supply was running well ahead of demand. Whereas 60 or 70 percent of eligible women might report in a survey that they were interested in limiting births, when they were provided with the services the majority did not use them. This striking lack of response, particularly in rural areas, forced a critical examination of the assumptions behind conventional family planning programs. At the same time it became obvious that birth-control programs were not the sterile, neutral biomedical exercises their designers had tried to make them. Behind the trappings of medicine critics saw disturbing elements of politics, ethics, and ideology. This combination of doubtful success and manifest contention touched off vigorous debates that peaked during the World Population Conference of 1974.

Aware of these crosscurrents of opinion, the Hastings Center in 1972 explored ways of studying the ethical and political aspects of population control in developing countries. The center had recently completed a project on similar questions in the United States and thought that the time was ripe to extend the analysis.[2] After several fruitless explorations with other donors, the center discovered common interests with the United Nations Fund for Population Activities (UNFPA). Through a preliminary grant from UNFPA, the center sought and found several colleagues in the developing countries who shared these research interests. An organizational meeting in May 1973 produced consensus on the broad outlines of a study and on ways of moving ahead with it. The result was the Project on Cultural Values and Population Policies, of which I was project manager.

The project was to move ahead on two interrelated tracks. The first involved a series of country studies on the formulation and implementation of

3

population policies. Each would be carried out by a scholar or institution from the country in question within a common framework of research topics. The second track entailed explorations of broad issues in population policy especially the role of donor agencies and the ethics of population control. This work would be done at the Hastings Center and linked to the results of the country studies. The center also agreed to be the overall coordinator of the project and to take responsibility for analyzing and interpreting the materials prepared.

CHOOSING COUNTRIES

The research plan called for four or five countries to be sites for major studies and for several other countries to serve as supplementary cases. Five criteria were used to select countries for the major studies. First, for adequate geographic coverage there should be at least one country from Asia, Africa, Latin America, and the Middle East. Second, each country chosen should have an explicit population policy and an organized national population program. To pursue our interests in policy formulation and implementation, it was necessary to have countries that had both policies and programs. This criterion ruled out almost every country in sub-Saharan Africa and much of Latin America. Third, the countries should be in the middle or low rather than high reaches of economic development. Nations within this range were more representative of conditions in the Third World than were their more affluent counterparts. Fourth, at least some of the countries should be characterized by internal ethnic, cultural, or religious differences. Because one goal of the project was to study the interactions between population policies and local cultures, it was important to have some internal cultural diversity. And finally, the research should be feasible in the country. There should be local social scientists qualified to handle the research and enough freedom of expression to permit honest inquiry into population policy.

The final list of possibilities was short: Egypt, Kenya, Mexico, Indonesia, and the Philippines. Other options were considered but for various reasons did not prove viable.[3] In the final negotiations Indonesia had to be dropped because the social scientists interested in the project decided that they were already overextended. Hence the roster of country directors included Saad Gadella of the Social Research Center at the American University in Cairo; Kivuto Ndeti, then at the Sociology Department of the University of Nairobi; Luis Leñero of the Mexican Institute of Social Studies (IMES); and Maria Elena Lopez of the Institute of Philippine Culture at the Ateneo de Manila University.[4]

Despite the care exercised in selecting the sites for major studies, we cannot claim that these four countries are representative of the developing countries in general or of those with population policies and programs. These nations include none of the success stories in family planning, such as Taiwan or Korea, nor do they include any of the most hostile settings, such as several countries in West Africa. As is almost always true with cross-national studies of this kind, the sample is of unknown generalizability. But the four countries do cover a range of situations and have proved to be valuable in raising generic questions about population policy. If their coverage is less than optimal it is certainly greater than the single-country approach that dominated much earlier research on population policy.[5]

The research design also specified less intensive studies in several other countries. For those studies no attempt was made to seek typical countries. The aim was to find unique or special situations that would expand the range of complexity in the project. The final list included Lebanon, Haiti, the Dominican Republic, and India, together with anthropological research to complement the main study in the Philippines. The rationale for those choices is given in the next chapter. In addition, we commissioned a study on Iran that could not be completed and proposed another for Brazil that was vetoed by the local resident representative of the United Nations.[6]

RESEARCH STRATEGY AND TOPICS

Under our contract with UNFPA the overall design and specific topics for the research were to be worked out by an executive committee made up of the four country directors, the project manager, and the director of the Hastings Center (Daniel Callahan). At its first meeting in 1974 this group decided that each major study would blend two elements: common topics to be explored in all four countries and aspects of population policy unique to a particular country. The aim of this strategy was to achieve cross-national comparability while concurrently recognizing the uniqueness of each national situation. The 1974 discussions also led to a document called "Core Topics for Country Studies." The country directors agreed to answer, to the extent they could, the research questions posed there. The following is a brief outline of those topics:

1. Historical background: What distinctive or formative historical events, if any, shaped the values underlying the country's population policies?
2. The formulation and presentation of population policies
    The process of policy formulation
    Elements in the formulation process: facts, values, and interests; key actors; degree of attention to ethnic, religious, and other cultural differences
3. Policy implementation
    Overall considerations: Were the programs carried out as intended? If so, who and what were the moving forces? If not, who and what were the main obstacles?
    Value conflicts in implementation: conflicts arising from what was done, who did it, how it was done, to whom it was done

Key actors in implementation: top-level officials, field implementers, opinion leaders
4.   The "fit" between family planning programs and their clients

Within this set of topics, primary emphasis was to be put on implementation. We felt that in previous studies too much attention had been given to the formalities of policy and not enough to its execution. One guiding hypothesis, amply confirmed by the research, was that policies as stated and programs as implemented may be substantially different.

The researchers concluded that no single method of data collection would be adequate for this study. Several members had considerable experience with the Knowledge–Attitude–Practice survey and were painfully aware of its limitations for policy analysis.[7] Hence we decided to use the methods and sources most appropriate to a given question. For the sections on history, the sources might be public documents and other published materials, supplemented by interviews with key participants. To investigate policy formulation and implementation, the most suitable method might be a combination of personal interviews and field observation. Because three of the study directors had also been active participants in the development and evaluation of population programs, they were encouraged to use their own observations as a further source of data. The document "Core Topics for Country Studies" made various suggestions about methodology, but in the end it was the responsibility of each team to work out its own blend. Although the cost of these procedures was some noncomparability across studies, this eclectic approach was strongly favored by the country directors and generally proved workable. Field visits by the project manager and annual meetings of the researchers helped to keep both the substantive and methodological perspectives equivalent across sites.

FOCUS AND ORGANIZATION OF THIS BOOK

The guiding concept in the following chapters will be implementation – whether or not programs were actually carried out. The discussions will pursue two interrelated questions about the implementation of population programs: First, whatever the nominal policies and stated intentions of governments, what really happened when family planning programs went into action? Were they carried out at all? Were they carried out in the manner prescribed by official policy? What were the political, social, and cultural side effects of execution? And were there any cases in which programs were implemented without a corresponding policy? Second, what do we learn from these cases and other literature about the conditions favoring and hindering implementation? When is a family planning program most and least likely to be carried out, and why?

Implementation has several advantages as an organizing focus. Most important, it directs attention to organizational behavior rather than to formal proclamations. Too much of what passes for policy analysis is not analysis at all but a mere recounting of what governments say that they intend to do. We found that governments rather consistently have lofty intentions for population policy. They want to enhance freedom of reproductive choice, promote maternal and child health, and raise the country's level of economic development. But a close look at their implementation record shows a very mixed picture. Governments whose stated aim is to promote freedom of choice have instructed field implementers to take steps denying clients that freedom. Only by looking at what is actually done can we make a fair assessment of any public policy. The implementation perspective also forces analysis to move beyond the capital city. Many earlier studies seemed to assume that the most critical actions on the population front took place in the office of the president, the Ministry of Health, or the central headquarters of the Commission on Population. Those offices are indeed important, but as programs move from concept to operational reality the action shifts to the countryside, for it is there that the majority of the people live. Finally, an emphasis on implementation not only does not preclude but actually requires analysis of other aspects of population policy, including its history, the process by which it is developed, and its various settings. Thus although implementation was not the only concept that could have been used for this analysis, it had distinct advantages over the competition.

The book as a whole both summarizes and interprets the voluminous materials gathered for this study. It is divided into four sections: an overview, a discussion of the process and contexts of policy formulation, an analysis of factors immediately influencing implementation, and conclusions. In addition to this chapter, the overview contains an essay on the centrality of theory for implementation and on the pervasive influence of international donor agencies in this field. Chapter 5 then considers the power of process in policy formulation, Chapter 6 examines the import of the political context, and Chapter 7 looks at the significance of cultural settings.

The section on implementation argues that a population program's chances of success depend on four critical factors. Chapter 8 examines the impact of the bureaucratic context, including interagency relations as well as intraagency conditions. Chapter 9 reviews the impact of implementer commitment at all levels, but particularly in the field. Chapter 10 then explores the influence of opinion leaders outside the implementing bureaucracy, and Chapter 11 shows the power of clients in affecting program outcomes. The book concludes with essays on two larger issues raised by the study. Drawing on the empirical findings and interpretations of earlier discussions, Chapter 12 proposes that implementation be viewed as a transaction rather than as a mechanical execution, a game, or programmatic evolution. Finally, Chapter 13 pleads for an ethics of respect in population policy and proposes a number of specific guidelines for implementation.

The reader should remember that the country studies are limited in time. Field research in Egypt, Kenya, the Philippines, the Dominican Republic, Haiti, and Lebanon took place mainly in 1976 and 1977, and sometimes continued into 1978. The Mexican project completed its field research in 1976 and submitted its report in early 1977. My main research on donor agencies was likewise carried out between 1975 and 1977, although some parts continued until 1981. Hence the material presented should not be generalized beyond the limits indicated. The Mexican program appears to have changed substantially since the research was completed, and the study itself may have prompted some of the changes. Accepter rates have also risen in the Philippines, and presidential commitment seems to have increased in Kenya. In other words, the research should be taken for what it is: an analysis of certain countries at a given point in time.

2   The country cases in capsule

To cover a reasonable range of diversity and yet not become mired in hetero-geneity, this study selected four countries for major studies and four others for secondary studies. The countries comprising the major studies had two common characteristics: official policies favoring reductions in population growth, and government-sponsored family planning programs. Despite wide geographic, cultural, and political diversity, these shared features permit useful comparative analysis across the four cases. By contrast, the countries in the secondary studies were chosen more for their singularity than for their comparability. Three are special situations, whereas the fourth (India) has been the single largest site of previous research on population policy in the developing countries.

MAJOR STUDIES

The countries serving as major studies were Egypt, Kenya, Mexico, and the Philippines. They span four continents, disparate political systems, distinct cultural traditions, and diverse historical experiences with population and allied issues. Yet they show numerous similarities in the way in which they defined their population problem, in their approach to population control, and in the problems that arose during the course of implementation.

Egypt

Egypt was the first of the four countries to announce an explicit policy for reducing population growth. In 1965, president Nasser established a Supreme Council for Family Planning, and in 1966 the government followed with a hurriedly assembled family planning program. These actions stood in sharp contrast to the slow pace of birth control before 1965 and to the tortuous path of implementation after 1966.

Warnings about the perils of population were sounded well before 1965. In 1930, several social-work professors founded a group called Al-Ruwad (the pioneers) to discuss Egypt's social and economic needs. One such need was family welfare, which the group members saw threatened by repeated pregnancies. Although they did not press for any specific action on birth control, they did ask the mufti of Cairo for a *fatwa* (edict) to interpret the Islamic stand on contraception. Issued in 1937, this statement gave nominal but not enthusiastic support to contraception.

9

Also catalyzing concern about population growth was a 1936 book by Wendell Clelland, *The Population Problem in Egypt*. Clelland claimed that people would soon outrun resources unless something was done to check Egypt's numbers. In 1937 the Egyptian Medical Association held discussions on population, and by 1939 the government had asked the Ministry of Social Affairs to look into the problem. But until the overthrow of the old order in 1952, there was simply no impetus for action on population growth.

With the advent of Nasser, the population question began to be taken seriously, but for a decade little was done. In 1953 Nasser stated: "In fifty years the population of Egypt will reach 44 million. . . If we are earnest about raising our standard of living, we should not be forgetful of this fact." That same year the minister of social affairs prepared a memorandum showing the many dangers of rapid population growth, especially for public services and housing. His statement led to the creation of the National Population Commission, an advisory body and study group, but to no governmental programs.

Two forces worked against explicit action on population growth in the 1950s. The first was the government's fear of kindling religious opposition. After the revolution, the subject of birth control was delicate in itself and was made more so by mounting tensions between secular reformers and champions of religious orthodoxy. Islamic leaders had given limited approval to contraception, but they were far from enthusiastic about governmental initiatives on family planning, and there was division in their ranks. In such a volatile atmosphere, caution seemed to be the best strategy. Second, like many nationalist leaders of his day, Nasser was confident that the population problem could be overcome by economic development. Many of his closest associates were skeptical about devoting scarce resources to birth control, and some were ideologically opposed to it. In 1959 Nasser himself stated: "In my opinion, instead of concentrating on birth control, we would do better to concentrate on how to make use of our own resources." Through the 1950s the government pinned its hopes for population control on agrarian reform, land reclamation, industrial expansion, and like measures. The Aswan Dam stood as an emblem of optimism for all fields of development.

By 1962, this developmentalist flush had turned into demographic depression. In May of that year Nasser was forced to declare that "population increase constitutes the most dangerous obstacle that faces the Egyptian people in their drive toward raising the standard of production in their country in an efficient and effective way." The main problem was that Egypt's economic performance had fallen far short of the goals set for it. Whereas population growth continued unabated, agricultural and industrial productivity were disappointing. Hence in 1965 Nasser installed the Supreme Council for Family Planning and urged it to act quickly. Three months later, in February 1966, the council launched a National Family Planning Program.

The program itself was stunningly simple in concept. Almost overnight, all health clinics were to add family planning to their list of services. Social workers from the Ministry of Social Affairs were to work with the clinics in motivating and educating potential clients. The pill was to be the program's mainstay, and sterilization and abortion were explicitly ruled out. Fees from the sale of pills were to be divided among physicians, social workers, and other staff members as an incentive for the additional work. The Supreme Council for Family Planning would be the national policy-making body, and the Executive Family Planning Board would handle program implementation, including the supervision, training, and payment of personnel. The program was based on the assumption that Egypt had a receptive consumer population whose demand for birth control could be met by supplying contraceptives.

The implementation record from 1966 to 1972 was disastrous. Far from flocking to the clinics to pick up the supplies of pills, many intended clients stayed home. Some who did venture forth found the buildings closed or staffed by janitors dispensing pill cycles. Doctors, nurses, and social workers squabbled over the apportionment of incentives and generally did not regard this line of work as of high priority. Confusion at the bottom was paralleled by chaos at the top. The program's first four years saw five different chairmen of the Supreme Council on Family Planning and a succession of powerless acting chairmen. The 1967 war with Israel dealt a lethal blow to the family planning effort, which quickly took a back seat to defense and then reconstruction. The Supreme Council did not meet for months at a time and provided no direction or leadership. And the structure of the program turned out to be largely unworkable. From top to bottom implementation was bedeviled by bureaucratic warfare and motivational inertia. By the early 1970s the number of new pill accepters was declining, dropouts were mounting, and in rural areas the program was not reaching much more than 3 percent of the eligible women. Some clinics attracted no new clients, and many served fewer than ten contraceptive users per month.

This dismal record pushed the policy emphasis from contraceptive supply to motivational demand. In 1972 the government changed the name of the Supreme Council for Family Planning to the Supreme Council for Population and Family Planning and appointed a new chairman, Dr. Aziz Bindary. Without delay Bindary proposed a National Population and Family Policy, which was approved by the Supreme Council in 1973. Its scope was broad and its thrust developmentalist. Nine factors were to be promoted simultaneously: family income, education, women's employment, mechanization of agriculture, industrialization, reduction of infant mortality, social security, communication of information about population and family planning, and the provision of family planning services. The first eight were to be stimulators of demand; family planning services would meet that demand. Bindary's model thus joined the developmentalist emphasis of the 1950s with the family planning focus of the 1960s. But however lofty the Supreme Council's ambitions, the council did not run the government. In Egypt, as in most countries, it is not easy for a unit charged with population policy to promote mechanization of agriculture, women's employment, or public health services. Either the population body steals the turf of other agencies, with the danger of causing bureaucratic brawls, or it does nothing on development, with the risk of losing credibility. As of 1978 there was no evidence that the Supreme Council had seized the reins of Egyptian development or even that it had been effective in supplying family planning services.

Kenya

In 1966 Kenya became the first country in sub-Saharan Africa to adopt an official family planning program. The government in that year announced its intention to "pursue vigorously policies designed to reduce the rate of population growth through voluntary means." The active ingredient in this policy was a family planning program to be implemented under the Ministry of Health. Given the political turbulence in Kenya at the time and the extreme delicacy of the birth-control issue, many were amazed at the speed with which this new policy came into being.

The period surrounding Kenya's independence in 1963 was marked by exceptional turbulence. The preceding five years had seen the Mau Mau rebellion, tribal rivalries, constitutional haggling. The country's image in the foreign press bordered on the barbarous as correspondents played up the Mau Mau massacres and then the exodus of European settlers. In the wake of this publicity, foreign investment ceased, and the international community kept a wary eye on President Kenyatta and his fledgling nation. Hence one of the paramount challenges for the new government was to win the confidence of overseas investors and the trust of Western governments.

A second striking feature of the postindependence years was the pervasive presence and influence of expatriates. Many key areas of development policy, including health and population, were under the direct influence of British civil servants who were continued in their posts or foreign advisers brought in after independence. In some fields both line officials and their advisers were expatriates.

These two contextual features came together in the development of Kenya's population policy. Anxious to repair the government's image in the West, Kenyan leaders relied heavily on the counsel of foreign advisors. As it happened, an emerging precept of development in international circles was the need to contain rapid population growth. The Coale–Hoover thesis about the detrimental effects of demographic growth had become fashionable by the early 1960s and was being propagated to the developing countries.[1] It found a receptive audience among the expatriate advisers, mostly economists, in Kenya's Ministry of Economic Planning and Development. Influenced by the projections of J.G.G. Blacker, the government demographer before and after independence, the Ministry issued Sessional Paper Number 10 in 1965. Following the Coale–Hoover argument, it concluded: "A high rate of population growth means a large dependent population, reduces the money available for development, lowers the rate of economic growth and makes exceedingly difficult the task of increasing social services."[2]

The confluence of Blacker's calculations and the conventional wisdom on development moved the expatriates to press for action on population. They persuaded the minister, Tom Mboya, and the permanent secretary that Kenya's development was being held back by excessive population growth and that the situation would deteriorate over the decades. Following extensive staff work by the advisors, in April 1965 the permanent secretary invited the Population Council of New York to send a team of experts to look into Kenya's "population problem." The Population Council accepted the invitation and sent a team of four Americans in 1966. After a three-week visit, this mission prepared a report that gave eleven specific recommendations to the Kenyan government. Kenya was urged to make a clear declaration of population policy and to embark on a nationwide family planning program. Action should begin with a Knowledge–Attitude–Practice (KAP) survey and with appropriate training of program personnel. The program should involve all government agencies but also allow for cooperation with private agencies. The recommended form of contraception was the intrauterine device (IUD), whose cost was exceedingly low and whose use required only a single motivation and acceptance. The report was accepted by the Ministry of Economic Planning and Development and became the foundation for the government's population policy. Announcement of the new policy immediately raised Kenya's credit rating among international donors, who saw such action as eminently "responsible" and as a model for other African countries.

The National Family Planning Program was launched by the Ministry of Health in 1967. Its task was to provide family planning information and services in all government hospitals and health centers. Services were to be wholly voluntary and linked to the delivery of maternal and child health care. Although the guiding objective of national policy was to reduce Kenya's birth rate, the publicly announced rationale for family planning was the spacing of births for improved health. Sterilization, abortion, and financial incentives were excluded from the program. The program was defined as a basic health service and nominally granted the same facilities as any other health service.

As international cheers for the new program subsided, domestic protest began to swell. The economic rationalism behind the government's policy had overlooked four critical features of Kenyan life: a lingering fear of colonialism; cultural values that emphasized fecundity; a political system threatened by tribalism; and an administrative apparatus given to territorialism. Critics soon charged that Kenya's efforts at population control were colonialism in economic clothing and might even have genocidal intent. The Catholic archbishop of Nairobi claimed that there was no population problem in Kenya, for there were vast lands yet to be inhabited. Oginga Odinga, once Kenyatta's vice-president, stated during parliamentary debates on the health budget: "We oppose family planning and don't even want to hear of family planning in Africa." Yusuf Eraj, a gynecologist active in establishing private family planning services, charged that too much attention was being paid to population when the real issue for Kenya was a poor distribution of resources. Cultural leaders charged that the idea of limiting rather than spacing births was essentially foreign. Others criticized the speed with which the Population Council report had become national policy, especially without public hearings or debate. And the Ministry of Health, which was responsible for carrying out the program, seemed to resent the fact that it had been developed by the Ministry of Economic Planning and Development without lateral consultation.

Before long, key figures pulled back from their espousal of family planning. In 1968 Tom Mboya told the National Assembly that a growth rate of 3 percent was not higher than normal. A month later he stated that the government was providing family planning for health reasons rather than for population control. The minister of health, J. D. Otiende, also retreated from an initial acceptance of the economic rationale for family planning. At a press conference in 1967, he referred to the dangers of Kenya's high dependency ratio but added, "I think the population growth at present is quite normal."

From 1967 until 1978 the family planning program suffered from weak commitment by senior government officials. From independence until his death in 1978, Jomo Kenyatta never once spoke out in favor of population control or even publicly mentioned his government's family planning program. The minister and the permanent secretary of health were widely thought to oppose the family planning program and in this study simply refused to speak about it. Politicians found birth control an easy target for potshots and felt little compunction in pulling the trigger. Sensing the ambivalence, indifference, and even hostility at the top, middle-level administrators did not give their all to implementation. In fact, the only individuals who seemed to believe in the program as presented to the public were the field implementers. In their candid moments most knowledgeable observers conceded that the Kenyan family planning program had fallen far short of the government's initial expectations. KAP surveys to the contrary, demand in many areas was weak and supply was shaky.

The paramount problem of the Kenyan program was that it was seen as foreign in inspiration and out of tune with national values on fertility. The early emphasis on population control proved disastrous, as it conjured up images of a white plot to limit African numbers or a Kikuyu design to consolidate power. The heavy commitments of funds by international donors, the heavy-handed lobbying by certain agencies, and the extensive presence of expatriate advisers on population accentuated the foreign image of family planning. In 1977 the government took a firmer hold of the program, especially by insisting on a closer integration of family planning into maternal and child health services. Although some donors objected, the government's take-it-or-leave-it stance carried the day. But in 1978 there were no signs that the government was about to throw its full weight behind a program that was still enmeshed in political complexities.

Philippines

Although private family planning activities in the Philippines date back to the 1920s, the government did not adopt an explicit policy on population growth until 1971. The development of that policy and the family planning programs that followed were very much a joint venture between national figures and international agencies. Foreign donors, particularly the Agency for International Development, influenced almost every aspect of policy formulation and implementation, but usually through willing collaborators or dependent organizations within the country.

As a colony of the United States from 1898 to 1946, the Philippines had long been exposed to North American values and practices. In addition to implanting such notions as the separation of church and state and the need for strong public education, the American presence sowed the seeds of legitimacy for birth control. Long before the government spoke about population matters, private citizens and organizations were busily and successfully promoting family planning. When the Marcos government moved on to the scene in 1971, its policy was less of a decisive break with the past than an incremental shift into the future.

The first family planning activists were Protestant missionaries. Beginning in the 1920s, they carried out a discreet motivational campaign for smaller families. Their efforts were hampered by strict laws prohibiting the importation of contraceptives or even reading matter on birth control, but they continued nonetheless. After World War II, a Protestant institution, the Mary Johnston Hospital in Manila, began to help the motivators with clinical support and contraceptive supplies. In 1957 the Philippine Federation of Christian Churches (now the National Council of Churches of the Philippines) started a family planning clinic for the greater Manila area. Also under Protestant auspices, a group of women concerned with problems of family life set up the Family Relations Center in 1961. With a grant from the International Planned Parenthood Federation (IPPF), it was able to include family planning among its services. Further expansion of these private efforts set the stage for the founding of the Family Planning Association of the Philippines in 1965. In that same year, the Family Relations Center became the Planned Parenthood Movement in the Philippines (PPMP). These developments were a portent of the organizational fragmentation that was to hamper the government's program in the 1970s. Under apparent pressure from the IPPF, which funded both groups and saw no advantages to their separate existence, the FPAP and the PPMP merged in 1969 to form the Family Planning Organization of the Philippines (FPOP).

Around 1964 a loose confederation of interested national and international agencies tried to push for public awareness about the "population problem" and the need for birth control. The newly established Population Institute of the University of the Philippines (UPPI) played a critical role in developing the intellectual rationale for an official population policy. Among international donors, the IPPF and the Pathfinder Fund tried to demonstrate through live programs that family planning was viable even in this Catholic country.

AID came on stage in 1966 and quickly stole the show. Its strategy was simple: Buy in, buy out, and buy around. Its goal was to stimulate as much action as possible through local intermediaries and allies. When existing agencies were willing to move, they were given help. Where there were no suitable organizations, some were created. If the government could not act because of religious and political counterforces, its environment should be changed by adding potent partisans. With the lure of easy program grants, travel funds, equipment, and supplies and in a setting full of bureaucratic entrepreneurs, AID had no trouble finding takers. Its efforts were supported by the Pathfinder Fund and IPPF, both of which received generous AID funding. By 1969 AID and its allies had built enthusiastic constituencies for population action in both private and public organizations. The resulting network clearly helped to move the government toward an explicit population policy but it also created an organizational structure that would impede the national family planning program.

The first signs of explicit government interest came in 1967, when President Marcos signed the world leaders' statement on population and human rights. In 1968 he asked his executive secretary, Rafael Salas, to convene a group of prominent citizens to discuss the population question. Then in February 1969 Marcos issued an executive order creating a Commission on Population. Its mandate was to "recommend policy, make program recommendations, and undertake research." Recognizing the political pitfalls of birth control, he tried to head off opposition by naming commission members from every major interest group, including the Roman Catholic church. The commission lost no time in acting, and seven months after its founding it presented Marcos with a clearly formulated Statement on Population. The following were among the main policies proposed:

1.　　　To establish and adopt specific quantitative population goals on the basis of reliable demographic data and expected demographic trends.
2.　　　To promote the broadest understanding by the people of the adverse effects on family life and national welfare of unlimited population growth and to provide the means by which couples can safely, effectively, and freely determine the proper size of their families.
3.　　　To make family planning part of a broad educational program oriented toward the harmonious development of individual personality, the family, and the nation.
4.　　　To examine legal and administrative policies and measures affecting family size and, if deemed essential, to revise such policies and measures to bring about a balance between family size and social and economic goals.[3]

Reflecting the active participation of the church in the commission's Committee on Religion and Culture, the statement emphasized the voluntary nature of family planning and the individual right of conscience. Specifically, it stated that

the programs will be educational and persuasive, not coercive. In the provision of services, nothing shall be urged on the individual clients and service personnel which is contrary to their conscience.

The statement also rejected abortion and discouraged sterilization.

When the statement was issued, Marcos was more concerned about politics than demography; therefore, he did nothing about it until after his reelection in November 1969. In his state of the nation message in 1970, he proposed legislation making family planning programs an official part of government services. Shortly thereafter, he reconstituted the Commission on Population to carry out that policy. Although there was some congressional and popular criticism of his population bill, it passed with no opposition (but numerous absences) in 1971. After the election, the president's wife, Imelda Romualdez Marcos, personally took up the population cause and by the late 1970s had become the country's leading advocate of family planning. Indeed, rivalries between the private population agency under her tutelage and the official Commission on Population came to be a major issue in implementation.

The family planning program established in 1971 had four key administrative features:

1.　　　*Integration.* The program would rely on existing organizations to do its work. It would also be merged into health and other services rather than left to stand alone.
2.　　　*Multiagency participation.* The forty-three organizations then on the scene would divide up responsibilities for clinical services; information, education, and communication; training; and research.
3.　　　*Partnership of public and private sectors.* The national program would include and fund private as well as public agencies.
4.　　　*Coordination.* The Commission on Population (POPCOM) was to formulate policy and manage program implementation for the participating organiza-

tions. However, its authority vis-à-vis the line agencies, and particularly the Ministry of Health, was not specified. Jurisdictional conflicts between POPCOM and other units later proved to be a serious obstacle to implementation.

On September 21, 1972, Marcos put the Philippines under martial law and disbanded the Congress. Three months later he installed a more muscular population policy. The Revised Population Act of 1972 (P.D. 79) used less lofty language than the 1969 statement and emphasized effective means of fertility control. Aside from the "get tough" attitude that often accompanies martial law, one reason for the change was a computer simulation showing that the government's demographic targets would never be reached without more effective methods of birth control. In response to P.D. 79, the Commission on Population pressured its subsidiary organizations to promote three methods: sterilization, the pill, and the IUD. The threat of funding cuts from AID and the prospect of little or no increase in national support enhanced POPCOM's bargaining position with these agencies. Soon afterward, fieldworkers began to press for the more effective methods, with results that will be discussed in later chapters.

From 1969 on, the main source of overt resistance to the government's population program was the Roman Catholic Church. Before P.D. 79, church leaders refrained from an all-out campaign against artificial birth control and even endorsed the principle of responsible parenthood. The government for its part respected Catholic sensitivities by using the language of responsible parenthood, endorsing freedom in the choice of methods (including rhythm), banning abortion, and adopting an educational approach to family planning. But after the imposition of martial law, the church hierarchy strongly criticized the campaign for effectiveness and specifically the emphasis on sterilization. The bishops of western Visayas issued a pastoral letter condemning the promotion of pills and IUDs and the accepter quotas set for fieldworkers. They and other clerics soon became the national conscience on the ethics of program implementation.

The implementation record for the Philippine program was spotty, at best. Perhaps the greatest single problem was conflict and tension among the many implementing agencies. The program was unquestionably hampered by the proliferation of many organizations that did much the same work, and especially by their competition for clients in a shrinking market. This problem can be traced directly to the manner in which the program developed in the 1960s. The situation was not helped by running battles between the Commission on Population and the agencies it was supposed to coordinate. Here as elsewhere, coordination proved to be a euphemism for power; it was so perceived by line agencies such as the Department of Health. The Philippine study also showed significant differences in perspectives between field implementers and national administrators and between POPCOM and AID. A second major obstacle to execution was a high rate of dropouts brought on by fears, rumors, and actual experience of contraceptive side effects. Anxious to deliver its services as quickly and effectively as possible, the Philippine program often over-looked the economic exigencies, cultural milieu, and individual psychology of its intended clients. Having sampled the program's offerings, many clients decided that it was not in their interest to continue. As of 1978 the family planning program in the Philippines had the nominal backing of the Marcos government but little of its funds, and an unimpressive input–output ratio. The tactical triumphs of the 1960s brought on the strategic failure of the 1970s.

Mexico

The most striking feature of Mexican population policy is the abruptness with which it changed in 1972. From the pre-Columbian period through the 1960s, growth had been the leitmotif of Mexican proclamations about numbers. The Latin refrain "to govern is to populate" was often heard, and the idea behind it was taken for granted by generations of Mexican rulers.

Many conditions supported the pronatalist tradition in Mexico. Among the tribes inhabiting the region before the arrival of Cortes, large numbers of people were needed for food production as well as military purposes. The abundant casualties produced by continual wars put a premium on equally abundant reproduction, and the maize-based agriculture needed many hands. The Spanish conquistadores had even greater reasons to favor a large popula-tion. Their haciendas, the gigantic mining industry, and colonial construction projects all required manual labor, and household needs called for a multitude of servants. Also fostering pronatalism was the colonial belief that open lands should be filled with people.

Heavy losses of people and territories reinforced the bias for growth. Mas-sacres, disease, and the sheer exploitation of the conquest produced an abso-lute decline in numbers. The war of independence from Spain (1810–21) brought still more casualties. Then in 1848 Mexico lost about half of its total land area to the United States. The fact that the conquered territories were only sparsely settled confirmed the belief that small numbers encourage ex-pansion from the north. When efforts to attract European immigrants failed, the policy makers of the day concluded that the only answer was natural increase through high fertility. A final wave of losses, amounting to some 10 percent of the population, came with the Revolution of 1910. The nationalism born of this struggle raised political barriers to foreign immigration, so that the only answer was again more people born in Mexico.

From 1910 to 1972 pronatalism was a staple element in the nationalist populism of the ruling party. The government often made statements leading to headlines such as these: "Land Without Men: Weak and Backward Country," or "Our Biggest Problem is Depopulation." In 1932 Gilberto Loyo, a prominent politician and demographer, published a treatise called "The Quantitative Deficiencies of the Population of Mexico and a National Population Policy." His basic message was that if Mexico wanted to be a modern nation, it had to have the large population size and density required by modernity. Loyo said specifically that "Mexico's plan is to expand and improve its national population" and indicated that his views were shared by ministers and other key officials. Dozens of other press items for that period made the same point. As late as 1970, the ruling party's presidential candidate, Luis Echeverria Alvarez, proclaimed himself in favor of greater numbers and against birth control. It was this same Echeverria who two years later reversed the nation's policy.

Why the turnabout? Because the decision was made behind closed doors and has never been discussed openly by those involved, it is difficult to know the exact reasons. But most observers agree that the overwhelming actuator of change was concern about the socioeconomic consequences of rapid population growth. Demographic research during the 1960s produced dramatic evidence that economic expansion was not keeping pace with population growth. By 1970 Mexico was faced with a series of fiscal crises and the long-term prospect of inflation. Also at work was distress at the burgeoning size and mounting deterioration of Mexico City and the massive exodus of Mexicans to the United States. There were likewise fears about the political risks in a swelling population of unemployed young people. The grim possibilities of discontent were brought home with particular force by the demonstrations and subsequent massacre of students at the 1968 Olympics. Although student revolts were scarcely new to Mexico, the public slaughter of hundreds of young people set off a national crisis of conscience and shattered the government's optimism about caring for its growing "revolutionary family." The myth of boundless triumph fell with the students at Tlaltelolco.

Although Echeverria's policy reversal was almost instantaneous, there had been premonitory signs of change over the previous decade. On August 26, 1961, the daily *El Nacional* carried a story with this headline: "Population growth may call a halt to economic development; the productivity of our agriculture is insufficient." On December 26 of the same year, *Excelsior* proclaimed: "Demographic explosion and economic development." By 1965 family planning began to be discussed in public, usually under the rubric of responsible parenthood. With the euphemistic name of Foundation for Studies of Population (FEPAC), Mexico's first private family planning organization appeared in 1965. This same period saw several significant pieces of research on Mexican reproductive behavior, including studies by the Latin American Demographic Center in Santiago, Chile, and the Mexican Institute for Social Studies (IMES). The first government-sponsored family planning program was established in 1968 as part of the postabortion program of the Mexico

City Women's hospital. Debates in Catholic circles about the morality of birth control, many prompted by the 1968 papal encyclical *Humanae vitae*, also brought the family planning questions to the fore. But until 1972 the government remained officially opposed to birth control, and in the 1970 presidential campaign Echeverria made a point of affirming the traditional populist position on growth.

The new policy emerged in several stages. The first came in 1972, when Echeverria publicly stated that Mexico had a population problem and established a family planning program within maternal and child health-care centers. In 1973 the Ministry of Health and the Mexican Institute of Social Security began to provide family planning services in their centers and hospitals. The sanitary code was changed in that year to permit family planning in public and private organizations, and a Council of Maternal and Child Health was established to coordinate programs in this area.

Toward the end of 1973 the government presented a draft population law to the Congress and capitalized on the subsequent deliberations to express its concern about population growth. Mario Moya Palencia, secretary of the interior (*gobernación*) and later a candidate for the presidency, appeared before the legislators and, in a televised session, offered a brilliant defense of the bill, which passed without difficulty. A key provision of the law was the formation of a National Population Council (CONAPO), an interministerial coordinating body to be headed by the secretary of the interior. It was created and went into operation in 1974.

In developing its population policy, the Echeverria government had a double challenge: to avoid destruction in the minefield of birth control and to build support among potential allies. Most to be shunned was the wrath of a Catholic hierarchy opposed to artificial contraception and vigilant of its prerogatives in moral education. Nor could the government afford the taint of American imperialism, a real risk because of unbounded *yanqui* enthusiasm for family planning. To assuage the Socialists, the government could not appear to be substituting birth control for development, while to satisfy the liberals and hold off the church it had to avoid any hint of coercion. In the end the government showed great political acuity in developing a population package that won the maximum feasible backing and evoked minimal antagonism.

The politics did not stop with policy development. As early as 1972 the shift to birth control became entwined with the choice of a successor to Echeverria. The formal unveiling of the ruling party's candidate was not scheduled until 1975, but the race was underway well before then. The heir apparent was Mario Moya Palencia, who, like Echeverria before him, was secretary of the interior. Moya's unannounced but widely recognized candidacy quickly became inseparable from the population effort. Political entrepreneurs soon saw unexpected promise in family planning. As a result, electoral politics began to shape the policy options chosen and rejected, the language used in presenting the policies to the public, and the directions of implementation (see Chapter 5). And needless to say, when Moya was not the party's choice in 1975 the instant converts to the cause of population control sought new outlets for their devotion.

During the delicate stages of policy formulation, Mexico kept its distance from international donors. The Ford Foundation had been on the scene for some time, but its primary role was to raise consciousness about population questions through research and conferences. The International Planned Parenthood Federation helped to support FEPAC but was not involved with the government. To maintain both the image and the reality of national self-determination, policy makers avoided any direct contact with the ubiquitous AID. Even so, there were rumors that in his 1972 policy reversal Echeverria had capitulated to pressures from the World Bank, whose president had visited the country shortly before. Once the new policy was safely installed, the government opened the door to more foreign assistance, especially from the United Nations Fund for Population Activities. Still, compared to the other countries covered by the major studies, the Mexican family planning program had the highest percentage of funds from national sources.

From 1974 to 1976 the program moved ahead as specified by the population law. Under the general policy guidance of the National Population Council (CONAPO), the government set up family planning programs under several entities, particularly the Secretariat of Health and the Mexican Institute of Social Security. Clinics offered services under the rubric of maternal and child health care. As in Egypt and the Philippines, the administrative system was complex. Coordinating agencies included not only CONAPO but also the Interministerial Commission on Maternal and Child Health and Family Planning, a body made up of representatives from public agencies and the private sector. To complicate matters, family planning programs had to pass through another bureaucratic layer connecting federal to state programs.

The implementation problems under Echeverria were partly unique and partly shared with other countries. Original to Mexico was the marriage of population policy with the presidential aspirations of the official most responsible for program execution. This fortuity drew to the program a host of aides whose heart was not in family planning and also produced some political detours in implementation. But most important, it gave the family planning program an aura of politics that cast doubt on the seriousness of its intentions.

Other barriers to implementation were more familiar. As in Egypt, Kenya, and the Philippines, the assumptions behind the program were middle-class, whereas most of the clients were not. Shyness in discussing sexual matters, female aversion to disrobing before male doctors, discomfort at the brevity and paternalism of contacts with clinic staff, a poor understanding of contraceptives, fears as well as real experience of side effects – all arose from a poor fit between programs and clients. Further, many clinic heads with broad responsibilities for health care saw no reason why family planning should come before other services. Some had never been given an adequate explanation of the program, and about one in ten were opposed to family planning. Hence by the end of 1976 the Mexican government had managed to gain political legitimacy for its announced population policy but was hampered by the usual obstacles to implementation.

SECONDARY STUDIES

To broaden its coverage, our project commissioned four smaller studies of national experiences with population policy in Lebanon, Haiti, the Dominican Republic, and India. The pivotal question for Lebanon was why it could not mount even a population census, much less a national family planning program, in its strife-ridden environment. The Dominican Republic was chosen to explore the policy repercussions of fears about an expanding but disparaged racial minority, the Haitians. Haiti was included partly to see if there was any reciprocity in its reactions to the Dominican Republic and partly to probe the interactions between voodoo and family planning. Finally, it seemed essential to include India, if only because it had been the single most common source of theories and illustrations about population policy and the subject of hundreds of prior studies. We did not want to add to the literature on India but thought that a review of its experience would round out the present picture.

Lebanon

Sectarian rivalries in Lebanon have created an environment that is sensitive to any overt discussion of population control. The country is nominally pluralistic, with Christian, Muslim, and Druze sects living close together. But there has long been a crucial line of political cleavage between the Christians, whose largest group is the Maronites, and the Sunni and Shi'ite Muslims. After the first episodes of confessional conflict in the 1840s, the numerical distribution of these communities became an issue in governance. To avoid the political subordination of one group to another, successive governments juggled administrative divisions and the numerical basis of representation. The partition scheme of 1843 divided Mount Lebanon into a northern district headed by a Maronite governor and a southern district headed by a Druze. Other attempts to institutionalize religious representation followed in 1845 and 1860.

With the creation of the State of Greater Lebanon in 1920, the numerical distribution of the sects became an even more delicate political question. Using data from the 1932 census (the last ever conducted), the National Pact of 1943 devised a formula in which parliamentary seats, cabinet positions, and civil service appointments would be allocated at a ratio of six Christians to five Muslims. Under this agreement, the Maronites, the largest sect, were given the presidency, the Sunni Muslims the premiership, and the Shi'ites the speakership of the chamber of deputies.

This confessional accord lasted for three decades but with constant strain and sporadic outbursts of violence. And throughout it was undermined by social and demographic changes of explosive proportions. The two most important were fertility differentials that gave the edge in population size to the Muslims and socioeconomic shifts of principal benefit to the Christians. Although Lebanon had shown a general drop in fertility, this was more rapid for Christians than for the other sects. As a result, the Shi'ite Muslims came to have the highest birth rate, followed by the Sunnis, the Druze, and then the Christians. The relative position of these groups on key socioeconomic indicators was just the reverse: Christians, Druze, Sunnis, and Shi'as. This coupling of increased size and reduced advantage for the Muslims led to the rupture of the political pact and the devastating civil war of 1975. There was no census to prove what everyone knew, but the game had changed and the demographic fiction of the previous decades could not be sustained.

Caught between an untenable myth and an unmentionable reality, the government chose the only path open: silence. A review of policy statements by the cabinet since 1943 showed a consistent avoidance of population issues. There was occasional mention of migration and rural–urban imbalances, as well as the problems of Palestinians, but there was no direct comment on matters at the heart of the national dilemma. Nor were population questions discussed in Lebanon's development plans and policies.

Despite these restraints on public expression, the Lebanese government did work quietly and often circuitously to support private family planning programs. Politicians, religious leaders, government administrators, and other public figures openly endorsed the Lebanese Family Planning association (LFPA), which has been active and visible. In 1977 the prime minister himself inaugurated a conference on population policy sponsored by the association. And in 1978 the secretary general of LFPA was also the full-time head of the Office of Social Development for Southern Lebanon. Indeed, LFPA often used the centers of this office as bases for offering medical advice on the side effects of contraceptives, inserting IUDs, giving injections, and referring clients for sterilization to a hospital in Beirut.

But the major government contribution to private family planning was its nonenforcement of severe legal restrictions on birth control. Lebanon's penal code sets down both imprisonment and a fine for those who use, spread, sell, stock, or "propagandize" contraceptive methods. During the 1960s contraception was practiced primarily by upper-class married couples who received supplies from private physicians. Although the law was being violated, the class background of the offenders together with the silence of the offense removed any pressure for strict enforcement.

The scene shifted in 1969, when the International Planned Parenthood Federation sent the LFPA twenty-five crates of Eugynon contraceptive pills. Hardly an unobtrusive gift, this shipment was blocked in customs on the grounds that it violated Lebanese law. However, a sympathetic minister of health came to the rescue by passing the pills through as medicament for regulating menstrual cycles. The letter of approval stated: "This Ministry wishes to inform you that it approves, as an exception, your request to import 25 thousand boxes of the medicament Eugynon, being a gift to your Association by the International Planned Parenthood Federation, on the condition that it will be distributed *gratis* by the clinics of your association." Subsequent health ministers have issued essentialy the same reply, changing only names and dates. Before long, pharmaceutical dealers also began to clear their contraceptive supplies as medicament with no interference.

The emergence of a de facto but never-articulated policy on family planning was a direct response to confessional conflicts in Lebanon. Fearing that it would be impaled on any public declaration of a population policy the government shunned positive statements or overt efforts to change the laws on contraceptives. At the same time, its sympathies were clearly on the side of family planning. Under those conditions, the safest course was to offer tacit support to the LFPA and disregard infractions of the laws on birth control. It was also symptomatic of the national scene that fieldwork for the present study was cut short by an Israeli invasion into southern Lebanon.

The Dominican Republic

Three historical events conditioned the development of population policy in the Dominican Republic. One was the military occupation of the country by the United States from 1916 to 1924. The public works program during this period led to the recruitment of a black labor force from neighboring Haiti and other Caribbean Islands. The second was the continuation of Haitian immigration, much of it illegal, from that point on. The growing presence of a black population speaking a foreign language (French) created a continuing fear of Haitian inundation and occasioned a brutal massacre in 1937. Generalized prejudice against blacks as well as specific fears of cultural deterioration were later to shape Dominican reactions to the government's family planning program (see Chapter 7). The third event, which was directly linked to the establishment of this program, was the U.S. invasion of the country in 1965. Coinciding with AID's active entry into the population field, the resulting American control paved the way to a national family planning program. With assistance and often nudging from AID, the government soon adopted the family planning model then in vogue among donor agencies.

The first organized attempts to introduce birth control into the Dominican Republic came under American Protestant auspices in the early 1960s. In 1962 the Church World Services (CWS) asked Reverend Donald Dod, a Presbyterian minister with experience in Puerto Rico, and his wife to assess the need for family planning in the Dominican Republic. The Dods reported "an immense need" and urged action programs through the Social Service of Dominican Churches (SSID). CWS accepted their recommendation and moved to help SSID. The Dods themselves established a family planning base at the International Hospital in Santo Domingo; but by 1965 it was clear that the long-term success of family planning required greater Dominican and smaller American participation. Hence, Reverend Dod and others called a series of meetings to stimulate local interest. Out of these came first an ad hoc group called Friends of Family Planning and later the Family Planning Association.

The U.S. invasion in April 1965 eclipsed family planning and every other aspect of the country's life. In the ensuing chaos, the Family Planning Association ceased to function. However, the resolute Dods kept at their work and in July even managed to open the first clinic devoted exclusively to family planning. In that same month an AID representative arrived and asked the Dods to continue existing activities until better arrangements could be worked out. By March 1966 the original group of Friends was transformed into the Dominican Association for Family Welfare (ADPBF), an organization that continues to the present time. It quickly requested and received funds from AID and sought affiliation with the IPPF. The ADPBF then took over the clinic established by the Dods and established working relations with other family planning units.

After the invasion, the government had no population policy and was primarily concerned with survival. The interim president believed in family planning, but with a shaky government in a fractured society he could offer little support. Other government officials were open to the idea but feared opposition from the church or the left if they took action. The government's attitude toward population matters in 1966 and 1967 was laissez faire – do nothing and stop nothing.

As the country moved toward peace, population advisers moved toward Santo Domingo. In 1966, representatives of the Population Council joined AID in pressing for government action. A crucial challenge was to convince the new president, Joaquin Balaguer, to support an explicit population policy. Balaguer was wary at first but was eventually persuaded by the AID consortium. Meanwhile, IPPF was trying to make the ADPBF became more Dominican in appearance and management. Under new leadership it became more assertive in its public campaigns as well as in its private lobbying for birth control.

On February 14, 1968, Balaguer created the National Council on Population and the Family to be the government's coordinating body for population activities. Since then, with substantial support from foreign donors, the government has established a large family planning program within the framework of maternal and child health services. Its mandate is to introduce family planning throughout the country's health services, to establish new family planning clinics and centers for maternal and child health care in the outlying areas of urban centers, to provide birth-control information and services to small villages and scattered populations in rural areas, to develop a postpartum program in hospitals and other public maternity centers, and to distribute contraceptives for the prevention of venereal disease. One part of the rural program is the community-based distribution of contraceptives under the supervision of the government's Basic Health Services. The postpartum program also offers sterilization and injections of Depo Provera, both of which are considered experimental. The ADPBF likewise continues with its family planning services but in the late 1970s concentrated on information, education, and communication services and experimentation with the newer contraceptives.

Despite its genesis in the American occupation, by 1978 the Dominican program seemed to have won the government's support. There were, however, numerous implementation problems: poor staff training, weak commitment among field implementers, unreliable service, and mismatches between local understanding of contraception and the services delivered. The issue of racial contamination by Haitians continued to resonate but at a lower level than when the public program was first announced.

Haiti

Haiti occupies the western third of the island of Hispaniola, the rest of which belongs to the Dominican Republic. In 1975 the estimated populations of the two countries were quite close – 4.6 million for Haiti and 4.9 million for the Dominican Republic – but their population densities and overall economic levels were strikingly dissimilar. Haiti's density of 200 persons per square kilometer was among the highest in the western hemisphere and double that of its neighbor. By contrast, gross domestic product per capita was about five times larger for the Dominican Republic than for Haiti. The inescapable realities of land and income plainly enhanced the appeal of Dominican residence for many poor Haitians.

Our picture of population policy in Haiti is the least clear of any of the country studies. Respondents seemed unwilling to move beyond official statements of reality, and the government's actions were difficult to interpret. Given limited resources and an environment hostile to this line of research, the country team could not probe very deeply into the dynamics of family planning. Still, several points emerged from their report.

If Dominicans were worried about racial adulteration from Haitians, the latter seemed unconcerned about any aspect of population in the Dominican Republic. The two nations have long had border disputes and other conflicts, but these do not seem to have shaped the Haitian mind set about population. Although neither this mind set nor the depth of the government's interest in birth control is easy to fathom, the country has had a national family planning program since 1971. The activities of the responsible organization, the Family Health Division, are geared to two main objectives: promoting maternal and child health care with a family planning component and carrying out related educational activities, including courses on child care, radio programs, home visits, and the training of midwives. The Family Health Division started its family planning work in Port-au-Prince, then moved to other cities, and finally moved into the rural areas that contain 80 percent of the country's population. Overall, the program has not been effective in reaching its intended population. In this tightly controlled political environment there has been little open opposition to the program.

A key question about Haiti is the impact of voodoo on family planning programs. Although voodoo is practiced by 80 or 90 percent of Haitians, the researchers were unable to learn much about its precise impact on these programs. Potential clients do seem to consult the local voodoo leader (*houngan*) before going to the clinics. Also, once a clinic is established in the countryside, its administrators lose no time in trying to win the *houngan*'s cooperation or at least neutrality. There are hints that modern methods of fertility control clash with voodoo and other aspects of traditional culture, but the evidence is sparse.

India

India has been the world's proving ground for birth control. Almost every policy innovation, from incentives to workers on tea estates to sterilization booths in railroad stations, has been tried, applauded, and abandoned. The country has alternately been the darling and the downfall of the donors, a prototype to be emulated and an antitype to be shunned. The government has veered from dormancy to militancy to restraint. Yet despite the enormous investment in birth control and the myriad policy experiments, family planning has not caught on in India. Buffeted by uncontrollable natural forces and squeezed by feudal landlords, villagers often find life more other-determined than self-initiated and birth control beyond the realm of the plausible. The assumptions behind family planning – that procreation is a conscious process and that fertility can be regulated by simple technologies – fly in the face of common experience and religious belief. To those who master nothing in their daily existence, the idea of consciously manipulating their most intimate behavior is not self-evident. For many, birth results from a process in which choice is irrelevant, if not precarious, and having numerous children, especially sons, is often the only hope for escape from destitution.

After independence in 1947, India's leaders showed little interest in birth control. Nehru not only accepted the socialist premise that development is the

best contraceptive but also had more pressing matters on his agenda. The first
central health minister, a woman who held the position for ten years, was a
Christian Gandhian who opposed artificial means of limiting births. The first
five year plan noted the problems posed by rapid population growth but
included very little money for activities to check this growth. The government's emphasis during this period was on child spacing rather than on birth
control. The second five year plan showed greater concern about curbing
population growth and allocated thirty times the funds devoted to this purpose
in the first plan. Family planning centers were rapidly expanded, and allied
educational efforts were intensified. In 1959 the Central Family Planning
Board added sterilization to the permissible means of birth control but hemmed
it in with various regulations. The 1961 census produced an even stronger
awareness of the consequences of rapid population growth and also suggested
differential growth rates across religious groups. These data strengthened
fears that Hindus would eventually lose ground to the more fertile Muslim
minority. In 1962 the government introduced financial incentives for persons
undergoing sterilization, although these were carefully billed as compensation
for transportation and lost work.

With Indira Gandhi's accession to power in 1966, India shifted from strict
voluntarism to program targets. A report from the Ministry of Health, Family
Planning and Urban Government stated that the objective of the family planning program was now to reduce the birth rate from forty-one to twenty-five
per thousand, but the target was vague as to time. Beginning in that period
and continuing to the downfall of her regime in 1977, Mrs. Gandhi increased
the tempo of population control, sometimes in desperately hurried fashion.
During 1967 and 1968 the sterilization program was accelerated, with mounting pressure placed on workers for results. The combination of pressure from
above and vagueness about limits on means inevitably led to abuses. Sterilizations were performed without informed consent and often without any consent. As Mrs. Gandhi laid her prestige on the line for family planning, lower
officials abandoned bureaucratic neutrality for programmatic effectiveness.
By 1969 the Ministry of Health could announce that family planning was "to
be given highest priority and to occupy a pivotal place in the economic
development efforts of the country." The dilemma from that point on was how
to combine freedom of choice with the demand for results.

In the late 1960s misadventures with the IUD and the general failure of the
family planning program set the stage for two new policy directions: a preference for sterilization and a tolerance of coercion. Ironically the states that took
the hardest line were the two with the best record in family planning, Madras
and Maharashtra. In September 1968, Maharashtra introduced a scheme of
disincentives, including such measures as higher rent and fewer medical
services for those with large families. This tough realism impressed Mrs.
Gandhi and her associates, but they held back until the declaration of the

emergency in 1975. Then, under the leadership of Sanjay Gandhi but with no legal recognition of compulsion, India's family planning program embarked on a path of coercion that eventually helped to bring down the government. Spurred from above, government officials used force and fraud to drive up success rates on sterilization. In the general elections of 1977, however, family planning became an electoral issue second only to the emergency itself. Mrs. Gandhi was thrown out and replaced by the Janata government. Although Indians did not seem to be rejecting family planning per se, they were outraged at the abuses perpetrated during the emergency. When the new government took office, the prime minister took pains to emphasize that family planning would thenceforth have no element of compulsion. The program did continue but in a much lower key and with a dramatic shift back to voluntarism. Even so, many would-be clients would not go to clinics or other sites of local atrocities during the previous regime. By 1978 few government officials were willing to press the case for birth control.

This, then, is a capsule summary of the eight country studies. More details will follow in later chapters. We turn now to the role of theory and to the ubiquity of donor influence in this field.

3   The centrality of theory

The psychologist Kurt Lewin once said that there is nothing so practical as a good theory. This research suggests that there is nothing so impractical as a bad theory. Every social policy rests on some theory of how individuals, societies, governments, and organizations operate. A good theory is practical because it points to areas of intervention likely to produce the desired results, correctly indicates how those results can be brought about, and warns of undesired consequences. A bad theory is impractical in that it provides no guidance or the wrong guidance on points of intervention, sheds no light or the wrong light on the dynamics of change, and overlooks or mispredicts harmful side effects of interventions. Policies built on sound theories may fail because of barriers to implementation, but they stand some chance of success at the beginning. Policies based on no theory or erroneous theories usually fail, no matter how open the implementation track.[1]

The country studies aptly illustrate the pitfalls of poor theories of planned change. Beclouding the possibility of sound theory was deep confusion and manifest equivocation about the purposes of family planning programs. Were they a means of helping individuals to exercise freedom of reproductive choice, or were they disguised instruments of government control? When theory did enter, it tripped over questionable assumptions about the general conditions of fertility decline and about the role of family planning programs in that process. And once family planning programs were installed, they all worked from an implicit theory of how organizations do and should operate. A brief review of these domains of theory will set the stage for the more detailed analysis of implementation in later chapters.

CONFUSION OF PURPOSE

National governments and international donors have been ambivalent, uncertain, and often devious about the purpose of population policies. The equivocation begins with the term "population policy" itself. Governments and donors regularly proclaim that this term is not synonymous with family planning programs and that it can embrace a variety of other initiatives. Yet a close look at what governments do shows that, in most cases, the heart of population policy is birth control and that other elements are either introduced to diminish its prominence or not implemented. Several of the present cases show that governments expanded the scope of population policy only in the

31

face of criticisms about excessive attention to birth control and then gave little funding or real attention to the new elements. In the 1970s both Egypt and the Philippines announced efforts to integrate family planning programs with other efforts to promote development. But neither government was able to bring about such integration, partly because their population units lacked the power necessary to control other development agencies, but largely because there was no real government commitment to the proposed merger.

Even greater confusion surrounds the purpose of family planning programs. Most governments try to advance two objectives through these programs: population control through reduced fertility, and individual welfare through the provision of voluntary family planning services. In all the relevant cases covered here, the government's foremost reason for establishing family planning programs was to bring down the birth rate. Donor agencies supporting the programs were typically even stronger advocates of population control. Yet when policies were presented to the public, national leaders almost always billed them as vehicles of welfare and played down the control theme. This is understandable, for people the world over prefer freedom to control, especially in reproduction. But beyond the rhetoric of presentation, in the 1960s and early 1970s donors and governments alike were confident that freedom for individuals and control for the state were fully compatible. According to the prevailing theory of fertility decline, women of reproductive age were already motivated to practice birth control and lacked only the means. If family planning programs provided these means, women would accept them, put them to good use, and thereby bring down the birth rate. In a happy convergence of private choice and public good, government actions to promote social control would actually enhance individual liberty.

But individual motives and public policies did not mesh. As the results of family planning programs fell far short of even realistic targets, the issue of welfare versus control did arise, sometimes violently. Caught between their intentions and their rhetoric, government officials began to divorce public proclamation from program action. They insisted ever more loudly that the purpose of family planning programs was individual and family welfare rather than population control. At the same time, program administrators went on acting as they had all along, and they sometimes moved even closer to outright control.

Kenya and the Philippines nicely exemplify both the dilemma and its practical resolution. The Kenyan government's initial decision to set up a family planning program was premised on the need to bring down the birth rate. As late as 1972, an official from the Ministry of Economic Planning and Development stated to the press that "Kenyans must believe in family planning if the explosion of population growth is to be checked, serious unemployment contained, and general economic growth stepped up."[2] Yet not long after the family planning program was established, in 1966, the government received a barrage of criticism for talking of control. Politicians raised the specter of genocide and lambasted birth control as an outcropping of neocolonialism. Religious leaders and intellectuals charged that whereas the notion of child spacing was well established in African culture, the concept of birth limitation was foreign. Others saw evidence of a plot by one ethnic group to limit the size of its rivals. Even the minister of health, who was at first enthusiastic about the new program, quickly backed away from any implications of control. Gradually family planning officials began to handle the dilemma of welfare versus control by compartmentalization. Privately they admitted that the basic purpose of the program, and the reason that it was so generously funded by foreign donors, was to lower the birth rate. Publicly they affirmed that its aim was to promote maternal and child health.

The gap between public declaration and the reality of the program was even greater in the Philippines. Faced with continual challenges from Roman Catholic clerics on the question of coercion, Filipino leaders issued soothing affirmations about freedom. At the same time, the government's family planning program was under pressure for results from its principal donor, AID. Hence, while they gave public assurances that voluntarism was the order of the day, program officials established acceptor and method quotas for fieldworkers and urged them to motivate clients for the so-called more effective methods (sterilization, pill, and IUD).

This seesawing between control and welfare stirred suspicions about family planning programs. Politicians intercepted the mixed signals and unscrambled them in the light of their own interests. Religious leaders, often skeptical about government intentions and wary of birth control, warned their followers about the perils of contraception. Ordinary people, including potential clients, were suspicious that here, as elsewhere, things were seldom what they seemed. And not least, program planners and donor representatives became so engrossed in moving their merchandise that they did not step back to reflect on their basic theory of marketing. In the end, confusion of purpose proved to be the nondoing or the undoing of more than one family planning program.

FERTILITY DECLINE AND FAMILY PLANNING PROGRAMS

What was the theory behind the conventional family planning program? The theory to be reviewed flowed from two key premises: that rapid population growth retards economic development and the government's ability to supply public services; and that a reduction in the rate of population growth facilitates economic development and the provision of public services. According to the first premise, a high rate of demographic growth prevents increases in per capita income, creates unemployment, reduces food supplies, and, by siphoning off resources for other purposes, hinders the government's ability to provide housing, schools, sanitation, and similar services. Debate on this argument is complex and need not be reviewed here.[3] The critical point is that both premises were widely accepted by recipient countries and international donors when family planning programs were being developed. The second proposition is an extension of the first: If the dampening effect of rapid growth is removed, the forces for economic development will be stronger. This is not a tautology, for it does not necessarily follow that a reduction in the birth rate will spur more economic growth or increased public services. For instance, by reducing fertility or by doing so differentially across ethnic groups, a country might aggravate political tensions, which in turn might set off domestic conflicts requiring larger expenditures on internal security.

Leading directly to the creation of family planning programs was an added assumption about the links between government action and economic development: that the most effective way to reduce population growth is to provide voluntary family planning services. In the developing countries, individuals are already motivated to limit birth but lack the means to do so. When these means are supplied, the eligible population will use them and thereby control fertility. The best way to provide such means is through a large-scale voluntary family planning program.

Beguiling in its simplicity and appealing in its politics, this master idea was sold to the developing countries as the answer to their population problems. But even simple ideas need to be fleshed out before they can be implemented, and it was here that pivotal assumptions about organization began to be added. Before long, international donors and their national counterparts had worked out an embodied theory of how family planning programs should be introduced, organized, and executed. Running the gamut from the measurement of motivation to the final delivery of services, this theory was exported to dozens of developing countries and became the foundation for the typical family planning program. The core elements can be summarized in twelve propositions, the first six dealing with individuals and the remaining six with programs.

1. *Irrespective of their social, cultural, and economic circumstances, women of reproductive age want to limit their fertility.* This is the assumption of universal demand. In all regions of every country, women of child-bearing age want to have fewer children than they would have without some kind of fertility control. This assumption is clearly stated in the 1966 annual report of the Population Council, the leading organization in developing and promulgating the present theory:

It is often argued that in the traditional societies people are not really ready for or interested in family planning. The experience of the council is that people are amazingly ready and that the difficulty lies in the failure of governmental personnel to realize that fact.[4]

Thus illiteracy, poverty, fatalism, pressures from relatives to have a large family, the notion that one is not fully a man or a woman without many offspring – these and other contextual factors may increase or decrease the basic desire, but that desire will still be present among most individuals everywhere.

2. *The motivation to limit fertility can be accurately measured through survey research.* Although most people want to practice birth control, there will be enough variation to merit research on levels of interest. Such variations can be measured within reasonable limits by the Knowledge–Attitude–Practice (KAP) survey. With generous support from international donors, hundreds of these surveys were carried out in the developing countries. Their methodology ranged from acceptable to atrocious, with the average inclining toward the latter. Although they were ostensibly concerned with gauging demand, these surveys often had the latent purpose of persuading national leaders that family planning was the people's choice. According to one eminent practitioner, "The most important function of (KAP) surveys is similar to any market research project: to demonstrate the existence of a demand for goods and services, in this case birth control."[5] In a set of guidelines for establishing national programs, Bernard Berelson, later president of the Population Council, was quite explicit about the political value of KAP data:

A survey should probably be done at the outset of any national program – partly for its evaluational...use but also for its political use, in demonstrating to the elite that the people themselves strongly support the program and in demonstrating to the society at large that family planning is generally approved.[6]

Chapter 7 will argue that the KAP survey was often methodologically misguided and sometimes a travesty of social science research. By ignoring the cultural context of reproductive decisions it violated rules of survey research known at the time and produced results that were profoundly misleading. Yet partly on the basis of such flawed data national programs were erected to satisfy the "demonstrated" demand for family planning services.

3. *People motivated to limit fertility will take action to carry out their desire.* Most family planning programs were premised on the idea that individuals who want a certain end state will act in ways necessary to produce that state. This rationalistic assumption, which violates fifty years of research on human motivation, was not borne out in practice.[7] Two flaws in logic are worth noting. One is the general premise that people who want something will act to get it. Human beings have innumerable wants, needs, desires, and wishes, but they work to obtain relatively few of them. If the barriers to action are formidable for everyone, they are doubly so for the very poor in the developing countries. For individuals who have little objective control over their lives and who feel that their destiny is shaped by God's will or by fate, the idea of planned action to implement one's goals may seem preposterous if it is considered at all. In the case of birth control, a second fallacy is that people will overcome any and all obstacles to realize their desires. Whether or

not they need children to work on their farms, whether or not their mothers-in-law badger them to have a son nine months after marriage, whether or not their husbands will send them home if they are not fertile, women will make the leap from wish to action on family planning. That some women go to heroic lengths to limit fertility does not negate the fact that many do not. Chapter 7 explores some of the reasons why simple attributions of rationality in action are theoretically and empirically mistaken.

4. *People acting to limit fertility will make use of organized family planning services.* Individuals who feel the pinch of unwanted fertility not only will act to do something about it but also will act by using family planning services when they are provided. The 1966 annual report of the Population Council reflects this assumption:

A substantial majority of couples want to limit the number of their children and experience with pilot projects has demonstrated that they will come for help to any well-organized family planning service even in the face of surprisingly adverse situations. There is no dearth of patients whenever a reasonable service of information, supplies and medical assistance is available.[8]

Later chapters and other studies provide overwhelming evidence that family planning services are not always eagerly embraced by waiting clients. Motivators in rural areas are often given quotas of acceptors – itself a sad commentary on client interest – and even with diligent work may not meet them. The reasons why motivated people may not accept the services offered are many, including resistance to the impersonality of the typical clinic, unwillingness to disrobe before a male doctor, fears of side effects, distrust of anything coming from the government, and the inconvenience of travel and clinic schedules.

5. *Individuals not motivated to practice family planning can be made interested through information–education–communication (IEC) programs.* In the guiding theory of family planning, no one is considered unreachable. IEC programs typically beam their messages at three kinds of individuals: the uninformed – those who want to practice birth control but do not know how to do so; the holdouts – those who do want to limit fertility and are aware of services provided but will not accept them; and the unmotivated – those who, for whatever reason, lack the requisite interest. The first group needs information about the opportunities available and perhaps assurance that the methods are safe. The holdouts need to be persuaded of the value or safety of the services; for example, to be convinced that the pill does not cause cancer. The unmotivated need even stronger persuasion to show them that family planning is in their interest. A crucial element, and a critical flaw, in the IEC approach is its assumption that change can be brought about by messages to individuals. Like the broader theory of which it is a part, the IEC component sees the situation in which individual people find themselves as either irrelevant or immutable. In its most blatant form, it tries to bypass developmental changes,

such as reduced infant mortality and higher income, by trying to convince destitute people of the objective benefits of smaller families – even when no such benefits exist. Sometimes such messages have an effect, but most often they fail when other conditions are not ripe for change.

6. *Individuals who once make use of modern family planning methods will continue to use them until they no longer need them.* The prevailing theory of the 1960s was astonishingly optimistic about the continued use of family planning services, and for a long while the problem of dropouts was not even seriously discussed. Birth-control methods were supposed to have such universal value that, once discovered, they would be used until the underlying problem disappeared. In a field dominated by demographers and medical doctors, little credence was given the idea that perceptions of birth control methods would be vitally influenced by traditional notions of health and illness, economic insecurities, and even witchcraft. The scene changed only after large numbers of users – sometimes more than half of those who started in a program – dropped out. A closer look showed that these defections often followed adverse physical reactions to pills and IUDs, fears about the dangers of contraceptives for both mothers and children, revulsion against the impersonality of clinics, and contrary advice from midwives, mothers, mullahs, and other trusted sources in the community. To make matters worse, in many countries the most potent assault on continuation came from that most elusive of sources, rumor. Unable to attack openly, detractors took to whispers, insinuation, and tale telling. Chapter 11 shows that many clients tried family planning and found it wanting, often because of insensitivity at the point of delivery.

Whereas the first six propositions deal with the motivations and behavior of individuals, the rest have to do with the development and execution of family planning programs. Concerning individuals, there are many writings illustrating each of the propositions stated, most notably the journal *Studies in Family Planning* and other publications of the Population Council in the 1960s. At the level of programs, explicit statements of theory and concept are sparse. Hence the following propositions are based more on what program designers did and did not do than on what they said they were doing.

7. *In developing population policies product is more important than process.* What emerges as policy is more important than how that policy is generated. Although in different countries there were marked variations in the degree to which the process of policy formulation was taken seriously, most countries and most international donors seemed far more concerned with the what than the how of policy. Yet as the next chapter shows, defects in process impeded more than one program. The heavy input of international donors, coupled with the failure to touch local political bases, created widespread perceptions that Kenya's population policy was foreign in origin and inspira-

tion. Egypt's overnight decision to add family planning to the country's existing health services also did little to foster understanding and commitment among health workers. Overall, the country studies reveal that process is linked to the initial legitimacy and ultimate implementation of population policies.

8. *Population policies are best developed by the central government.* Most policy makers and their international advisers assumed that population policies should be worked out by central authorities with little participation from local constituencies. This belief reflected the conventional wisdom in public administration, which saw the central government as the proper locus of policy making. But also at work was the belief that on a matter as sensitive as birth control the fewer the decision makers the better. In Kenya, open discussions might become a forum for debates about tribalism; in Mexico, they would almost certainly stir controversy about church–state relations. Donor agencies likewise favored centralized decision making, partly to avoid needless delay and controversy and partly because donor representatives had their best and sometimes their only contacts in the capital city. Centralization did have the advantage of speed, but its cost in several countries was insensitivity to varying cultural contexts and the alienation of individuals critical to implementation.

9. *Family planning programs should be mounted with standard parts and uniform methods of assembly.* In the formative period of the 1960s, the literature spoke of a semistandard "family planning delivery system," usually built in or around a health clinic. Standardization had the twin advantages of ready applicability to all parts of a country and smooth integration into an existing bureaucracy. Clinics could be built almost anywhere, staffed with doctors, nurses, and other health professionals, and fitted into the organizational structure and operating procedures of the Ministry of Health. Donors also liked the standardized approach, for it allowed large loans and grants to be made for familiar kinds of construction and promised rapid diffusion of services to the countryside. The question of whether such uniformity was the best way to reach rural populations was rarely raised in the 1960s. Only later, when the clinic-based system showed serious deficiencies, were more flexible approaches tried.

10. *In the development and implementation of population policies sociocultural and economic contexts are largely irrelevant.* Governments often did recognize that political and related historical contexts had a bearing on the viability of population policies. The same cannot be said for sociocultural and economic contexts. The typical program was developed and implemented as if the occupations and income levels of clients made no difference and cultural variations within the country could be disregarded. Tailoring family planning programs to local understandings, traditions, or economic realities was almost never considered. One reason was that such adaptation would reduce both

centralization and standardization: How could one have a stock delivery system that was different in each cultural region? But the main reason that the notion of regional tailoring was given short shrift was that it was considered unnecessary. If people are already motivated to control their fertility and lack only the means to do so, why bother with minor details about how those means are to be delivered?

11. *Once harnessed to the structures of government, family planning programs can be implemented through the force of top-down authority.* The machine model of program design was logically tied to the machine model of implementation, which will be discussed in the next section. The guiding notion was that the foremost requisites for successful execution are a sound policy; an efficient administrative apparatus, such as the national health bureaucracy; and clear directives from above. No credence or even much thought was given to the possibility that the minister in charge might not believe in family planning (as happened in Kenya), that clinic directors might be caught between pressures from superiors and the expectations of local leaders, or that field implementers are human beings whose personal values and needs for self-esteem might influence their willingness to carry out orders from above. Typically, national administrators issued orders fully believing that the weight of their authority, bolstered by effective monitoring and control systems, would be enough to bring about implementation. Yet in several cases this authority lost its impetus within a few kilometers of the national family planning headquarters.

12. *The paramount need of clients is for modern family planning services; other needs are either secondary or irrelevant.* The tensions between population control and individual welfare were most acute in decisions about how to deal with client needs. For instance, how much attention should program personnel pay to client concerns about the side effects of contraceptives? From the standpoint of control, time spent on side effects is largely wasted. In practice, most clinic workers covered by this study struck a compromise that favored control over welfare but that made some concessions to the latter. They were generally willing to provide assistance with overtly medical difficulties, such as bleeding from the IUD, but not with psychological reactions such as fears about cancer or a generalized feeling of weakness. The tendency to dismiss such complaints arose from several causes: a medical rationalism that sees the only real problems as those of a directly physical nature; the paternalistic belief that the staff knows what is best for clients; and more immediately, from piecework incentive systems and pressures for results. The overwhelming impression left by this research and the literature of the 1960s is that client needs for anything other than birth control counted for very little. Chapter 11 shows that such narrow treatment of clients was counterproductive even for population control.

THE MACHINE THEORY OF IMPLEMENTATION

A final area of theory has to do with the implementation of population programs. The guiding approach adopted in many countries can fairly be called
the machine theory of implementation. This theory views implementation as a
quasi-mechanical exercise in which organizational units and individual
implementers form a delivery system and program clients become receptacles
for the services delivered.

A curious feature of machine theory is that, although it is widely espoused
in principle, it is almost always diluted in practice. In designing organization
charts and drawing up program specifications, administrators the world over
use the metaphor of machine, sometimes lightly, sometimes heavily. Individuals enter the system not as persons but as incumbents of positions. These
positions are articulated to produce efficient action toward a specified goal.
Hierarchies are established to provide the requisite articulation; and rules are
written to ensure standardization of parts and operation. Managers speak of
the goods to be moved and the services to be delivered by means of the
system. The cruder adherents of machine theory talk about cranking elements
into the system or pulling levers to get action at the other end. At the same
time, few managers really act as if the machine model were sufficient to bring
about implementation. But the important point here is that many designers
and managers of population programs do take the machine metaphor seriously, and some come close to accepting it in pure form.

This discussion presents machine theory as an ideal type, in the sense used
by Max Weber. According to Weber, "an ideal type is formed by the one-sided
accentuation of one or more points of view and by the synthesis of a great many
diffuse, discrete, more or less present and occasionally absent individual phe-
nomena."[9] Although it is rarely or never encountered in pure form, the ideal
type nevertheless includes characteristics that are examplary or prototypical in
that sphere of action. Hence if the machine model described here does not exist
anywhere in the form indicated, the model does contain elements that are
present to some degree in many programs. Few managers subscribe completely
to its precepts, but the very fact that machine theory is held up as a model and
used as a metaphor suggests its potential influence. When in doubt about how
to design a family planning program, a government official may unconsciously
draw on the model that is closest at hand, and when under attack for poor
results administrators may tighten up the system with guidance from machine
theory. The following are the four major components of this ideal type.

Basic structure

An implementation machine is a set of organizational positions designed to
attain certain preordained goals, such as the delivery of family planning

services. Like all machines, it produces force and controls the direction and motion of that force but cannot generate energy. The required energy is supplied by laws, policies, executive orders, or other manifestations of legitimate authority. Individuals enter the system as incumbents of positions. Like the teeth on a spur gear, they are interchangeable and replaceable. An efficient administrative machine should be designed so that employees can be replaced without special attention to quirks of personality or other idiosyncrasies. Once he or she is in the system, the employee's task is to move in the ways indicated by rules, regulations, and instructions from superiors.

The implementation machine should be judged by two basic criteria: effectiveness and efficiency. Effectiveness is attained when the apparatus yields the results necessary for meeting the goals set by the organization, such as a given number of family planning accepters. Efficiency is the ratio of the resources put in and the resulting output. Inefficiency arises from defective parts, such as family planning workers who do not know their jobs; from slippage in the connection among parts, such as poor coordination in a family planning clinic; and from friction, such as that produced by workers overlapping on the same job. The task of the manager is to remove all correctable sources of inefficiency and to provide the lubrication necessary to keep the machine going.

The machine should be structured to attain the maximum feasible effectiveness and efficiency. The science of organizational mechanics argues for two structural features: a vertical hierarchy and straight-line connections. A vertical hierarchy is the proven means for ensuring that all parts in the machine work toward a common goal. With a clearly specified chain of command, slippage is reduced, coordination facilitated, quality control maintained, and friction minimized. The main advantages of straight-line connections are clear accountability and efficiency of communication. In bureaucracies, as elsewhere, the straight line is the shortest distance between two points. Circuitous communications and information networks are not only inefficient but also subversive of the chain of command. These two organizational principles come together in the typical organization chart, which has units structured by hierarchical levels and connected by straight lines.

Machine theory notwithstanding, this study suggests that effective implementation demands at least as much horizontal as vertical communication, that some of the transactions most critical to program success fall outside the chain of command, and that key interactions are more often serpentine or circular than rectilinear. These points are taken up in Chapter 10.

Management

And what is the task of management? In orthodox versions of machine theory, the word *management*, which carries overtones of initiative and flexibility, would not appear at all. Instead we would find the term *administration*, which suggests doing what one is told by superiors. The basic task of administrators is to make the decisions and give the orders necessary to move their parts of the machine. The administrator at the top of the hierarchy takes a policy and translates it into a workable set of actions to be carried out by the machine. Supervisors at lower levels do essentially the same thing, but with decreasing scope for judgment. The basic direction of movement is from the top down, but room is left for communication from the bottom up. If the driving force is orders from above, the essential lubricants are instructions on the details of implementation and close supervision. Friction is reduced by showing implementers precisely how their positions fit together and by monitoring their actions to ensure compliance with orders. Employee motivation to obey can be assumed, but it is also inconstant and thus in need of reinforcement by careful supervision. In short, good administration means doing all that is necessary to ensure faithful performance of the actions ordered by those at the top. A turn of the crank by the head office should produce roughly the same amount of motion in the same direction at each level to which those gears are connected.

This gearbox model of administration surfaced in several of the country studies, most notably in the Philippines:

There is a high degree of centralization in decision-making among family planning agencies. The strong authoritarian orientation of Filipinos supports this type of structure where agency heads (and not only those in population) make decisions for all but minor details. Lower level personnel also depend on higher authorities for decision-making and comply with their decisions to avoid error.[10]

Machine theory does not rule out administrative discretion but allocates it in direct proportion to an employee's authority in the hierarchy. Officials at the top have the greatest scope for interpretation, for they are in the best position to see how the machine can be used to execute policy. Employees at the bottom need little discretion. It is their lot to be moved rather than to move.

Implementers

The doctors, nurses, motivators, and midwives on the front lines of family planning are left in an odd position by machine theory. They are portrayed as the terminal gears in a delivery apparatus. Their movements are to be programmed, their time clocked, and their progress charted by standard procedures. Where it is recognized at all, field discretion is considered a necessary evil, an expedient required by constraints on efficient organization. Yet in practice, field implementers must use considerable ingenuity in delivering the family planning product. Because they are outside the organization, potential accepters are often difficult to locate and even more difficult to convince about the merits of birth control. Only rarely are they waiting at the end of the delivery system. Hence implementers are defined by machine theory as standard parts in a bureaucratic instrument whereas they expected to act as flexible agents in the pursuit of program goals. Chapter 10 shows that machine theory was very much in evidence in several family planning programs and that it clashed sharply with the human situation in which implementers found themselves. Understanding how field personnel handled the tensions between standardization and discretion will provide an important key to the appreciation of implementation realities.

Clients

If implementers are the gears moving the belts of service transmission, clients are the receptacles into which the products are dropped. The term "accepter" itself suggests passive receipt of goods delivered by others. After an initial assessment of aggregate holding capacity through the KAP survey, the system is activated to deliver set quantities of the family planning product to the waiting receivers. Should holding capacity fall below the amounts specified by the production targets, it can be enlarged through information–education–communication programs. Resistance arising from anxiety, fear, or shame can be overcome through such lubricants as interpersonal persuasion. And if, as in India during the Emergency, the pressure to deliver is substantially greater than the capacity to receive, the product can be forced into the receptacles by any means available.

This image of the client as receptacle has two key implications for program design. First, the delivery system should be structured so that accepters come to the supply points to collect the product. Programs requiring delivery agents to locate accepters are not only inefficient but also hard to control through standard bureaucratic means. (How can you supervise a family planning fieldworker who rides around the countryside on a motorcycle?) Because according to the guiding theory of fertility control individuals are already motivated to use family planning, a delivery system constructed in this way should be viable. Second, the delivery system need not and probably should not pay attention to the personal needs and social context of service recipients. An efficient program should concern itself with getting the product to the accepter and not with the accepter's worries about the product. Client fears and cultural norms may well be a source of friction, but it is not the task of the family planning engineer to redesign the system to remove that friction.

The statement of machine theory presented here is an ideal type. In none of the country programs did it appear in pure form, but in none was it completely absent. The main use of the model is to suggest a major source of tension and obstacles to implementation in family planning program. As later chapters show, the greatest single problem faced by several programs was reconciling the dictates of machine theory with the demands of common sense. The negotiations made and the compromises reached in this struggle provide grist for the transactional model of implementation presented in Chapter 12.

4   The ubiquity of donors

International donors have had an incalculable effect on the origins, shape, and direction of population programs in the developing countries. Of all the spheres of national development, population has been the most donor driven. Governments do not usually have to be prodded hard to grow more food or to build more roads, but many had to be persuaded to act on population control. Toward that end, dozens of donors stepped in with grants, loans, scholarships, advisers, exhortations, backstage deals, and even clandestine interventions.

The specific areas of donor impact included the initial idea that the country had a population problem – something that was not evident to many governments; the precise definition given to that problem; the broad strategies used for dealing with the problem, such as voluntary family planning programs; the number, location, and organizational structure of population agencies; the strategies they followed in pursuing their mission, including the promotion of specific family planning methods or the use of targets; the kinds of personnel used at all levels; the level of commitment from top to bottom; the criteria used in judging programmatic success of failure; and the program's image in the country. Donor influence is not unique to population programs, but it is especially important in this area because of the domestic delicacy of birth control and the perceptual links between foreign influence on that matter and such broad political issues as genocide and neocolonialism.

Population donors differ greatly in their size, style, and impact. Some organizations, including the Agency for International Development and the Ford Foundation, were primary in almost all respects. Not only did they have a substantial direct impact through their own work in the developing countries, but they supported many other organizations as well. Others, such as CARE, worked mainly on other aspects of development but accepted funds for small programs related to population. Still others, most notably the Pathfinder Fund, were distinguished less by their size and funding power than by the speed and boldness of their initiatives abroad. To convey a sense of the diversity and yet coherence of donor activities, this chapter considers three main-line agencies with unquestionable impact in many countries and then the donor underground, which is made up of agencies that supply aid for abortion. This discussion blends the author's own research on donor agencies with material from the country studies. The primary focus is on donor activities between 1960 and 1976, the formative period for the programs under review, but where possible material will be added on more recent developments.[1]

THREE MAIN-LINE AGENCIES

During the 1960s and 1970s the main-line agencies for population assistance were the Agency for International Development (AID), the World Bank, the Ford Foundation, the Population Council, the International Planned Parenthood Federation (IPPF), and, especially in the 1970s, the United Nations Fund for Population Activities (UNFPA). Many other donors were involved in population work, some with major impact, but these names would appear on almost anyone's list of influential agencies. The three chosen for analysis here – AID, the Ford Foundation, and the Population Council – differed in many ways, but all were important for the development of population policy in the countries covered here. These agencies can fruitfully be compared by considering their respective origins, mission, strategies, values, and value conflicts. An understanding of their internal dynamics and their own interrelationships leads to a better appreciation of their transactions in the developing countries.

AID

If one had to pick the donor agency with the strongest total impact on population programs in the developing countries, the choice would be AID. Not only was AID a vigorous promoter in its own right, it also bought into and used numerous intermediaries. In the early 1970s AID contributed about half the budget of the International Planned Parenthood Federation (IPPF) and the UNFPA, over 90 percent of the funds for the Pathfinder Fund, and substantial amounts to the Population Council, Church World Service, Family Planning International Assistance, university programs in population, and other organizations. And AID was not timid about using its funding leverage to promote desired action by these recipients. The following discussion deals with AID mainly from 1966 through 1976. Significant changes made after 1976 will be noted later.

Background. The major impetus for establishing a strong population unit in AID came from a coalition of congressmen and outside lobbyists rather than the agency itself.[2] In the early 1960s officials in both AID and the State Department were nervous about moving into population assistance. From the beginnings of foreign aid after World War II until that time, the prevailing attitude was that birth control was not the business of government. The two individuals who spearheaded the campaign for government action, Senator Ernest Gruening and General William Draper, were both from outside the executive branch. In 1959 a presidential committee headed by Draper had recommended specific action on population "in order to meet more effectively the problems of economic development."[3] The Draper committee report and lobbying by private groups did bring attention to the population question, but it was not until congressional hearings in the mid-sixties that barriers to population aid began to drop.

Piotrow argues that "no single government undertaking had greater impact in publicizing birth control as a legitimate public policy issue in the mid-sixties than the Senate subcommittee hearings chaired by Senator Gruening."[4] Over three years (1965–8) Gruening called in 120 witnesses, including Draper, John D. Rockefeller III, and almost every major figure from the population lobby. Aided by activities in the House and the Senate, these hearings did help to change the climate of opinion about voluntary birth control.

In 1967 Congress added Title X, Programs Relating to Population Growth, to the Foreign Assistance Act. Three individuals were particularly influential in facilitating this move: General Draper, who was ubiquitous on all matters relating to birth control; Reimert T. Ravenholt, the recently appointed director of AID's population activities; and Philander Claxton, the special assistant for population in the State Department. Together they formed a triangle linking the State Department, AID, and the population control lobby, led by Draper. Not only did the bill pass and Congress authorize $35 million for population assistance, but the funds were earmarked for this sole purpose. The AID administrator objected to this decision, fearing that the agency could not properly spend $35 million on population in the time specified. But Draper prevailed then and later, and Ravenholt was given a secure base of funds that could not be diverted by the AID administration. From then until his death in 1974, Draper continued to be the leading and most effective advocate of increased budgets and earmarked funds for population.

With a clear mandate and a generous helping of funds, the population unit lost no time in seeking outlets for spending. At the same time, it created antipathies in AID. Many saw the population division as a nouveau riche intruder and Ravenholt as an arriviste upstart whose power base was outside the agency.[5] Senior administrators resented the independence provided by earmarked funds and Ravenholt's brashness in using that independence, and the economists in the Bureau of Program and Policy Coordination were never fully converted to family planning. Mission directors in AID's overseas offices also complained of pressures to sell family planning in settings where the subject was still delicate. But whatever the ambivalences, Ravenholt's unit pushed ahead.

Mission. AID's Office of Population had a single mission: to reduce the levels of fertility in the developing countries. The principal means of attaining this mission was voluntary family planning. Because some countries were not in a political, social, or economic position to undertake family planning activities, AID was prepared to help them move in that direction through research or other means, but the ultimate objective was still fertility reduction.

The population unit's mission was premised on a simple definition of the population problem: that demographic growth retards economic development and needlessly eats up foreign aid. An AID report stated in 1973:

Population growth in the past decade has already limited or threatens to reduce to futility key development actions in a number of LDC's [less-developed countries]. This growth, unless checked, may prove to be one of mankind's chief limiting factors, leading to exhaustion of resources, overcrowding, inflation, breakdown in services, idleness of large numbers of people, frustration, demoralization, unrest, tension and warfare.[6]

Dozens of other reports emphasized the detrimental consequences of population growth for economic development.

Programs. AID's population program rested on two main assumptions: that population growth can be brought down by voluntary means and that the most effective voluntary means is the direct provision of family planning services to interested clients. As a senior official put it in a 1975 interview: "At this point in time in every country there are couples and individuals who want to control their fertility and would use means of fertility control if given access to them."[7]

AID's spending priorities reflected its belief in the efficacy of birth control. In 1973, 47 percent of its budget of over $125 million went into the delivery of family planning services. This category included contraceptives, experiments on low-cost delivery systems, training, and technical assistance. In second place with 12 percent of the budget was staff and institutional development, partly in the United States but mostly in the developing countries. The development of adequate demographic and social data came next, with 8 percent, followed by contraceptive research, which also received 8 percent. AID devoted 7 percent of its budget to work on population policy and population dynamics and another 7 percent to information, education, and communication programs related to family planning. Although the population unit often affirmed that there was great unmet demand for birth control, it also believed that at least some people must be educated before they become accepters. Finally, 4 percent of AID's resources for 1973 went to the UNFPA and 7 percent to support the central office in Washington.

Strategies. The population unit was far from a lifeless bureaucracy pursuing its mission by the force of authority. It was an entity defined as much by its leader as by its legislation, and one that quickly made its mark in the bureaucracy. With secure funding inside and powerful backing outside AID, Reimert Ravenholt forged an organizational strategy that was as controversial as it was consequential.

A focal element in the Ravenholt strategy was program autonomy for population. As one of his associates put it in an interview, "the best way to deal with population is to deal with population." After the World Population Conference in 1974, AID came under pressure to integrate population and other development activities. Ravenholt saw this move as disastrous. An AID official in the Philippines echoed his belief in this picturesque analogy:

My fundamental worry is that if you integrate family planning into all the other things that need to happen like better health, better nutrition, better maternal and child health, or even agricultural development, cottage industries, liberating roles for women, etc., you run the risk of making what we call Polish horserabbit sausage. You use one horse and one rabbit; the rabbit is family planning, and you don't get much family planning out of that kind of sausage factory.[8]

AID officials in the Philippines specifically objected to the Total Integrated Development Approach (TIDA) devised by the Commission on Population. Although they eventually approved some funds for this purpose, they feared that family planning would be merged into a larger scheme before it was strong enough to stand on its own. Some Washington officials also considered such integration illegal and counterproductive. They felt that Congress intended population funds to be used strictly for population rather than for development activities covered by other parts of the AID budget. One senior administrator said that, as there was not enough money to meet existing demand for family planning, "why should we waste it on other activities?" He added that the health route to family planning was very slow, and that AID had been supporting health programs for over thirty years without much visible impact on population. If anything, health activities aggravated the problems by lowering death rates. He also noted that it costs about ten times as much to introduce family planning through maternal and child health programs as with a "direct sell" method, so that "if you have only 100 million you don't go the route that is ten times more expensive." His conclusion: "We tend to our own knitting."

A second hallmark of AID's population strategy was promoting contraceptive technology. The population unit classified birth-control methods into five tiers of technology, running from the least to the most effective: (1) abstinence, coitus interruptus, delayed marriage and nonmarriage, crude vaginal barriers, douching, and illegal abortion; (2) the previous methods plus condoms, diaphragms, vaginal chemicals, rhythm, and surgical sterilization; (3) the previous methods plus oral contraceptives and intrauterine devices; (4) the previous methods plus legal surgical abortion; and (5) the previous methods plus "a non-toxic and completely effective substance or method which when self-administered on a single occasion would ensure the non-pregnant state at completion of a monthly cycle."[9] From 1965 to 1976 AID placed high priority on developing "fifth-tier" technology. During this period Ravenholt himself became the world's foremost salesman of contraceptive technology. At open meetings and private gatherings he often caused a stir by pulling multicolored condoms from his pocket, or, before 1974, by demonstrating the use of the "menstrual regulator" kit.

A third element in Ravenholt's strategy was emphasis on results. He and his staff thought that the best way to advance their mission was to show Congress that action was possible in the short run. Hence the population unit pressed funding recipients to provide concrete evidence of performance effectiveness. An official in the Office of Population commented: "Here there is tremendous pressure to show results, and to attribute it to program action." The effects of this output orientation were apparent in the Philippines, where an AID memo stated that

it is of the utmost importance in justifying future AID funding, particularly of local costs, to identify AID funds with promising new initiatives and program acceleration. By contrast, mundane program overhead costs, however necessary, have little appeal to AID/W [Washington] decision-makers and are to be avoided wherever possible as a support component.

As a final incentive to adoption of the proposed target, I would mention the AID/W reaction. We could not ask for better AID/W support to date. But the competition for Title X resources is growing, and it becomes increasingly important to show progress in the only terms which ultimately matter – births averted (or declining growth rate).[10]

An AID official in Manila put the point more simply: "I'm a pragmatist; whatever works gets the money."

As a concrete manifestation of this emphasis on results, AID officials in the Philippines pressed not only for family planning accepters but also for promotion of the more effective methods – sterilization, IUDs, and the pill (in that order). AID's passion for performance did generate results, but it also spurred complaints about heavy-handedness. With obvious reference to AID, an official of the Philippines Commission on Population remarked:

But some of our well-meaning foreign donors and expatriate advisors, though it is not their nation that is at stake, react with greater feeling than we do – or so I have observed. They seem to harbor either fear of failure or genuine impatience with "slow moving success."[11]

Others complained about "nosy Americans sniffing into their operations" and about AID's penchant for "quick and dirty results." Moreover, pressures from AID were passed along the implementation route to the final supply points, where field implementers found themselves caught between demands for results and expectations from self and community (see Chapter 9).

A fourth component of AID's strategy was action through intermediaries. From its earliest days, the population unit saw the constraints on its own operations and the advantages of working through others. AID officials cited IPPF as particularly helpful in this regard. When the population unit could not, for political or bureaucratic reasons, enter a country, it could still channel funds through IPPF to the local family planning association. After the Helms amendment, which prohibited the use of AID funds for abortion, IPPF indirectly supported Ravenholt's desire for action on this front by distributing the vacuum aspirators developed by the agency. Because AID's contributions to IPPF were comingled with funds from other sources, IPPF could claim that AID money was not being used for abortion. Other organizations mentioned by AID officials as helpful to their mission were UNFPA, the Population Council, the Pathfinder Fund, the World Assembly of Youth, World Education, Inc., the Council on Social Work Education, the American Public Health Association, and the American Home Economics Association. In 1975 Ravenholt summarized his view on intermediaries in testimony before the House appropriations subcommittee:

There are many countries where we can move much more quickly and efficiently on a bilateral basis than the multilateral agency is able to move. On the other hand, participation of the multilateral organizations, particularly the U.N. and the IPPF, have been indispensible for the rapid development of population programs during the past decade. Had we not had multilateral activity as well as bilateral, there would have been unfortunate polarization against the United States, particularly. Yet in some ways they are limited in how fast they can move. We need both instruments. It is analagous to the needs of a boxer; he needs both arms.[12]

A final part of AID's strategy was, simply, spending money. The population unit had to convince both Congress and the agency administration that it could make good use of earmarked funds allocated for its activities. If the money could not be spent, claims about the massive demand for family planning would be undercut and AID's senior leadership would have a strong case against earmarking of funds. Ravenholt and his associates rose to the challenge and became the best spenders in AID. During a 1975 interview a staff member remarked: "A core value for the Office of Population is showing that you can spend money faster than other organizations in the field." He added that the spending ethic was often combined with a bias for activism: "Look how quickly we act, how outrageous we dare to be." The pressure to spend sometimes produced a frantic search for new projects and pieces of action in intermediary organizations. Even a few funding recipients found such activism embarassing. The director of a private family planning association in Latin America – someone whose work had profited from AID funds to IPPF – charged the Office of Population with spreading "projectitis."

Value Conflicts: Although there were some differences of opinion within the population unit itself, its main value conflicts involved disagreements with other parts of AID and with groups outside the agency. Even in the 1960s, but especially after the World Population Conference in 1974, critics charged that Ravenholt and AID held simplistic beliefs about the value of contraceptive technology and ignored the broader cultural and developmental context of planned change. In a direct slap at the approach taken by the Office of Population, a 1973 report of a staff survey team to the House committee on foreign affairs made this recommendation: "The United States should broaden its approach to the worldwide population problem by linking family planning, health and nutrition in a coordinated program of assistance for the less developed countries."[13] One of the authors of this report, John Sullivan, later became head of the Asia bureau in AID and was instrumental in Ravenholt's ouster. Ravenholt also came under attack from right-to-life groups for his active support of abortion and from the regional bureaus in AID for excessive enthusiasm about population control in countries that were not ready for it. The key value conflict, then, was between vigorous but narrow action on birth control and a broader, less direct, more nuanced, and longer term view of the problem. Ravenholt held tenaciously to the first view and went down with it in the AID bureaucracy.

Opposition to Ravenholt was present almost from the beginning, but it came to a head during the Carter administration. In 1977 a coalition of internal and external figures worked to rein in the Office of Population and then tried directly to remove Ravenholt as office director. Pieces of responsibility in the population unit were transferred to other bureaus, often in the name of integrating population and development. Ravenholt's immediate superior, Assistant Administrator Sander Levin, asked for his resignation, and when Ravenholt refused to resign, Levin repeated the invitation several times. Levin then sought and obtained the help of Administrator John Gilligan and later Acting Administrator Robert Nooter. On July 2, 1979, Nooter finally sent Ravenholt a letter demoting him from director of the Office of Population at the supergrade rank of GS-18 to supervisory population advisor, Office of Population, at GS-15. After many months of appeals Ravenholt resigned from AID in late 1980 to take a position at the Center for Disease Control.

Ravenholt feels that his downfall was due to hostility from three officials with right-to-life sympathies: John Gilligan, John Sullivan, and Congressman Clement Zablocki, chairman of the House international relations committee.[14] In Ravenholt's view, Sander Levin and his assistants were brought in to execute the will of this trio so that the political-religious connection would not be too obvious. But almost certainly at work was the feeling in AID that Ravenholt had become too powerful and was too difficult to control. Whatever the case, Ravenholt left behind a program that had shaped the paradigms and supplied the materials for family planning programs in dozens of countries. Its mark was indelible.

The Ford Foundation

The major donor most different from AID in its style of operations was the Ford Foundation. Both AID and Ford sought to bring down the birth rates in the developing countries and both supplied funds to other organizations, but there the similarities ended. Whereas AID favored rapid action and short-term results, Ford was open to research and other long-term activities. Whereas

AID pressed funding recipients for concrete evidence of an impact on fertility, Ford allowed them great autonomy. Yet both organizations were effective in pursuing their objectives.

Background. During the 1950s and early 1960s the Ford Foundation was the largest single source of funds for population activities. Its commitments began with $60,000 in 1952, rose to $1 million in 1957, $4.4 million in 1961, $8.2 million in 1963, and crested at $26 million in 1966. Between 1972 and 1977 the spending leveled off to between $11 and $14 million per year and then dropped even further. Ford is considered a trailblazer in population and family planning, especially for its support of biomedical and social science research and its training activities. Often it was the first donor on the scene but then drew back as more affluent organizations came to the fore. By the late 1970s Ford was no longer a towering presence in the field, but it continued to play a catalytic role in selected areas of assistance.

The initial impetus for the Foundation's entry into population came from its trustees or, more accurately, their wives. Strong urging in this direction came especially from John Cowles, whose wife was a family planning activist. At the beginning, Ford's emphasis was on the values associated with planned parenthood, including family welfare and the liberation of women from excessive childbearing. In 1958 Oscar Harkavy was asked to do something about population to satisfy the trustees. He responded by organizing three conferences: one on demographic data, another on behavioral science research, and a third on reproductive biology. These meetings laid the groundwork for the Foundation's work over the next twenty years. One of the scholars at the conference on reproductive biology was the late Gregory Pincus of the Worcester Foundation for Experimental Biology, the organization most responsible for developing the contraceptive pill. Later Pincus offered a proposal for postdoctoral training at his center, and Ford accepted. This step marked the beginning of Ford's substantial commitment to research on human reproduction and contraceptive technology, a departure from its general policy against medical research.

The other early priority was basic demographic research. Ford's initial funding in this field was heavily skewed toward the United States. That picture began to change when Douglas Ensminger, Ford's representative in India, regularly wrote New York that population was a critical issue for that country and one that should be addressed by the Foundation. Ensminger's urgings led to approval of Ford's largest and most controversial venture in direct technical assistance for family planning. Ford's India effort became a visible pilot project in foreign aid and a training ground for some of the more prominent figures on the population scene. But it also proved to be a bone of contention in India and eventually within the Foundation itself.

Mission. In the 1960s and 1970s Ford's mission in population was to bring about a reduction in population growth as a means of promoting economic development. The chain of reasoning was as follows: The primary aim of the Foundation is to advance human welfare. In the international division, human welfare is best promoted through assistance for national development, and one key area of aid for development is the reduction of population growth. Oscar Harkavy, the Foundation's population officer for over two decades, stated its rationale in these terms:

The concept of development puts major emphasis on improvement of human conditions. Within this context the control of fertility must be considered not only as it affects national economic development, i.e., as it helps increase gross national product per capita, but also as it affects the welfare of the individual family. This focus on individual family welfare is a powerful, and I believe unassailable, rationale for population work, whether in the industrialized or the developing world.[15]

Until the World Population Conference in Bucharest in 1974, Ford paid primary attention to the reduction of fertility and showed little interest in mortality, migration, and other population variables. After Bucharest the Foundation kept its commitment to fertility reduction but became more open to integrated development programs and other indirect means of achieving this goal. In West Africa, for example, it approved the use of population funds for public-health programs on the grounds that family planning alone was not viable in that region.

Activities. Between 1952 and 1973 the Foundation's top spending priority was in reproductive biology and contraceptive development. In second place was training and research activities in population and family planning. Ford provided grants, for instance, to the Population Council, the University of Chicago, the University of Pennsylvania, Cornell University, the University of North Carolina, the Demographic Institute of the University of Indonesia, and the Latin American Demographic Center (CELADE). Third came technical assistance to family planning programs in the United States and abroad. The largest recipients of funds for this purpose were India, Pakistan, and the organizations working with them on family planning. Fourth, Ford supported numerous informational activities, ranging from large general-purpose grants to the Population Reference Bureau to seminars on specific topics held across the world. Among the countries covered by this study, Ford provided grants to the Philippines, India, Mexico, Haiti, Kenya, Egypt, and Lebanon.

Strategies. Although its overall objective was roughly the same as that of AID, Ford's programmatic strategies were strikingly different. Published literature, internal documents, and especially, interviews with Ford officials brought out four elements in the Foundation's population strategy.

The first element was the advancement of knowledge. Of the major donors, Ford consistently took the broadest view about the value of research. It supported studies in nearly every corner of the population domain, from pure research on demographic history to highly applied work on contraceptive development. Its paramount research priority over the years was reproductive biology and contraceptive development, followed by demography and population studies more broadly defined. In the late 1970s it supported research in demographic history, economic factors influencing decisions about family size, motivational aspects of contraceptive use, and the sources and effects of urbanization in the developing countries.[16]

A second strategic approach was to build institutions with strong capabilities in population. Initially, Ford concentrated on American universities and the newly founded Population Council. From 1954 through 1976 the Population Council was the single largest institutional recipient of Ford funds. The Foundation also contributed millions of dollars to a dozen university centers in the United States. By 1968 it could claim that "these and other centers have trained many of the individuals now holding responsible positions in national family planning programs."[17] Beginning in 1968 Ford tried to do the same in the developing countries. By 1977 it had supported twenty-five institutions in Africa, Asia, and Latin America, sometimes directly and sometimes through the institution-building programs of the Population Council.

A strategy that became more important as revenues slumped was catalytic program innovation. Whereas in earlier years Ford could lay out huge sums to start new fields of activity, with diminishing funds in the 1970s, it sought to mobilize the resources of other groups. Respondents spoke of the Foundation's role in "levering funds" and in "filling in holes" left by the larger donors. Asked when the organization felt it had done a good job, one staff member replied: "They are happy when they prove an ability to get new things going, and to get others to support them." As a specific example of such innovation Foundation officials cited the International Committee on the Management of Population Programs (ICOMP). This body grew out of a meeting of managers of national family planning programs and some donor representatives. Ford provided the initial funds to bring the committee into existence and was pleased when other sources later agreed to help.

Fourth, the Foundation emphasized collaborative relationships with other donors. As one official said, "If nobody is interested, you can't do it, but if there is a potential for collaboration with others, we are interested." This preference brought Ford into contact with many agencies, especially the Rockefeller Foundation, the Population Council, and the International Development Research Centre of Canada.

Values and value conflicts. The Ford Foundation is first and foremost a foundation, and it must act as such. It has the distinct advantage of having its own funds, but it must pay attention to style. Frantic campaigns to spend money, crude pressure tactics to produce results, exaggerated claims of accomplishments, and other signs of unbridled entrepreneurship would hardly be acceptable in the community of philanthropists. Moreover, "the Ford Foundation, like other large foundations, justifies its role less by the size of its resources than by the institutional qualities which give it special opportunities for independence, flexibility, persistence, professionalism, speed of action, and the capacity for innovation, experimentation, and action."[18] Central among its organizational values during the period under study were flexibility, continuity, and sensitivity to cultural differences.

Ford showed flexibility by avoiding stock solutions to the "population problem." Although it favored family planning programs, it did not push them aggressively and was open to other action alternatives. As a staff member put it: "The Foundation has a real commitment to decentralization – identifying needs, problems and program opportunities at the field level. We support the idea of having program activities be responsive to local needs and priorities." A review of the programs actually receiving Ford support shows that the Foundation was not open to every possibility but that it was not narrow.

Serving as a counterpoise to flexibility was Ford's belief in program continuity. Because it had its own funds, the Foundation could and did stay with certain institutions and lines of activities. It was not under pressure to take up the latest fashion or to diversify for political reasons. When asked why Ford chose the particular set of population activities it then supported, a senior executive replied:

It had to do with our comparative advantage. One is our willingness, compared with other organizations, to be patient in institution-building and capacity-building. The payoff, if any, is far down the path. We don't have to come before a committee and say what we did last week.

A third value cited by Ford staff was sensitivity to varying cultures and political systems. Many would agree with this observation by a staff member:

I really feel that the Foundation staff are extremely well-informed and culturally sensitive. I can't think of examples where we've pushed things down people's throats or where it was against the culture. We have tried to integrate with the culture.

Aiding cross-cultural sensitivity was the fact that Ford used its own funds, did not take on many gargantuan projects, and was not part of its government's foreign policy apparatus. With a project running $10,000 or $20,000 one can be much more creative and flexible than with one involving a $100 million.

Ford's value conflicts grew from the tension between mission and welfare, between the zeal to improve the human condition and the desire to do so in established ways. Ford entered the population arena with a broad concern about poverty but with some specific ideas about its causes and solutions. Among these was a belief that reducing population growth would promote development and thereby advance welfare. Acting on that belief, the Foundation supported a broad range of activities designed to bring down fertility.

Then, at the World Population Conference in Bucharest, critics challenged the assumptions underlying the Ford strategy and called for a greater integration of population and other development activities. As a philanthropic organization concerned with welfare Ford felt obliged to heed this challenge, but as an institution with certain programmatic responses in place it did not want to change without viable action alternatives. When interviewed two years after the 1974 conference, Ford officials were generally positive about the idea of integration but unsure about what it really meant, how it should be accomplished, and how far it should be carried. The first value conflict, then, was between integration in the interests of welfare and independence for population in the interests of program effectiveness.

A second dilemma concerned reproductive freedom versus birth prevention. The World Population Plan of Action approved at Bucharest stated: "All couples and individuals have the basic right to decide freely and responsibly the number and spacing of their children and to have the information, education, and means to do so." But the same document also called for countries to "ensure that family planning, medical, and related social services aim not only at the prevention of unwanted pregnancies but also at the elimination of involuntary sterility and subfecundity." The balance to be struck between birth control and reproductive freedom posed a genuine ethical quandary for the Ford Foundation. Its initial and continuing reason for being in the field was to bring about a reduction in fertility. Taking steps to aid the infertile would obviously work against that mission. But the Foundation's larger commitment was not to birth control but to human welfare. If the alleviation of sterility was, as many argued, a matter of welfare, the Foundation could not dismiss it as counterproductive. And as a practical matter, in some regions, particularly Africa, providing birth control without some attention to sterility gave family planning programs a bad name. In the late 1970s the Foundation was still ambivalent on this question, but it leaned toward supporting services for infertility when they would enhance the legitimacy of family planning.

Overall the Ford Foundation was one of the most influential and yet least controversial international donors. It played a leading role in drawing world attention to population questions, preparing the ground for national programs, developing new contraceptives, setting the directions for and actually supporting academic research, developing the major training institutions in the field, and facilitating the entry of larger donors such as AID and UNFPA into this field. For various reasons, including declining resources, Ford's involvement in population tapered off at the end of the 1970s. In 1981 the Foundation's president announced that this area of foreign assistance would be ended, partly on the grounds that Ford's contributions were no longer as necessary as in earlier years.

The Population Council

Founded in 1952, the Population Council quickly became the world's most respected organization on questions of population policy in the developing countries. If one were to rate population donors on a scale running from hard to soft sell, AID would be on the hard end, Ford on the soft, and the Population Council somewhere between the two, but closer to Ford than AID. The Council tried to become a global center of knowledge, research, and policy analysis and at the same time to remain open to direct action abroad. It managed to do both, but not without some strain.

Background. The Population Council grew out of the personal concerns of John D. Rockefeller III. During a trip to the Orient after World War II, Rockefeller was struck by the degree to which population growth might affect the destiny of that region. He saw that war had brought with it easy access to the technology of death control, with mortality rates often falling by 50 percent, but that birth rates were remaining constant. In 1952 he called a conference of prominent persons from several fields to consider the impact of population growth on human welfare. After two and one-half days, the group recommended the establishment of a permanent, unofficial, international council working on population at a high level of professional competence and public esteem. Five months later the Population Council was formally incorporated, with Rockefeller as its first president and chairman of the board of trustees. He held the latter position until his death in 1978, and throughout that period he remained a dominant force in the life of the Council.

At the beginning, the Council was little more than a fund, operating with a budget of about $200,000 a year. It started by building research capacity and assisting demographic studies at other institutions, such as Princeton University. Soon it attracted support from the Rockefeller and Ford foundations, which were interested in population but chary of launching their own programs. As its budget hit $1 million a year, the Council added biomedical research to its demographic studies, with a strong emphasis on developing better contraceptives.

Beginning around 1958, the Council came under pressure to provide technical assistance. A former staff member observed: "The Council got into technical assistance by default; it filled a vacuum left by a refusal of the UN, WHO, the U.S., etc. to get involved." As requests for assistance poured in, the Council took one external and one internal step. Externally it tried to promote international public health as a discipline, with emphasis on family planning administration. Internally it created a separate Technical Assistance Division. This unit soon became the largest area of revenue and expenditure in the organization, and a prime source of value conflicts.

The Council's widening circle of activities was matched by a growing budget. The figure rose from $200,000 in 1953 to $15.5 million in 1974. The main contributors to the Council, which had no independent funds, were the Ford Foundation, the Rockefeller Foundation, the Rockefeller Brothers Fund, John D. Rockefeller III, the Scaife/May family, and other foundations. The Council also received large amounts from AID, which at one point accounted for 32 percent of its budget, and later from UNFPA.

Mission. The mission of the Population Council was to promote knowledge and action leading to a reduction in fertility. The main conception of a population problem in early Council documents was excessive demographic growth. Other aspects of population policy, such as migration, distribution, mortality, and morbidity, received only slight emphasis. In 1968 Frank Notestein, then Council president, summarized the trustees' views in these terms:

Believing as they did that the mounting tempo of growth among the world's poorest people represented a major threat to social-economic development, to political stability, and indeed to human freedom, they were concerned with problems of population growth at home and abroad.[19]

Although the Council was always committed to the reduction of population growth and carried out few activities that were not somehow related to that end, it adopted no single set of means. In its first years the organization thought that its greatest contribution was in demographic and biomedical research as well as in the sponsorship of training. Its operational goals in that period were to promote public awareness of population issues and to legitimate discussions about family planning. In the 1960s the Council shifted from a predominantly research role to a mixture of research and advocacy. During this period the organization came to espouse one particular means of limiting demographic growth – family planning. A senior official summarized the Council's trajectory as follows:

During the initial period, say eight years, the emphasis was on basic understanding. However, the Council went into the 1960's with a rather vigorously defended stance of promoting one particular line of attack, which is family planning. The degree of consciousness varied. The organization, however, was fairly clear about why it is in this business. The view was that people do not have access to cheaper, safer, contraceptive devices. If society made these devices available, people would utilize the services, people would be lifted to a higher level of happiness, and society would benefit by the aggregate behavior changes.

Hence the mission of the Population Council was to work for fertility reduction, and for at least a decade that mission included a strong commitment to voluntary family planning. In comparison with the methods of AID, this commitment was relatively soft and tentative. But when it came time to offer advice to countries such as Kenya and the Dominican Republic, family planning was the recommended course in the 1960s.

Strategy and activities. The Council's strategy involved four cardinal elements: advancing knowledge, training, developing contraceptives, and technical assistance. The primary element was the advancement of knowledge. This emphasis is well stated in a Council document:

The aim of science is to advance knowledge and as a scientific institution the Council has constantly sought to do so in the field of population. It has done so indirectly by providing for scientific training and by helping to build up research and training centers in various parts of the world. It has also tried to add directly to the fund of established knowledge in demography, in the implementation of family planning programs, in the physiology of reproduction.[20]

The specific kinds of knowledge included basic demographic studies, biomedical research, methodological aspects of both biomedical and demographic research, descriptive information on population policy and family planning programs, and program evaluation.

At the same time, certain kinds of knowledge were largely ignored. The Council published little on the politics of population control or on the cultural aspects of population policies and programs.[21] As one staff member reported, the Council was mainly interested in knowledge about "how to provide services more effectively and efficiently – how to do a better job of making contraceptives readily available to all people in the country." But even there it leaned toward a politically neutral, culturally universal technical view.

The second major element in the Council's strategy was professional training.

At the time the Council began its work, there were few skilled people in the field of population throughout the developing world. Yet the analysis of national problems is best done by a nation's own experts, especially on a politically sensitive subject in a period of emerging nationalism... Accordingly, from the very outset and continuing to the present [1965] the Council has stressed the training of skilled personnel, particularly for the developing world.[22]

The Council supported two kinds of training activities: institutional development and individual fellowships. In its first decade it assisted United Nations regional demographic centers as well as demographic training programs in various developing countries. But by far its most successful training venture was its fellowship program, which included North Americans and candidates from the developing world. Today the roster of fellows reads like a who's who in population. And the presence of alumni in the developing countries led naturally to invitations for collaboration and technical assistance in those countries.

A third ingredient in the Council's strategy was contraceptive research. Its Biomedical Division, housed at Rockefeller University, became a world leader in both basic research on reproductive physiology and on the development of new contraceptives. Its most notable accomplishment was the development of one form of the IUD.

The fourth and most controversial element of strategy was technical assistance to the developing countries. Among the specific projects of the Technical Assistance Division were the International Post Partum Program, an effort to introduce family planning after women have delivered children; the Taylor–Berelson program, an extension of the postpartum concept to rural areas; and the assignment of resident advisers to countries undertaking family planning programs. In addition to the four elements noted, the Council served as a clearing house for information on population matters and tried to increase public awareness of population issues.

Values and value conflicts. Durings its first twenty-five years of existence, the Population Council was guided by three organizational values: institutional autonomy, professionalism, and political caution. Institutional autonomy was a salient value because of the Council's dependence on outside bodies for funds. Although donors and recipients regularly proclaim that money is given and taken with no strings attached, financial dependence does limit autonomy, often in subtle but powerful ways.

The Council's experience with its funding sources was varied. The Ford and Rockefeller foundations shaped the directions of the Council's work through what they funded, but they did not put explicit pressure on the organization beyond the terms of the grants made. However, as one trustee pointed out after reading the last sentence, "They have not needed to. The Council knew what it had to offer to get money from these sources." A staff veteran also commented: "There are many examples scattered over the years that could conclusively demonstrate that both foundations, and other Rockefeller interests, have been successful in 'bending' the Council." But such bending was indirect.

Pressures from AID were more direct and not especially subtle. In the mid-1960s, when there was no single locus of population activities in AID, the Council received generous grants without pressure for specific results. But when Ravenholt built a single Office of Population, the arm twisting began. A senior staff member recalled that "when AID became centralized the Population Council found itself at odds with Ravenholt. The Council wouldn't play their role with abortion and sterilization, and it wouldn't play a cutting-edge role." Because the Council had independent support from other sources it was not in such a subservient position that it had either to bend before AID or collapse financially. But the sheer fact of such pressures convinced the Council leadership that, with over 30 percent of its budget from AID, it was simply too dependent on that source. By 1975 the figure dropped to 15 percent and the funds were all in projects of mutual interest. Overall the Council fared rather well in maintaining its autonomy, in good part because of an internal sense of professionalism and diversity of funding.

A second value was to follow professional standards in research and other activities. The words "professional" and "professionalism" came up often in our interviews and seemed to reflect a genuine organizational commitment.

"The Council," said one staff member, "has come through the years basically as a very professional organization." But there were disagreements on just what professionalism meant in that setting and tensions between that value and the quest for action. The third value reflected in the Council's work was political caution. This was particularly evident in the organization's approach to sterilization and abortion, both of which were fraught with political and moral conflicts. A senior staff member observed:

The Population Council is a conservative organization because of the professionals in it, and the concentration on professionalism. This is quite different, for example, from the Pathfinder Fund where [Clarence] Gamble was willing to go in and do any damned thing to get started. The Council weighed the pros and cons. The conservatism showed up on the question of abortion. One reason was that family planning was controversial enough, so why should we get involved there?

A former president also argued that the Council avoided direct policy advocacy on the grounds that an organization of this type would not be effective in that role.[23]

Given the Council's mission, strategy, and values, internal rifts were almost inevitable. The two most basic revolved around knowledge generation versus technical assistance and scientific objectivity versus mission advocacy. For the Council, as for most organizations, it was hard to marry the pursuit of knowledge with the provision of technical assistance. Those of a scholarly bent seek knowledge for its own sake, even when it may not be practical, whereas practitioners seek action, even when it may not be scholarly. One senior official felt that mixing these two aims in the same organization produced an "unholy marriage" that was bad for both. The practical constraints of program design impeded the kinds of experimentation necessary for new knowledge, and the niceties of knowledge generation often contaminated technical assistance by making it too academic.

The tension between objectivity and advocacy grew directly from the Council's entry into technical assistance. Action projects can help to advance knowledge, but they also carry the temptation of salesmanship. If a pilot project in family planning works well, the organization may report the results and, also as happened with the Council, hold the project up as a model for replication. When criticisms are then made of the intervention, as they inevitably are, the organization may defend not only its findings but also its image. Thus the Population Council found great difficulty in criticizing the Knowledge–Attitude–Practice (KAP) survey while it was the foremost exponent of this method as well as in objectively evaluating family planning programs while its leaders were heralding their success. Time and again in its annual reports the Council cited KAP data as a prime reason for governments to move ahead on family planning. But in so doing it compromised its scientific goals by overselling KAP data (see Chapter 7). Instead of openly criticizing this method and its results in a scholarly manner, the Council worked quietly for better methodology but publicly used KAP results to promote family planning. The same thing happened with the council's evaluations of family planning programs. A staff member reported constant tension between those who wanted to show the usefulness of family planning and those who favored objective analysis of results no matter what their direction. Another individual was even more critical: "The evaluation is hogwash – it is like the KAP surveys. There is a conflict of interest between research and mission . . . There are strong pressures to slant the results toward selling the program." The point of these criticisms was not that the evaluators were dishonest, but that in an organization with a mixed mission they were caught between conflicting expectations.

Since 1976 the Council has generally continued along the lines it followed before, but with four notable changes. First, it now gives more explicit attention to questions of population and development. The Council has a Center for Policy Studies that "seeks to deepen our understanding of the complex behavioral forces that lie behind demographic change and of the impact of demographic change on social and economic development."[24] This Center is responsible for the *Population and Development Review*, a new and respected journal in the field. Second, the Council has demonstrated greater interest in the question of women in developing countries, particularly programs related to food production, nutrition, health, and contraception. Third, the Council has modified its earlier opposition to programs involving abortion activities in the developing countries. And fourth, the Population Council is now much less of an advocate than it was in the 1960s of the conventionally designed family planning delivery system. Partly because family planning programs are now installed in many of the developing countries and partly because of its broader focus on issues of population and development, the Council now seems more a student and less an advocate of specific policy solutions.

THE DONOR UNDERGROUND: FOREIGN AID FOR ABORTION

A discussion of donor agencies confined to AID, the Ford Foundation, and the Population Council would give only a partial picture of foreign aid for population. And the picture would not be completed by including more mainline agencies, such as the World Bank or the United Nations Fund for Population Activities. The key elements missing are the smaller private agencies, including those using clandestine operations. To broaden the coverage of donors, I will now consider several agencies that provide foreign aid for abortion.[25]

A look at clandestine activities is useful for two reasons. First, it helps to explain the widespread suspicions in the developing countries that there is more to population assistance than meets the eye. Observers from many countries, but particularly from Latin America and Africa, are sometimes wary of accepting aid for population precisely because they fear that abortion, sterilization, or unsought activities may be smuggled in without their knowledge. Often these fears remain unvoiced, but their presence can pollute the atmosphere for foreign assistance. Also, one of the reasons that several of the smaller agencies took up aid for abortion was that the main-line donors would not, or, in the case of AID, could not, act in that field. Hence in an environment marked by the strong desire for action on population control, the failure of the population establishment to provide aid for abortion prompted others to fill the vacuum.

The major donors and abortion

Before turning to these other agencies, it is worth asking how the major donors have dealt with abortion. AID was an ardent promoter of abortion until it was stopped by the Helms amendment of 1973. This amendment stated that none of the funds used to carry out the Foreign Assistance Act of 1961 "shall be used to pay for the performance of abortions as a method of family planning or to motivate or coerce any person to practice abortions." In a policy determination issued in 1974, the administrator of AID interpreted this language to mean that AID funds could not be used for the direct support of abortions, for the promotion of abortion as a family planning method, or for paying women to have abortions. AID funds could be used for training programs with abortion as one element in the curriculum and for research on different methods of abortion. In practice, the amendment not only drove AID itself out of supporting abortion but also affected its monitoring of abortion-related activities among its funding recipients. Sensitive to the political dangers at stake for themselves and the government, administrators, lawyers, contract officers, and auditors in AID and other federal agencies have kept a close watch on abortion and abortion-related activities. As a result, funding recipients such as IPPF and the Pathfinder Fund, have been under strong pressure to maintain detailed records showing that AID monies have not been used for abortion.

The major philanthropic organizations, including the Ford and Rockefeller foundations, have shied away from abortion projects for other reasons. Despite some urging from AID to fill the gap left by the Helms amendment, Ford and Rockefeller apparently concluded that abortion projects were not in their interest. Two reasons were cited by persons familiar with those organizations: a fear that association with abortion would contaminate their work in areas of higher priority, such as agricultural development; and squeamishness among the professional staff about the furtive operations that seemed necessary in this field. The Population Council, for its part, endorsed aid for abortion in 1976 but did little in the field thereafter. The reasons were probably the same as those of the Ford and Rockefeller foundations.

The only two major donors that have operated openly in this area – although without publicity and on a very small scale – are the World Bank and UNFPA. UNFPA's policy is to respond to country requests for assistance with all kinds of population programs, provided that they are within the Funds' terms of reference and do not violate UN standards on human rights. UNFPA has been willing to entertain requests for abortion assistance and did provide such aid to Tunisia. The World Bank operates under similar policies.

The abortion activists

The four main agencies providing aid for abortion have been IPPF, the Pathfinder Fund, the Population Crisis Committee, and International Projects Assistance Service (IPAS), formerly called the International Pregnancy Advisory Service. These agencies vary markedly in the balance they maintain between overt and covert activities, in their commitment to abortion as an area of foreign assistance, and in their overall style of operations.

IPPF is the central office for several dozen private national planning associations. As such, it receives funds from international bodies, including AID, and passes money and supplies along to the local associations. Its stated position is that all forms of family planning, including abortion, should be legally available to those who desire them. Over the years IPPF has operated mainly above ground, but it has also provided clandestine aid for abortion. As of 1978 it had carried out specific abortion projects in ten countries in addition to various regional and global efforts, particularly the training of personnel.

In the Philippines, where abortion was both illegal and explicitly against the national population policy, IPPF supplied 20 "menstrual regulation" kits for demonstration purposes.[26] Although the government had laws prohibiting the importation of abortive devices, these kits were brought in as medical instruments" to obtain "sample tissue for examination." And though it was aware that these vacuum aspirators had been imported and were being distributed to private doctors, the government's official body in this field, the Commission on Population, did not take action. Because the IPPF affiliate, the Family Planning Organization of the Philippines, did not take a public stand favoring abortion, and because it did not use these devices in its own clinics, the commission apparently felt that its regulatory powers were limited. Others concluded that commission officials were in fact not opposed to the use of the kits so long as no public uproar was generated. In addition to its activities in the Philippines, IPPF has also supplied vacuum aspirator kits to Bangladesh, Korea, Singapore, Hong Kong, Thailand, Vietnam, and India.[27] Although IPPF claims to be open about its assistance, it did not list these abortion activities in any of its published reports, even in its main report to donors.

A second activist agency, and one more willing to go public with its abortion work, is the Pathfinder Fund of Boston. A Pathfinder flyer from about 1975 stated:

Abortion – safe, legal, and available – is important as a backup for contraceptive failure, and as a way to bring women into programs of contraception at the moment they are most susceptible to persuasion. But because of the Helms amendment to the foreign-aid law, no AID money can be spent to promote abortion. Therefore we do this important work with money raised from the private sector.

In the 1970's Pathfinder engaged in two main kinds of abortion activities: helping to establish clinics in countries where abortion services were illegal but tolerated by the government, and distributing vacuum aspiration kits to interested clinics and private practitioners. It worked, for example, with a local doctor to open an abortion clinic in Colombia and took similar initiatives elsewhere in Latin America. When asked about the legality of such interventions, a staff member commented: "Where abortion is culturally acceptable we don't think the law is restrictive in an ethical sense. We are also concerned at the practical level – will it be enforced or not." Another commentator said that the clinic in Colombia was indeed against the law, but that prosecution was unlikely, if only because the daughters of public figures were using its services.

One of the most influential yet anomalous organizations in this field was the Population Crisis Committee (PCC). Long a significant lobbyist for birth control in Washington, PCC has been quite visible on the domestic scene. With its board made up of retired ambassadors and generals, prominent businessmen, and other celebrities, it would seem an unlikely supporter of illegal abortion overseas. And yet that is exactly what it has become outside the United States, although never under its own name. A United Nations document contains this description of the Population Crisis Committee/Draper Fund:

PCC/DF works to generate support for reducing world population growth in two basic ways: through high-level advocacy at home and abroad to increase government commitment to strong, effective family planning programmes; and through its highly selective support of innovative, cost-effective private family planning projects in developing countries.[28]

Although abortion was not specifically mentioned, closer checking revealed that this was the major form of "innovative, cost-effective, private family planning projects." The organization works as follows:

PCC has no overseas operations. Instead, it funds or finds funding for selected high-leverage projects initiated by or recommended to PCC by IPPF and other family planning/population organizations that have a proven track record in overseas operations. Projects are undertaken in collaboration with indigenous leaders and groups...Projects selected for support are those that promise exceptional return in lowered birth rates per dollar invested. Typically such projects involve one of the ten most populous Third World countries; they demonstrate or extend an approach to delivery of family planning services that has proven cost-effective in lowering birth rates in similar conditions elsewhere; they require private money because the government is not ready to accept a new approach until it has been proven successful; and they include a sensible plan for expansion or replication.[29]

In the late 1970s PCC leaned strongly toward programs involving local businessmen. PCC officials spoke of a three-legged stool made up of the doctor who provides the services, the woman who receives them, and the businessman who organizes them for a profit. They cited with pride an experience in Taiwan in which a loan for one clinic ultimately led to a total of nineteen clinics, all patterned after the first. Among PCC's other projects were a program in the Philippines to train doctors in the use of vacuum aspirators, a "pregnancy clinic" in Bogota whose aim was to treat incomplete abortions, and abortion training and supplies in Bangladesh. The agencies most often used for executing PCC projects were the Pathfinder Fund and the International Projects Assistance Service. As of 1979, PCC administrators felt that private abortion services had a bright future in the developing countries, mainly because they play into the profit motive. They also felt that the Helms amendment was a blessing in disguise, for it forced abortion advocates to rely less on large donors and the public sector and more on commercial ventures.

The most aggressive promoter of abortion services in the developing countries has been the International Projects Assistance Service (IPAS). Its policy was to move in wherever it could to start up projects. A former staff member said: "Our policy is that the more abortion is illegal, the more attractive it is because it is necessary. If it is legal other organizations can handle it." In the late 1970s IPAS worked in three areas: (1) providing loans for new abortion clinics; (2) manufacturing vacuum aspirators for sale to other organizations, including the Pathfinder Fund and IPPF; and (3) direct abortion services. Its strategy on this last front was to identify doctors interested in abortion, whether it was legal or not, and then help them provide new services. By 1979 IPAS was supporting clinics in some twenty countries, including Mexico, Brazil, and Indonesia, where abortion was illegal. In Bangladesh, Pakistan, Sri Lanka, Thailand, and Mexico IPAS also offered vacuum aspirator kits through a direct-mail program and provided training in their use. The organization's main problem in 1979 was in raising funds, mainly because the direct-action tactics left donors uncomfortable about supporting it. Hence IPAS had to depend on grants from the PCC and other private sources as well as revenues generated by a loan program and manufacturing operations.

Although nominally they were independent, these four organizations overlapped in several ways. The primary connector was the PCC, which provided funds to the other three. PCC also purchased vacuum aspirator kits from IPAS for shipment to the IPPF; Pathfinder acquired these kits directly from IPAS.

Moreover, all four organizations followed a common strategy of promoting "menstrual regulation" as the primary means of abortion and of distributing vacuum aspirators for that purpose.

In conclusion, international donors have influenced almost every stage of population policy in the developing countries, from the incipient sense that there is a population problem to be solved to concrete strategies for implementing family planning programs. The main-line agencies, including AID, the Ford Foundation, and the Population Council, were particularly influential in moving governments to develop explicit population policies and to establish voluntary family planning programs. Although those agencies differed greatly in their strategies, tactics, and operating styles, they were alike in promoting significant governmental action to reduce population growth. But for various reasons, including professional caution and prohibition by law, AID, Ford, the Population Council, and other main-line agencies could do little about direct action on abortion. To fill that gap, other organizations stepped in with clandestine assistance.

Part II

Policy formulation: process and contexts

1   The power of process

The way in which a policy is developed affects not only its contents but also its image in the political arena, the backing of key administrators, and other factors critical to implementation. No matter how sound its ingredients in theory and no matter how many economic cost/benefit analyses it passes, a population policy designed by foreigners with little attention to national culture may create antipathies by its very mode of formulation. Process, in other words, has effects that transcend the nominal product.

But what is process? In general, the term refers to a succession of actions leading to the accomplishment of some result. Here that result is a governmental population policy and the programs, if any, that it embraces. From the standpoint of implementation, critical features of the succession of actions are the strength and location of the initial demand for a population policy, the range of participants in policy setting and their characteristics, the extent to which policies are tailored to varying national circumstances, and the language used in presenting population policy to the public. This research considered the effects of seven specific aspects of policy formulation:

1. *Demand for a population policy*. In any policy area, one can ask who wants an explicit policy and how strong their interest is. Implementation problems are most likely to arise when the overall demand for a policy is low or when demand arises from persons with little responsibility for program execution. If the sense of a population problem is weak at the top levels of a government and pressure for a policy comes mainly from foreign sources, prospects for effective implementation are usually dim. And when the substance of the policy is inherently controversial, as is often the case with population policy in sub-Saharan Africa, the motivation for implementation is further weakened. This factor refers not so much to the process of policy setting per se as to the conditions in which policy development takes place. In many spheres of public policy these conditions are interwoven with process more narrowly defined.

2. *Extent of foreign influence*. In the developing countries it is always relevant to ask about the extent to which a given population policy reflects domestic or foreign initiatives. Often these are hard to disentangle, but the question remains salient even when the answer is complex. Overall, one would expect that the greater the foreign influence in policy formulation and the greater the sensitivity of foreign influence as a political issue, the stronger the obstacles to implementation. Where nationalism and fears of neocolonial-

71

ism are relatively weak, difficulties from heavy donor participation in policy setting may be muted. But where foreign impact raises the specter of genocide, colonialism, and other perils, as in Kenya, the damage to implementation may be severe. Although much depends on the historical, political, and cultural context, there is no developing country in which foreign influence is not a potential issue.

3. *Involvement of senior executives.* The question of who participates in policy setting and how is particularly relevant for senior executives in the national government, for implementing agencies, and for opinion leaders. This study explored the hypothesis that involvement of the nation's chief executive is crucial to the implementation of a national family planning program, especially when that program proves controversial. If the president or prime minister is excluded from policy formulation or chooses to stay at a distance from the resulting programs, senior officials below that level may find it risky to support that line of policy. If the chief executive targets population control as a prime area of interest and controls important aspects of the professional destiny of his or her subordinates, key administrators may think it folly not to become committed to implementation. From all indications, Kenyan President Jomo Kenyatta's noninvolvement in the formulation of his country's population policy and his persistent silence on the topic of birth control made some of his senior officials wary about vigorous implementation of the country's family planning program. Contrarily, in Mexico many former nonbelievers were converted to family planning when it was linked to the political fortunes of President Echeverria and his most likely political heir.

4. *Participation by implementing agencies.* In numerous spheres of policy the success of a program depends on coordinated action by several different agencies. Yet in the tradition of machine theory, policies are often set by one agency, such as a planning office, without the direct involvement or even concurrence of the units that will have to carry them out. We can hypothesize that the more implementing agencies take part in developing population policies and the greater their influence on the policies adopted, the more willing they will be to implement the resulting programs. Moreover, in countries with a central population unit that depends on line agencies for execution, the greater the participation and influence of the line agencies, the fewer the subsequent rivalries between them and the central unit.

These hypotheses reflect a core theorem of participative management: that workers are most likely to accept and carry out a policy and least likely to engage in bureaucratic subversion when they have been party to policy development.[1] As usual, there are important qualifications. In an environment riven with racial, ethnic, or political strife or one in which interagency hostilities are chronic, participation may be used for sabotage. In an atmosphere of warfare, combatants may use participation as a weapon for demolition rather than as an instrument of construction. But in more benign circumstances the involvement of implementing agencies often improves the substance of policy, builds goodwill, and forestalls mischief.

5. *Involvement of opinion leaders.* In most spheres of public policy, opinion leaders will count for the implementation of a given program. Sometimes, as with the Catholic hierarchy in Mexico, they are highly visible and their impact is somewhat predictable. In other cases, the true opinion leaders become known only when a policy is announced, or even in the advanced stages of implementation. Such might be the case with untrained midwives or local religious leaders opposed to family planning programs. We predicted that the more opinion leaders were involved in policy formulation and the more they felt that the resulting policy was their own, the greater would be their support for implementation. However, participation makes a difference for implementation only to the extent that opinion leaders are concerned about the policy at stake and can influence crucial aspects of implementation. Religious leaders in most countries have been explicitly concerned about population policies, because of the close ties between birth control and morality. No major religion has been indifferent to the ethics of contraception, sterilization, and particularly abortion. For this reason we expected religious leaders to be among the most critical opinion leaders for population policy in all of the countries under study. Business and industrial leaders, on the other hand, vary widely in their concern about population matters and are often unconcerned about family planning programs. Nor do these leaders often have much influence on program implementation. Hence, other things being equal, consultation with religious leaders on population policy should bring greater benefits for program execution than consultation with business leaders.

6. *Adaptation to national circumstances.* Implementation further hinges on the degree to which policies and programs are modified to fit different social, cultural, and economic circumstances in the country. The more policies are adapted in this fashion, the greater the willingness of field implementers to provide services and the greater the interest of clients in accepting them. Programs developed centrally with no thought for regional differences are likely to cause difficulties for local implementers. For example, rural family planning workers in the Philippines had trouble promoting vasectomy among villagers who had no word for that process and whose closest equivalent was the term for animal castration. Further, stock programs developed in the capital city or abroad may clash with client beliefs, attitudes, and understandings. Contraceptives certified by Western-trained physicians as safe and effective may be seen by village women as a source of cancer for themselves or of harm for their children. Even the venerable clinic, with all its trappings of modernity, may be poorly understood and even feared by persons accustomed to different modes of healing.

7. *Language of presentation.* The language used in presenting policy to the public can affect both the overall level of controversy about that policy and

the specific issues raised for debate. The effects of language are greatly conditioned by the political and cultural context in the country and in specific regions. In Kenya declarations emphasizing the theme of population control brought accusations that the program was foreign inspired and ill-suited to national traditions. In Egypt similar statements had little independent effect on national debate. The language used in Mexico was carefully chosen to avert political dissension and to create maximum resonance with the country's religious, cultural, and political environment.

Taken together these seven dimensions provide a lens for viewing policy formulation and its effects in a given time period. But such formulation is often a continuous process in which spurts of formalization are followed by intervals of adjustment. As the country studies show, dislocations produced by policy formulation or implementation or some combination thereof sometimes led to emergency repairs and, in the case of Egypt, to a complete shift in strategy. It would be a mistake, therefore, to treat policy formulation as a discrete process with clearly demarcated time limits. Formulation and implementation continually interact with each other and with the relevant societal and bureaucratic environments.

The seven dimensions of process will now be used to analyze policy formulation in the four countries serving as major studies. The emphasis will be on the process involved in formulating and declaring an official governmental population policy. Other aspects of policy formulation, including reappraisals stimulated by implementation problems, were mentioned in Chapter 2 and will be considered in depth in later chapters.

KENYA

What was the effective demand for population policy in Kenya, and where was it centered? From all indications, the felt need for an antinatalist policy was weak in all sectors of Kenyan society save two: the Ministry of Economic Planning and Development and the private family planning movement. Because in 1965 the former had numerous foreign advisers who were pressing for action on population and the second showed equivalent expatriate influence, neither could be considered a strong indigenous source of demand. Unlike debate in Egypt, Mexico, and the Philippines, where population control had been seriously discussed by national scholars, debate in Kenya had been scant and largely foreign inspired. The country's president and preeminent figure, Jomo Kenyatta, showed no overt interest in family planning, and most other political leaders avoided the subject. And even Kenyans active in the private family planning movement did not press for a governmental policy with the same vigor as their counterparts in other countries. On the whole, the demand for an official population policy from Kenyan sources would have to be rated as low.

Foreign influence, by contrast, was very high. Indeed, some commentators have argued that the main reason for Kenya's adoption of an antinatalist policy in 1966 was to improve its credit rating in international circles. That is probably an oversimplification, but to this day it is a view that is not rejected out of hand by informed Kenyans. Whatever the case, foreign influence coupled with limited domestic participation raised the specter of neocolonialism and created numerous other difficulties for implementation. A brief review of how the 1966 policy developed will explain why perceptions of foreign inspiration were well founded.

A key figure on the population scene after independence was J.G.G. Blacker, the government demographer and a British subject. Using data from the 1962 census, Blacker built a persuasive case for public policies to curb the birth rate. He argued that between 1948 and 1962 Kenya's population had grown from 5.4 to 8.6 million, with an estimated growth rate of 3 percent per year. With this growth rate, he claimed, the population would double in just eighteen years, and even with a 50 percent reduction in fertility it would still double in thirty-five years. Blacker's figures had particular resonance among expatriate economists advising the Ministry of Economic Planning and Development. They believed that a high birth rate coupled with a large dependent population would depress economic growth and make it increasingly difficult to provide social services. They convinced the minister, Tom Mboya, that quick action was needed. Hence in April 1965 the Ministry invited the Population Council to send a team of specialists to study the population question in Kenya and to make appropriate recommendations for action.

The Population Council sent a team of four Americans: Richmond Anderson, a medical doctor and director of technical assistance at the Population Council; Ansley Coale, a demographer at Princeton University; Lyle Saunders, a social scientist; and Howard Taylor, a gynecologist at Columbia University. The mission spent three weeks consulting with government officials and health centers, visiting villages, and studying available materials. But from all indications, the consultations were window dressing for decisions that had already been made. The Ministry that issued the invitation and the mission that accepted it started with the same general idea: that a government-sponsored family planning program was necessary. The question was not whether to have such a program but how, and it was on this latter question that the mission spent its time.

The Population Council's report, issued in August 1965, made eleven recommendations to the government. Five are worth quoting:

1. *Decision on programme*: We strongly recommend that government embark on a programme directed at a decrease in the rate of population growth...
2. *Declaration of policy*: We strongly recommend that as an initial and probably essential step the Government of Kenya clearly declare its policy regarding a reduction in the rate of population growth...

3.   *Government assistance*: It seems essential and we recommend that Government be willing to provide financial assistance, approve the use of national and local facilities, and promote the participation of government personnel...

6.   *Use of the intrauterine device*: We believe that the family planning programme in Kenya should rely heavily on the intrauterine device. Its cost is exceedingly low, a single insertion can suffice for years and it requires only a single motivation and acceptance on the part of the recipient...

11.   *Foreign advisers*: We therefore recommend that Government give early attention to the need for advisers and explore their availability from various potentially interested agencies.

The mission did not spell out why the government should make an open declaration of policy, nor did it seem sensitive to the politics of such openness. Given that Kenya was the first country in sub-Saharan Africa to be open to family planning, the consultants might have been thinking about other countries besides Kenya in this recommendation. The team's enthusiasm for the IUD reflected the then-current optimism about this method in the Population Council, which had sponsored its development.

In early 1966 the Ministry of Economic Planning and Development accepted the Population Council's report as the basis for national policy. Following the mission's advice, the Ministry openly stated that the purpose of the family planning program was to bring down the country's birth rate. The rationale set forth in the development plan for 1968–72 emphasized population control in the service of economic development:

Reducing population growth may, for several reasons, raise the rate of growth of Gross Domestic Product, thus giving an even greater life to per capita income.

As the program was getting underway in 1967, Minister Mboya was also explicit on its purpose: "Family planning in the context of development cannot be overemphasized at the present state of the country's development...People need to be aware of the direct link between population growth and economic development."

Depicting population policy as an instrument of control brought on a torrent of criticism. The policy's detractors credibly linked it to genocide, neocolonialism, tribal scheming, and other atrocities (see Chapter 6). During an interview for this study, a magazine editor remarked:

When it started people felt that it was meant to keep some tribes down. This was due to the way it was introduced. People came and advised people not to have children.

A member of the University Women's Association also noted the negative image created by the control theme:

For heaven's sake stop telling people that you want to "control" their reproductive powers. Stop telling them that they are too many and too poor. Try telling them that these days we have no traditional safeguards to ensure mother and child welfare.

An immediate and related implementation problem was that although it was formulated by the Ministry of Economic Planning and Development, the program was to be executed mainly by the Ministry of Health. With characteristic optimism, the Population Council report had recommended that "all ministries be intimately involved in the programme, though the direct service aspects may be largely the concern of selected ministries, particularly Health." In fact, not even the Ministry of Health was consulted about the language used to present the program. As often happens in health ministries, top administrators disliked the emphasis on control and preferred a rationale centering on health and welfare. When asked about the beginnings of the program, two program officials later listed the following problems:

– Reluctance of the people because at the outset, family planning was introduced wrongly, i.e., as population control and people did not like the idea. The wrong introduction to family planning could have been avoided by only mentioning the improvement of the health of the mother and the children.

– Family planning is misinterpreted to mean birth control. We should have convinced people that it need not mean birth control but child spacing to give the mother and child enough time to get strength.

In later years program officials in the Ministry of Health handled the presentation problem in two different ways. Privately they recognized that the main purpose of the program and the reason that it was so generously funded by foreign donors was to bring down the birth rate. Publicly they stated that its aim was to promote the health of mothers and children. By 1976 the early exuberance about population control had been replaced by caution, ambivalence, and circumlocution in public statements.

The formulation process in Kenya also did poorly in consulting with opinion leaders. Although consultants were flown from New York to Nairobi and expatriate advisers abounded, policy makers did not involve religious leaders and other influentials in Kenya. As a result, opinion leaders were taken by surprise and displeased when the policy was announced in 1966. Clergymen soon charged that birth control would promote promiscuity and otherwise pollute national morality. Others criticized the concept of population control and saw nefarious foreign plots behind it. Reactions in Nairobi traveled to the countryside, with negative effects on both clients and program administrators.

The design of the Kenyan family planning program almost totally ignored nuances of national culture and regional variations in cultural traditions. The program model recommended by the Population Council was presumed to be of universal applicability; therefore, tailoring was not deemed necessary. Beginning with the notion of strong existing demand for family planning services, the visiting mission suggested a stock service-delivery program available ready made in New York. Its basic ingredients – clinics, contraceptives, and family planning education – were considered to be so well tested that they required no modification for the circumstances of Kenya. The mission report did raise the question of culture, but only to dispose of it:

Traditional attitudes and values – although likely to change rapidly in the relatively near future – will probably be a hindrance to family planning for some time. Particularly relevant are value systems that assign a subservient status to women, that favour high fertility, that rely on land and family relations for social security, and that are oriented more toward maintaining the past then improving the future. . . . The extended family system tends to weaken the motivation for family planning by decreasing individual responsibility for children and spreading it over a large number of adults.

In other words, traditional norms are unfortunate relics from the past that should, and quickly will, give way to more modern and therefore better values. The extended family system, which many Kenyans regard as the center of their social relationships, is a particular nuisance, because it "weakens the motivation" for family planning. But all will be well, because worldwide (though not Kenyan) KAP results show "a widespread latent desire to have a smaller number of children than are actually born."

Failure to adapt the family planning program to Kenyan circumstances had two immediate implications. First, many administrators, particularly those in the middle and upper levels, were reluctant to push hard for implementation. Seeing the controversy touched off by the program and not seeing much evidence of enthusiasm in the Ministry of Health, many held back. Second, the program was poorly received by clients, particularly in rural areas. Women did not hesitate to approach clinics for prenatal and postpartum care, but the family planning sections were often underused. Moreover, the methods promoted, often poorly understood by the users, gave rise to rumors about harmful side effects and associations with witchcraft (see Chapter 11).

Finally, as far as we can determine, the Kenyan population policy was developed without the direct involvement of the chief executive. The most likely reason was that Jomo Kenyatta, the father of the country, wanted to keep himself above an issue that could easily work against national unity. Not only did he himself say nothing in public about family planning, he made it clear to others that they were not to use his name or photograph in this context. His avoidance of the topic, combined with his political stature in the country, dampened the enthusiasm of senior administrators.

In sum, on all seven aspects of process under discussion, Kenya scored poorly from the standpoint of implementation. Local demand for a policy was weak, foreign influence was strong, the chief executive was not involved in policy formulation, the main implementing agency and national opinion leaders were not consulted, the program was not tailored to varying cultural conditions, and the language of presentation raised issues damaging to the program's image.

MEXICO

The development of population policy in Mexico was strikingly different from that in Kenya. The perceived need for a population policy was stronger within the government, and it was centered in the presidency and rooted in research and pilot projects carried out by Mexicans. Although the demand for a policy to contain demographic growth was hardly widespread, it was strong in places that counted. Contributing to a concern about population policy was a series of studies showing that Mexico had one of the world's highest rates of demographic increase and one that showed no signs of abating. In the middle to late 1960s, research conducted by the Latin American Demographic Center (CELADE) in Santiago and the Mexican Institute of Social Studies (IMES) further showed an apparent interest in family planning among Mexican couples. Government-sponsored experiments in family planning conducted during the 1960s, together with the work of a private family planning organization, the Foundation for Studies of Population (FEPAC), provided tangible evidence to support the argument of client interest. Then, in the early 1970s, the country faced a series of economic crises together with the long-term prospect of inflation. At this point, national scholars, including several at the Colegio de Mexico, came forth with a variety of publications documenting the negative consequences of continued population growth. Other groups that contributed to a sense of urgency about population questions were the Mexican Society of Genetics and the Mexican Association for Studies on Fertility and Reproduction, as well as some journalists and editorial writers. Hence, when Echeverria made his abrupt policy shift in 1972, considerable intellectual groundwork had been laid, most of it by Mexicans.

Foreign donors did play a part in this policy transition, but in the background rather than the foreground. Probably the most influential agency was the Ford Foundation, which worked quietly with local institutions to increase the volume and quality of population research. Its grants to public and private organizations stimulated some of the pioneering research of the 1960s and opened the door to later undertakings. Ford representatives also played a catalytic role in bringing together key people at meetings and cocktail parties. These contacts both created an informal network of population specialists and provided psychological support for professionals moving into this controversial area. Other international activators included the Pathfinder Fund, the Population Council, the Pan American Health Organization, the Latin American Center for Demographic Research, the World Health Organization, and other United Nations agencies. One agency notable for its absence was AID, which did not maintain a mission in Mexico and did not try to buy into policy development in any direct way. AID did channel some funds to Mexico through such intermediaries as the Pathfinder Fund, but its overall impact was slight. Given the delicacy of the population question in Mexico, the topic's association with the United States, and lingering Mexican resentment of American intervention, both AID and the Mexican government probably concluded that distance was desirable.

Involvement by the chief executive in policy formulation was evident, although the details are still obscure. Unlike Kenya, where President Kenyatta said nothing about population policy, Luis Echeverria was visibly and firmly in command of the policy change. Given that he was reversing not only his own stated position on population growth but forty years of official policy, it is hard to imagine how Echeverria could have left this matter to a subordinate. Also critical to the next stages of policy development was the man widely reputed to be Echeverria's political heir, Mario Moya Palencia, secretary of the interior. It was Moya who became the kingpin of family planning, defending the new Law of Population before Congress and taking his place as the visible head of the National Population Council (CONAPO). Before long, dozens of political aspirants, including many who had previously opposed birth control, followed Moya into the family planning fold and were given key positions. State officials also heeded the call of CONAPO and quickly set up pilot projects on family planning in their regions. These instant conversions were closely linked to the perception that this minister of the interior, like his two immediate predecessors, would be the next president. The fervor dissipated when Moya lost out in the party competition of 1975, but in the meantime the government moved ahead to install family planning services. Without the explicit backing of Echeverria, only the foolhardy public servant would have become an avid booster of this cause.

Because of the secrecy surrounding the policy change, details are scant on how far Echeverria went in consulting national opinion leaders. Given the realities of Mexican politics, we can assume that he brought up the matter within his own party, the PRI. Little of importance happens in Mexico without the involvement of party and president, and much that might happen is stopped by the opposition of either. Because the party articulates the interests of various groups, including unionized workers, white-collar employees, and business elements, consultation with that source would provide some indication of a policy's political acceptability. Outside the PRI, there is no evidence that Echeverria made direct consultations with such opinion leaders as the Roman Catholic hierarchy, newspaper editors, or medical associations. There is very strong evidence, however, that he and his associates made every effort to have the new policy, including the specific language in the Law of Population, take account of the preferences and sensitivities of the most important interest groups. This point will be discussed further in connection with policy presentation. Thus although direct consultations apparently were few and secret, Mexican officials did try to determine the concerns of opinion leaders and to propose a policy that would be at least tolerable to those concerns.

The relationship between policy formulation and the implementing agencies was rather complex in Mexico. In some respects the Law of Population simply gave legitimacy to what some government organizations, such as the Social Security Institute, had already been doing in family planning. This was a case in which prior, covert implementation preceded overt policy formulation. (In the machine model of implementation such a sequence cannot occur, but it did in Mexico.) Beyond this meshing of experience and policy, we do not know how much formal consultation took place between the initiators of the new policy and the principal implementing agencies. The Mexican study does suggest, however, that there was considerable informal contact between key figures in the government's family planning operations and those developing the official policy. Unlike Kenya, where the government's policy took the Ministry of Health somewhat by surprise, the implementing agencies in Mexico seemed reasonably well prepared for the actions entailed by the Law of Population.

Mexico also shows a mixed pattern on the question of adaptation to varying social and economic circumstances. In one sense, the entire process of policy formulation was a massive attempt to develop programs that would be compatible with the values of the urban middle classes and not offensive to the church and the political left. The government's declarations about the nuclear family, responsible parenthood, equality of women, quality of life, planning, and child spacing all reflect middle-class values and aspirations. The same is true of the emphasis on clinics as the form of service delivery. And the predominantly urban location of the health clinics, the background of their personnel, and their reliance on a bureaucratic mode of interaction further suggest this class alignment. The government did, in fact, succeed in winning the support, or at least the tolerance, of its urban middle-class constituency, but at the expense of losing marginal populations in both urban and rural areas. As implementers found when the program moved to the field, persons living in a culture of subsistence respond poorly to a program organized around clinics and bureaucratized methods of service delivery. Overall adaptation, therefore, would have to be rated low, although it was higher than in Kenya.

Finally, Mexico went further than any other country covered by this research in using the language of policy presentation to generate support and forestall opposition. The Law of Population, adopted in 1974, was couched in terms calculated to make the policy seem thoroughly Mexican, amply Christian, fully progressive, and eminently libertarian. Reaffirming the traditionally strong Mexican nationalism and implicitly rejecting any hint of American influence, the law called itself "a policy based on sovereign self-determination of the nation, rejecting neo-colonial attitudes." Echoing the World Population Plan of Action, the law stated that its aim was "to pursue economic and social development and not substitute for it." This affirmation could serve to head off charges from the left that Mexico was controlling the fertility of the poor without promoting their development. The law further proclaimed "absolute respect for human rights and for our national cultural values." Some critics, particularly from within the church feared that if the government entered this delicate sphere it could easily resort to coercion or impose un-Christian values on the country's citizens. The language of presentation sought to allay such fears by underscoring the completely voluntary nature of family planning and a broad respect for Mexican culture. The law also spoke of balancing rural and urban development, preserving the environment, and collaborating with all social sectors, private as well as public, in carrying out the new population policy.

The themes stated in the Law of Population were repeated in congressional hearings and in other presentations to the public. This carefully orchestrated campaign had its desired effect. In the period following promulgation of the law public acceptance ran high, whereas attacks from the government's traditional adversaries, including the church and the Marxists, were muted. By contrast, the government reaped a mixed harvest with a subsequent campaign to promote family planning. Organized around the theme "Let's Make Ourselves Less," this effort produced suspicion of the government's intentions rather than new recruits for family planning. The government's very enthusiasm for birth control kindled old suspicions that if the rulers are eager, there must be something wrong with the programs they are advocating.

EGYPT

Serious public discussion of overpopulation in Egypt dates to the 1930s, but it mounted after the revolution of 1952. In 1953, both President Nasser and Dr. Abbas Ammar, minister of social affairs, spoke openly about the difficulties the country would face if rapid population growth continued. But in that period Nasser hesitated to arouse religious opposition over birth control and was also confident that the economic development being promoted by his socialist government would help to bring down the birth rate. By May of 1962 Nasser was forced to conclude that excessive population growth was a significant obstacle to Egyptian development and that organized family planning services were needed. In 1965, after considerable prodding by various domestic opinion leaders, he finally established the Supreme Council on Family Planning. Whatever his hesitation, it is clear that Nasser himself sensed a population problem and saw a publicly sponsored family planning program as a partial solution. As in Mexico, the demand for a population policy may not have been broadly based, but the perceived need was authentically national and centered at the top.

Direct foreign influence on Egypt's population policy was minimal. Although various donors were active in the country before 1965, their presence was muted and their lobbying discreet. Hence throughout the numerous debates about the wisdom of providing family planning services, the issue of birth control as a form of neocolonialism was not present. Still foreign influence was strong, if indirect. The intellectual paradigms within which the debate about family planning took place, particularly arguments about the links between demographic and economic growth, were identical to those in New York and Washington. The use of Knowledge–Attitude–Practice surveys to assess demand for family planning and the ready acceptance of the clinical mode of service delivery also reflected the conventional wisdom among donor agencies. Interestingly, however, even when the first version of the family planning program failed, critics did not pin the blame on its foreign inspiration or the failure of Egyptian officials to question the prevailing models. Because the issue of foreign domination was not salient to the Egyptian context at that time, the Egyptian debate about population control had a largely domestic cast.

Problems did arise, however, from a failure to involve implementing agencies in policy setting. In essence, family planning was simply added to the existing responsibilities of the Ministry of Health and other agencies, and such practical details as staff compensation were not thought out. As will be shown in Chapter 8, this initial error led to multiple and continuing tensions between the Supreme Council for Family Planning and the executing agencies. The switch to a developmentalist policy in 1973 did nothing to overcome the original interagency problem and may have added problems. By pegging fertility decline to education, women's employment, industrialization, and other areas outside of population, the renamed Supreme Council for Population and Family Planning implicitly claimed wide areas of bureaucratic jurisdiction that it in fact lacked. As of 1978 the other agencies had not subordinated their authority to that of the Supreme Council nor had they done much with the council on a collaborative basis.

At the national level, Nasser and his associates apparently did discuss the proposed official policy with opinion leaders, including Islamic leaders in Cairo. The issue had been debated for many years in Egypt, with open commentary by medical doctors, journalists, social work professors, Islamic scholars, and other academics. There is evidence that Nasser listened to this debate and was influenced by it. His reluctance to introduce family planning even in the face of his own conviction that it was necessary suggests considerable sensitivity to the crosscurrents of national opinion. Where there was virtually no consultation or even much attention given, however, was at the local level. It was here that the family planning program encountered its greatest obstacles to implementation. While Islamic leaders in Cairo issued statements supporting contraception, imams in the villages were proclaiming its immorality (see Chapter 10). And as medical authorities in the capital certified the health benefits of child spacing for mother and child, local midwives were spreading rumors about the dire consequences of pills for users and their children. In Egypt and in other countries, the centralist bias of planners and decision makers led to a severe discounting of opinion leaders outside the capital city. Yet it was these leaders who became influential when the programs finally reached their intended clients.

Despite some ethnic diversity and notable differences between rural and urban areas, Egypt made no serious effort to tailor its family planning program to regional and local conditions. The introduction of family planning services in 1966 was almost a paradigmatic example of the machine model of implementation. A stock pattern of service delivery was introduced with the assumption that it would be equally applicable to city and countryside, to Nubians and Bedouins, to Upper Egypt and Lower Egypt. Leaders thought that the force of top-down authority would be sufficient to install the new services throughout the country, even when those who were charged with implementation were skeptical of this effort and considered themselves overloaded with existing duties. This was a program that would have run into trouble even with considerable adaptation to local conditions, but without that adaptation its chances of success were dim indeed (see Chapter 7).

The manner in which Egypt's population policy was presented to the public was not a major issue in implementation. Unlike Mexico, where the political context was fraught with sensitivities related to birth control, in Egypt the atmosphere was more benign. Population control in general and contraception in particular were points of contention but not to the extent that they would be greatly affected by nuances of expression. The language used was straightforward, and opinion leaders did not shrink from mentioning the need for a reduction in numbers. Whereas in Nairobi the rhetoric of control touched tender nerves of history and culture, in Cairo such language seemed to make little difference. There was debate about population policy, but little of it would have been averted by the kind of verbal massage that occurred in Mexico.

THE PHILIPPINES

The most striking aspect of process in the Philippines was the extent to which both the sense of population problem and the subsequent structure of implementing agencies grew out of joint action between national advocates and international donors. In the mid-1960s a loose coalition of donors and interested nationals undertook a multipronged campaign to raise public awareness about the dangers of demographic growth and to increase the availability of family planning services. At the beginning, the critical actors were AID, IPPF, the Population Institute at the University of the Philippines (UPPI), and the mass media. It would be a mistake to view these as independent agents, for they were all linked by international funding and in other ways as well.

AID not only supported a variety of national population organizations but also made substantial contributions to IPFF, which in turn channeled funds to some of the same organizations. Established with help from the Ford Foundation, UPPI later received technical assistance from the Population Council, which was partly supported by AID. And some of the journalists who spoke out for population control attended training courses sponsored by the Asian Press Institute, which received funds from international donors and reported data from UPPI. The agencies worked neither as a single unit with a common guiding force nor as independent organizations. Connections were overlapping and intricate.

AID's strategy was to create a domestic constituency for family planning by funding as many national organizations as possible. Whereas its normal operating procedures called for institution building and counterpart funding, in population it offered almost total financing and overlooked institution building. AID gambled that Filipino interest would rise to the level of its funds and that local recipients would press for governmental action. Its first family planning grant came in 1966 and supported a pilot project run by the Manila Health Department. Then it gave funds and supplies to the Family Planning Association of the Philippines (FPAP) and to the Planned Parenthood Movement in the Philippines (PPMP). With AID support, FPAP set up fourteen family planning clinics as part of child-care centers in four of the country's poorer provinces. Because these centers were under the general jurisdiction of the Department of Health, that department also became involved in AID-sponsored family planning. For its part, PPMP began a comprehensive training program in family planning for both medical and nonmedical personnel. Also receiving generous support during this period was the Institute of Maternal and Child Health. At the insistence of the National Economic Council, this agency's family planning activities were also to be supervised by the Department of Health. Thus although AID had made no direct grants to the Department of Health, the latter was pulled into family planning through its supervisory role.

As the number of funding recipients mounted, AID pressured the government to create a coordinating organization for family planning matters. These negotiations eventually led to the establishment of the Project Office of Maternal and Child Health in the office of the secretary of health. Its mandate was to handle all AID assistance for family planning in the Philippines. In this way AID was able to channel funds easily and unobtrusively to private organizations. AID pressure also played a role in removing a legal ban on importing contraceptives.

Overall, AID had a pervasive influence on the development of population policy in the Philippines and on the organizational structure for executing that policy. By encouraging the creation of private organizations to promote family planning, providing free contraceptive supplies to public and private agencies, sponsoring research to show the existence of a population problem in the Philippines, using its leverage with the government to change rules and to create structures, and adopting tough performance criteria for agencies receiving its funds, AID plainly helped to put population on the agenda in the Philippines. The agencies that it funded did voice support of government action and did show that family planning services had a local market. But once the government announced a policy in 1970, these same agencies began to compete for scarce funds and to get in each others' way in the field.

Also important in convincing the government that it had a population problem was UPPI. Established in 1964, it quickly became the country's prime center of demographic research and a vector for an antinatalist policy. Its director, Dr. Mercedes Concepción, was a respected demographer with close ties to prominent figures in the international population movement. One specific source of UPPI's influence on policy formulation was a Knowledge–Attitude–Practice survey. A report on this study stated that women in the Philippines generally approved of family planning and wanted to learn more about it, preferred moderate-sized families and did not want to have more children than they already had, and were not greatly affected by the church's teaching on contraception.[2] The report concluded: "Many women will have more children than they want because of ignorance, lack of services and supplies."[3] UPPI and its director not only prepared the intellectual ground for the government's policy but also helped to shape its specific contents. By serving as the secretariat for the Commission on Population, UPPI was in a strategic position to press for an economic-demographic definition of the population problem and for voluntary family planning as a solution. And this it did.

In the immediate prepolicy period, the media further made the case that the Philippines had a problem of numbers. Typical of the many commentaries on population is this 1969 excerpt from the *Manila Chronicle*:

For now there is no escape from the frightening fact that unless something is done, the population of the country shall double in the next 20 years. This means that to feed these growing millions and maintain an average standard of living, the country must produce three times as much food and goods.[4]

Several columnists played up the threat to political stability from the poverty and unrest of the have-nots and argued that family planning is a form of protection for society. This theme arose later in legislative debates over the law on population.

In short, the perception of a population problem in the Philippines was closely tied to the activities of foreign donors but not the sole result of donor influence. Donors, especially AID, were active from 1966 through 1970 but made most of their policy impact through local funding recipients. During this same period, individuals and groups within the country likewise took up the population cause, often without any foreign support. Physicians, economists, journalists, and even Jesuits were concerned about population growth and made their views known in national forums. Although it is hard to disentangle domestic and foreign influences, this much is clear: (1) Much of the momentum for developing an explicit policy came from a combination of national and international initiatives; and (2) AID funding had a significant and direct impact on the organizational setting for implementation. Although there was no real backlash against the foreign cast of the program, AID's legacy of multiple and overlapping agencies became a major stumbling block to implementation in the 1970s.

The chief executive's involvement in policy development was relatively high in the Philippines. Population control was clearly not the highest political priority for President Marcos, but he took an active part in the deliberations leading to an official policy and stiffened that policy after his declaration of martial law in 1972. Marcos was accused by his critics of succumbing to World Bank pressure in announcing the 1970 policy, but he has never been charged with installing that policy as window dressing or of being uninterested in population control. And as the government moved into action, First Lady Imelda Marcos increasingly saw family planning as an arena in which she could stake out her own claims for influence. Top-level involvement thus included both husband and wife.

In contrast to Kenya, where consultation was minimal, Marcos made a sizeable effort to involve key opinion leaders in the development of population policy. To avoid the troubles encountered in other Catholic countries, he was particularly anxious to win the cooperation or at least neutralize the opposition of the church hierarchy. Before establishing the first Commission on Population in 1969, he had his executive secretary, Rafael Salas, convene a group of twenty-four prominent people to discuss the population question. Among these were several priests. For its part, the Catholic Bishops Conference had urged public discussion of all aspects of the population problem and had endorsed the notion of planned parenthood. But the bishops had also argued that fertility control is best left in the hands of private groups rather than the government. Given this situation, which was more favorable than that in many Latin American nations, Salas hoped to include the clergy in policy formulation. As a key informant described the official mood at that time, "The government would adopt whatever policy everyone could agree on, and if the only thing on which all could agree was rhythm it would confine itself to rhythm." This ad hoc group met several times and was later absorbed into the Commission on Population. When Marcos announced the commission's formation, he appointed members from almost every influential group in Philippine society, including the political, religious, health, and education sectors. In this first stage of policy setting, consultation was widespread and consensus the order of the day. Even though the church was not happy with the language of the Population Act and withdrew its representative from the Commission on Population, it could not claim that it was left out of the deliberations. But when, with the advent of martial law, the policy was revised, this quest for consensus was summarily abandoned in favor of the need for results. For procedural as well as substantive reasons, the good will of the church hierarchy soon began to diminish.

In one sense consultation with the implementing agencies was extensive, for it was these agencies that became a major force in establishing an official policy. But their lobbying had more to do with the broad content of the policy than with the precise structure of implementation, and it was in this latter area that problems mounted. By winning the battle to have the new programs carried out by the many existing agencies, these organizations set the stage for what is probably the world's most complex structure of implementation in family planning. But organizations concerned about their own short-term survival interests rarely think out the long-term implications of success, and the Philippine case was no exception.

As in the other three countries, population planners made no significant effort to adapt the family planning program to the unique sociocultural, economic, and geographic conditions of the country's different regions. The one major concession to local realities was the adoption of a complex, multiagency implementation structure. This, according to the authors of the Philippine study, did reflect the cultural values of personalism, accomodation, and smooth interpersonal relations. Partly because of donor influence but also because of a desire by decision makers to avoid conflicts, the government permitted the emergence of many overlapping organizations in family planning. Once formed and in operation, each agency centered its loyalties around the personality of its director:

The strong in-group orientation finds concrete manifestation in a common pattern of Philippine organizations, namely, a proliferation of agencies doing the same type of work. The organization or at least its style of work is identified with the person who runs it. Affiliation with the organization is as much with its universal aims as with its leader or clique in the forefront of activities. The growth of numerous volunteer family planning organizations in the mid-sixties is illustrative of this. In fact, one perceived difficulty of merging the FPAP and PPMP was the issue of board membership [Key Informant]. The concern was important because leadership in the Philippines functions on a personal basis and loyalty of followers is essential to program implementation.[5]

But beyond such passive adaptation, the basic model for the family planning program in the Philippines was the same as for a dozen other countries: a clinic-based service-delivery system. In the mid-1970s the model was expanded to include outreach workers and other innovations, but for the first several years of implementation the basic approach was nearly identical in all regions in which it was introduced.

Among the four countries under review, the Philippines comes second to Mexico in the extent to which it tailored the language of policy presentation to the exigencies of national culture and politics. In contrast to Mexico, which shunned even the overtones of population control, the Philippine government spoke openly about the need to limit numbers. At the same time, official declarations refrained from using language that would suggest coercion or otherwise offend the church. As in Mexico, public statements spoke of "responsible parenthood" (a term common in the papal encyclicals) and stressed the voluntary nature of family planning. A circular from the Department of Health to family planning trainers urged them to use the terms "family planning," "planned parenthood," and "responsible parenthood." Terms to be avoided were "population control," "birth control," and "contraception."

Some of the linguistic manipulation went beyond political paraphrase. In defending the government's program, family planning advocates claimed that it included measures for infertility as well as fertility control. A representative of the Family Planning Organization of the Philippines argued that "family planning works both ways: to help couples who have already enough children to limit births or space them, and to help sub-fertile couples beget children."[6] Despite these and other assertions of concern about infertility, the program was patently biased toward reducing the birth rate. Instructions to family planning workers urged them to press for the "more effective" methods of birth control. Quotas posted on clinic walls did not mention services for the infertile or subfertile. The Rural Health Unit of the Department of Health, a major supplier of family planning services, provided no assistance for infertility. Although the government was not unaware of infertility problems, they were certainly not significant or visible in the family planning program. And even while the government was privately telling field workers to push the "more effective" methods, its publicly stated position was that family planning methods remained available on a cafeteria basis with full respect for client choices. Eventually this gap between rhetoric and reality brought denunciations from the Catholic hierarchy and consequent debates about what was happening during implementation.

In sum, the four countries chosen for major studies show a mixed pattern on six of the seven dimensions of process. As shown in Table 1, the internal demand for population policy was low in Kenya and medium in the other three countries. Direct foreign influence on policy setting was high in Kenya and the Philippines, low in Mexico and Egypt. The involvement of senior executives, and particularly the chief executive, was low in Kenya and high in the other three countries. Participation by implementing agencies in policy setting was low in Kenya and Egypt, unknown in Mexico, and medium in the Philippines. The involvement of opinion leaders was low in Kenya, probably medium in Mexico (the evidence is not clear on this point), medium in Egypt, and high in the Philippines. Adaptation of population programs to national

Table 1. *Country positions on dimensions of the formulation process*

Process Dimension	Kenya	Mexico	Egypt	Philippines
1. Domestic demand for population policy	Low	Medium	Medium	Medium
2. Foreign influence in policy setting	High	Low	Low	High
3. Involvement of senior executive	Low	High	High	High
4. Participation by implementing agencies	Low	?	Low	Medium
5. Involvement of opinion leaders in policy setting	Low	Medium	Medium	High
6. Adaptation of program to national conditions	Low	Low	Low	Low
7. Manipulation of language of presentation	Low	High	Low	Medium

circumstances was low in all four countries. And manipulation of the language of presentation to promote public acceptance was low in Kenya and Egypt, high in Mexico, and medium in the Philippines. Given the political context of Egypt, this last dimension might not have been particularly salient to implementation.

If these dimensions of process were used as predictors of implementation, Kenya would have the lowest probability of success, Mexico and the Philippines the highest, and Egypt would be in between. On every dimension Kenya scores in the direction least likely to facilitate implementation. The effects of process are, of course, mediated by many other aspects of context, including overall commitment to implementation, but this brief analysis suggests some plausible directions of influence. In none of the countries studied was the process of setting population policy as favorable as possible for implementation, and in one it was close to the realistic limit of unfavorability.

6   The pervasiveness of politics

The political context of population policy, including its historical substratum, has a pervasive impact on policy formulation and program implementation.[1] The present studies suggest six broad effects. First, the political context affects whether a country has an explicit population policy. No matter what the preferences of its leaders, the sectarian conflicts in Lebanon were so severe and so closely intertwined with demographic questions that to have an explicit antinatalist policy was impossible. Second, political considerations likewise impinge on the process by which policies are set; they influence the actors involved and affect their specific role. The political and cultural sensitivity of birth control in Kenya undoubtedly underlay the decision to keep deliberations quiet and participation narrow. The decision of the Marcos government to involve church leaders in policy setting grew out of a different set of political considerations. Third, the political context often shapes the precise contents of a population policy as well as the language in which it is offered to the public. Pressures are strong in many countries to have a voluntary rather than a coercive family planning program and to exclude measures, such as abortion, that are offensive to large or powerful segments of the population. And as illustrated by Mexico and the Philippines, the anticipation of political reactions can lead government officials toward euphemisms or outright evasion in discussing population policy.

A fourth influence of the political context is on the organizational embodiment of program implementation – who gets the action and how much. Pressures from interest groups bear upon the decision to allocate responsibility to a new superagency or, as in the Philippines, to divide the task among many existing agencies. Politics further enters into decisions about whether a politician or a technician should head the national program and about the vigor with which that person is urged to pursue the task. Fifth, politics lies behind the imbroglios and outright conflicts set off by actions on population. Delicate issues from the past or present are often brought before the public as evidence of the government's ineptness or of the perils of population control. Finally, a current or conjectured political environment can either enhance or devastate a program's chances of implementation. Officials who discern political capital in rapid execution may pull out all the bureaucratic stops under their control. Those who anticipate political suicide or bureaucratic extinction from enthusiastic support may join the ranks of the minimalists.

Political contexts vary across regions and over time. Even in the same country the political environment for population policy is often quite different in the capital city and in rural villages. As Egyptian population planners found to their dismay, winning the support of religious leaders in Cairo is a poor predictor of comparable support among the imams in the countryside. In discussing contexts, it is thus essential to specify the locality involved and to indicate whether it is representative of the whole country. Political contexts also vary substantially across time. At any given time there is a manifest context that is visible to the naked eye and a latent context that requires careful scrutiny of the past. Particularly in highly charged areas such as population, issues that have been dormant for decades may suddenly erupt. Dominican concerns about racial pollution from Haiti are but one example of latent issues that may quickly become manifest. And even on the contemporary scene, the political context for policy formulation may be only partially the same as that for implementation, and the context for implementation at one time may be distinct from that at another. Those who consider their mission accomplished with the adoption of a formal policy may leave the scene and be replaced by others whose focus is on the flow of action thereafter.[2]

The political context has three interwoven elements: actors, issues, and conditions. *Actors* are the human element of context – the individuals, groups, or organizations with the power to influence a policy at any stage or place. They can be identified by asking who counts for a given policy or program. *Issues* are points of focus, debate, or contention. Their main effect on population policy is to shape the perceptions it evokes and thus the actors likely to enter the scene. *Conditions* are impersonal circumstances, such as uncertainty or threat, with significant repercussions for policy formulation or program implementation. Under the threat of war, for example, some actors become more salient than others for population policy and some issues, such as family planning, are eclipsed by the more pressing concern of national survival. This chapter will deal mainly with the political context for population policy at the national level. Local contexts will be taken up in chapters 9 through 11.

ACTORS

Who has counted most in the development of governmental population policies? The eight cases suggest that the specific answer depends a great deal on the country but that there are constant actors across countries. Foremost among these are the chief executive, domestic interest groups, and international donors.

The chief executive

Among the countries that were the subject of the major studies, the chief executive took an active part in formulating population policies in Mexico, the Philippines, and Egypt. The exact role of the president in Kenya is unknown, but he was certainly not active.

In Mexico the government's shift toward an antinatalist policy would not have occurred without the direct involvement of President Echeverria. Given the paramount and paternalistic role of the president in Mexican politics, it is hard to imagine a change of this magnitude taking place without his personal participation. Moreover, Mexico's population policy quickly became tied to the presidential aspirations of his reputed heir, Mario Moya Palencia. This development had two effects on the evolution of policy. First, because Moya was both a presidential contender and the official most directly responsible for population questions, he was personally motivated to handle this issue with care. In fact, Moya and his staff went to great lengths to develop a policy compatible with the country's political and cultural contexts. But the ambitions prompting that diligence also left the impression that population policy was inherently political and thus could not be taken at face value. During my stay in Mexico in 1974 and 1975, it was an open secret among population researchers that Moya wanted no trouble in this area. Ironically, the government may have won the battle of making population policy politically palatable only to lose the war of having it taken seriously as population policy. Significantly, when the Lopez Portillo government assumed power in 1976, it tried to depoliticize population by appointing staff members with a technocratic bent.

In the Philippines both President Marcos and his wife Imelda were significant actors in the development and execution of population policy. During the critical periods of policy setting, Marcos seemed to be personally interested in population control, but it was not among his highest priorities. As he stated in 1973, "We are, indeed, concerned that our population growth rate is high and poses possible problems to our transition into modernity, but the proportions of the problem do not demand that we institute drastic controls."[3] Indeed, many would argue that he gave over large parts of this policy area to the First Lady. At the time of this study, power contenders in the Commission on Population regularly sought to use her name in their quest for policy influence. One official commented: "All that [a staff member] has to do is put the First Lady's name...and that will immediately cut off 80 percent of effective opposition...And that is whether or not the First Lady really said what she was supposed to have said." The implications of the First Lady's influence for interagency relations are explored further in Chapter 8.

The Egyptian experience documents both the importance and the limits of presidential support. In a political system organized around a strong chief executive, that individual's backing was clearly necessary for instituting a population policy. And even in the face of some religious opposition, both presidents Nasser and Sadat gave family planning their full endorsement. Yet both found that wars with Israel made greater claims on their attention and on the country's resources, and neither had the time or the interest to disentangle the program's administrative system.

The role of the chief executive in Kenya was enigmatic but hardly energetic. As the country's dominant political figure, President Kenyatta must have been aware of what was happening with population policy and must have given it his tacit approval. But once the policy was adopted, he let it be known that he did not want his name associated with it. At one point a Kenyan family planning organization was about to launch a new journal and asked the president for permission to use his picture in the first issue. Word reportedly came back from the state house that Kenyatta did not want his picture used in that way and that if it was, the journal would be permanently shut down.[4] Presidential silence led to wariness at lower levels and consequent difficulties in implementation.

Domestic interest groups

Across the eight countries, the domestic interest groups with the greatest impact on population policy were religious leaders, private family planning activists, and, to a much smaller extent, political groupings. The Roman Catholic clergy was a crucial actor in Mexico, the Philippines, and the Dominican Republic but it had a somewhat different pattern of influence in each country. National religious leaders were also part of the political context in Egypt and, after the official policy was announced, in Kenya. Details on the role of religious leaders follow in Chapter 10.

In most of these countries, private individuals and organizations that promoted family planning prepared the way for a national population policy. The pattern was similar in several cases. In the first stage, concerned professionals, usually gynecologists, started to provide family planning services for their patients or clients. They typically came to know each other and then banded together in a loose association. This process was sometimes accelerated by public criticism of their activities from religious leaders and others. Usually at this point, but occasionally before, they came into contact with international organizations advocating family planning, especially the International Planned Parenthood Federation (IPPF), the Pathfinder Fund, and Church World Service. These agencies encouraged them in their efforts, supplied them with funds and contraceptives, and worked with them to expand the number of clinics available. The next stage, usually precipitated by grants from IPPF, was the establishment of a local family planning association. At this juncture, private promoters often joined forces with donor agencies to lobby for governmental action. By then other donors were on the scene, particularly the Ford Foundation, the Population Council, and the Agency for International Development (AID). Private groups played a pivotal role in demonstrating the acceptability of family planning in national circumstances and in creating an organizational base for future expansion. With the usual perversity of history, many of these crusaders were reviled for their initial efforts, hailed as pioneers when the government adopted a policy, and then brushed aside as new actors came to the fore.

Parties and other formally organized political groups played a small part in the development of population policy in these countries. In no case did the primary impetus for an explicit policy come from a political party, and in no case was a party in the forefront of implementation. Egypt did not have a competitive party system, so the question was irrelevant there. Before martial law there were active parties in the Philippines, but despite some comments during legislative debates, none seemed really interested in the population question. In Kenya politicians commented openly and often critically about the government's announced policy but the lineup did not follow any clear factional lines. Parties of the right and center seemed to favor family planning in the Dominican Republic, whereas those on the left were weak and did not see population control as a crucial issue. For Lebanon the question of confessional rivalries overrode all others, so there was not much scope for partisan influence, and in any event there was no policy to debate. Indian political parties likewise saw little payoff in family planning, at least until it came to symbolize the autocratic rule of Indira Gandhi. In several countries, left-wing groups attacked birth control as a distraction from development, but this criticism carried little weight. In most countries there were more wrangles between competing bureaucracies than contending parties.

Although parties as such were of minor importance, the Mexican study brings out the salience of broader ideological clusters. The study identified four major ideological tendencies that did, directly or indirectly, bear on policy formulation. The first was nineteenth-century liberalism, a school emphasizing the value of individual freedom and the nuclear family and opposing state intervention in personal and family matters. Adherents of this view would favor family planning only if it were offered as an aid to free choice. The second tendency is a set of disparate views held together by Christian ideology. Adherents of a conservative approach basically accept the Vatican line in opposing birth control. A larger group of progressive-liberal Christians believes in responsible parenthood, following the dictates of one's own conscience, the value of personal love in marriage, demystifying church authority, and some secularization of family life. Their core values are those of twentieth-century liberalism, but with a Catholic cast. Family planning is acceptable as an exercise of free choice and personal conscience but only so long as it rejects abortion and any form of coercion. Even further to the left are those of social Christian outlook. This group accepts elements of socialist ideology within a framework of Christian humanism. They are not opposed to family planning in itself, but they are skeptical of the alleged dangers of the population explosion.

The third broad tendency is socialism. The socialist movement in Mexico is not strong in numbers, but it carries intellectual weight. It is centered in the universities and its adherents include students, professors, intellectuals, a few journalists, and some groups of unionized workers and peasants. Its guiding values include the liberation of Mexico from economic and political dependence, prevention of North American cultural influence, promotion of Mexican and Latin American nationalism, collective planning, and, at the broadest level, social justice. Mexican Socialists have resisted birth control because of its association with North American imperialism rather than for any intrinsic reasons.

The final and most powerful tendency can be called officialism, for it represents the cental views of the ruling Institutional Revolutionary Party (PRI). Officialism is basically an amalgam of views rather than a unique ideological current. From liberalism it has taken respect for individual freedom and a tacit acceptance of capitalism. From socialism it has accepted nationalism, populism, the expropriation of basic industries, land reform, and provision of public services to the masses. And from Christian sources, especially the progressive-liberal current of Catholicism, it borrowed such notions as responsible parenthood and the secularization of family life. Even though the PRI itself was not a prominent actor in formulating population policy the government slanted both the contents of the policy and its public presentation toward the values of officialism. At the same time, it sought to make that policy as compatible as possible with the three other tendencies noted. The Mexican case thus illustrates the power of broad ideological currents in shaping public policy even when they are not articulated by any single pressure group. Echeverria and Moya and their associates knew that some policy lines would be consonant with the national environment and others dissonant, and they made every effort to stay with the former.

Other interest groups have also tried to influence population policy, often on specific issues. Medical associations in several countries opposed the nonmedical distribution of contraceptives and urged adequate standards of health care. The Dominican Medical Association argued against the country's narrow emphasis on reducing the birth rate and called for family planning to be part of a national health policy. The press likewise played some role in forming public opinion, especially in the stage of debate on an official policy. Mexican journalists were influential in building support for the government's population law, and newspapers in Kenya and India often served as outlets for criticisms of national programs. Finally, various private associations launched attacks on governmental programs, usually in response to what they viewed as flagrant abuses. Parent–teacher associations in Mexico lashed out at the government's program of sex education, and the Catholic Women's League in the Philippines vehemently protested a government-approved campaign for the commercial distribution of condoms. This latter protest was so strong that it came to be known as the condom war.

International donors

International donor agencies have had a direct or indirect influence on population policies and programs in every country under review. Even in Lebanon, which has no official policy, the International Planned Parenthood Federation supported the development of a private family planning association and provided it with contraceptive supplies. Donor influence extends from creating the conditions that lead governments to become aware of a "population problem," through defining the organizational forms and dominant emphases of family planning programs, to pressuring for specific results in implementation. Examples of donor styles and influence were cited in chapters 4 and 5, and others will be added in later chapters.

ISSUES

In addition to actors, population policies and programs can be strongly affected by a country's *issue context*, the set of matters on which there is significant conflict, debate, or attention in the society. Issue contexts germane to population vary markedly from country to country and region to region: The question of racial extinction from birth control is salient in Kenya and in some other African countries but is almost never heard in Indonesia or the Philippines. And even where the same issue is present across countries, it often differs in its political charge. The question of American imperialism arises throughout Latin America but with much greater intensity in Mexico and Cuba than in Paraguay. For population policy in any given country, two questions about the issue context are central: (1) What are the focal points of debate or attention in the society, and (2) how do these connect to population policy or programs?

Some issues are *energizing*, in that they spark interest or mobilize support for population policy. The question of toppling the agrarian elite was highly energizing to the land reform undertaken by the Peruvian military in 1969.[5] Because success in this effort was crucial to political survival, top-level commitment was strong. A common problem for population policies is that there are no energizing issues to push them forward. In most countries population control is not a popular item, and in some it is plainly despised. Nazli Choucri writes that "there is no public constituency for population intervention; as an issue, population is not a source of political support."[6] Because it cannot energize itself, it must seek support from some more appealing issue, such as economic development, health, or freedom of choice. But governments are sometimes reluctant to make this identification, because population may draw support away from the more popular issue and thereby lower its value. Among the countries studied here, Mexico went farther than any other in seeking energizing issues for its population policy, but the net effect was to defuse opposition rather than to kindle enthusiasm.

Issues are *debilitating* if they enervate or contaminate the programs to which they become attached. A Latin American family planning program would be harmed if it were plausibly linked to American intervention; a Kenyan program would be hurt by association with South African racism. A third set of issues are those that are *burning* but unpredictable in their consequences for population policy. The Haitian question in the Dominican Republic has alternately worked for and against the government's family planning program. On the positive side, it has lent impetus to birth control for poor Haitians in the border regions. At the same time, it has spawned fears that widespread adoption of family planning by Dominicans would ultimately give the demographic edge to the reputedly more fertile Haitians. This study brought out several clear examples of issues in national life that affected the development and implementation of population policies.

Racism and genocide

Questions about the racist or even genocidal intent of birth control programs have often been raised in Africa, and they surfaced when the government announced a family planning program in Kenya. Oginga Odinga, opposition leader in parliament, charged that black people were already being eliminated from a sparsely populated continent and that birth control would only speed up this trend. At a seminar held in 1967, the Kenyan author Grace Ogot said that "colonialism is still fresh in the minds of East Africans and it would, therefore, not be difficult to interpret the foreign experts' enthusiasm. . . as a kind of neocolonialist trick to keep the African population down."[7]

Why did the extinction theme arise in Kenya and not in the other countries studied? One obvious reason is the continent's experience with slavery, which many Africans still see as genocidal. Also at work in Kenya was the fairly fresh memory of an absolute population decline under British colonialism. The famine of the 1890s took thousands of human lives, and livestock was diminished by drought and rinderpest, a contagious cattle disease. Fatalities mounted with the spread of diseases against which the native population had no immunity. By 1890, smallpox, measles, polio, plague, influenza, and whooping cough had spread through East Africa and claimed scores of victims.[8] And more lives were lost in revolts against the British. Although estimates are unreliable because blacks were not included in the British census at that time, some place the population decline between 1890 and 1920 as high as one-third. Whatever the case, the net result for many Africans was a lingering sense that their numbers were plummeting.

Racial contamination

If fear of genocide from whites was important in Kenya, fear of racial pollution from blacks was crucial in the Dominican Republic. The origins of

Dominican antipathy to Haitians date back at least to the nineteenth century, when Haiti, under the French, became one of the world's richest colonies. In 1801, under the fabled Toussaint L'Ouverture, Haitians invaded the Spanish side of the island of Hispaniola (what is now the Dominican Republic). They remained there until 1809, when the Spanish returned. Shortly after Dominican independence from Spain in 1821, the Haitians invaded the country again and remained for twenty-three years. Their occupation was marked by a brutality that has never been forgotten by the Dominicans, and that may well shape current attitudes toward Haitian immigrants.

A more immediate source of concern was the large number of illegal immigrants from Haiti. Thousands of Haitian laborers were imported during the U.S. military occupation from 1916 to 1924 and again by the U.S.-financed sugar industry during its period of expansion. Dominican concern mounted during the 1920s as large numbers of Haitians entered the country illegally, and it culminated in 1937 when Rafael Trujillo ordered a massacre of Haitians, allegedly to end a border dispute.

But the Dominican fear of Haitians is more than a collective anxiety about threats to employment or border security. Beneath these apprehensions lies a deep-rooted racial and cultural prejudice that persists to this day. Joaquin Balaguer, vice-president under Trujillo and president from 1966 to 1978, made these revealing remarks in 1946:

Haitian population, for a biological reason, tends inevitably to flow over into the Dominican territory, which is much richer, much flatter, and much larger than their own. . . What were the consequences of this state of affairs? The Dominican Republic was rapidly becoming "Haitianized," and the common ties among the old Spanish part of the island were being destroyed. Voodoo, the national Haitian religion, a type of African animism of the worst origins, became the preferred cult of the entire frontier population. The Haitian currency, the *gourde*, replaced the national currency, even in markets in the central region of the country. Dominicans living near Haiti – who were the most exposed to the denationalizing influences of our neighbors – lost their sense of nationality, to the extreme where even today many families possess in their hearts an astonishing sentiment of ties to the country of Dessalines. The Dominican Republic was thus condemned to disappear, being absorbed by the Haitians, a race more prolific and homogenous than our own; in another couple of decades the country would have been irreparably "Haitianized."[9]

In 1973 Frank Marino published an empirical study of the Haitian problem.[10] He asked a sample of Dominicans where, aside from their homeland, they would most and least like to have been born. Haiti was not mentioned by a single respondent as a preferred alternative, and it headed the list of negative choices. When asked why they did not like Haitians, respondents gave justifications such as these: They damage our race; they have a low cultural level; they are corrupt; they aren't Catholic; they have a bad reputation.

This running antagonism to Haitians broke out soon after the Dominican government established a family planning program in 1967. A private group called the National Frontier Commission at first opposed birth control on the grounds that it would work to the numerical advantage of the Haitians. Later, the commission qualified its opposition in two ways. First, it would tolerate family planning so long as it was not introduced in the frontier regions, which needed more Dominicans. Second, it would favor family planning programs in the colonies of Haitians clustered along the country's western border. The following statements, made to researchers in this study, capture the group's feelings on the matter:

The Dominican frontier region should be populated, developed, and the object of a cultural campaign. In this way we can prevent them from saturating us with a foreign culture...

This scientific measure of family planning is very healthy for the economic and social development of the Dominican people, but at the same time it is dangerous as long as the government does not change its pernicious policy of tolerance regarding the thousands of Haitians who live in our country. The government should not sponsor birth control among Dominicans at the same time that it opens its doors to the uncontrolled migration of Haitians, because in a short while we will be a Haitianized nation.[11]

These views are not limited to one group. In his opening address to a 1970 seminar on population and development, President Balaguer stated:

There are zones in our territory which for deep historical reasons have to develop a sufficient population density so as to avoid absorption by the neighboring country. Our borders with Haiti must be increasingly populated by Dominican elements, and in these areas any practice aimed at reducing birth by artificial means will always be a senseless measure.[12]

As of 1978, the Haitian issue seemed to have lost much of its force on the population scene. It remained present but did not have much direct impact on the way in which the program was being implemented. But it is also one of those issues that, with a sudden change in the political climate, could quickly be recharged and come back to damage the program.

Sex and centralism

A Mexican debate over the content of school textbooks shows the interplay of historical resentments and contemporary power struggles in breeding political rancor. The case in point was a new series of free and obligatory textbooks issued by the Minister of Education in 1974. On February 3, 1975, the National Parents Union (Unión Nacional de Padres de Familia) published a full-page ad in the daily *Excelsior* lambasting the natural science and social science texts for grades 4 to 6. The assault had two specific targets: sex education and the teaching of evolution. Because material on sexuality was developed under the coordination of the National Commission on Population, the resulting conflict directly touched on the educational component of population policy.

The group's key arguments on sex education were that it should be carried out by parents rather than the state and that it should be set in the context of Christian humanism rather than biological materialism. On the question of who should be responsible, the ad was unequivocal:

The entitlement for sexual education resides, according to nature, in the family. The school is a complementary element of this formation and should never operate on its own without the knowledge and consensus of the parents, for this education should be individualized and personalized. Unilateral education should not be made as if we were dealing with the children of totalitarian or Communist countries.[13]

The sponsors came down even harder on the "biological and naturalistic" approach to sexuality in the textbooks. They specifically tore into passages condoning masturbation as a normal phenomenon among adolescents:

That something is frequent does not mean that it is natural; the fact that in many cases men have been able to give up their vice does not negate that in others it has had repercussions on their whole life.

Statements such as these tend to exonerate young people who masturbate from moral responsiblity.[14]

Further, they argued, sexuality taught by poorly prepared teachers is a cure worse than the disease, for many childhood and adolescent neuroses are caused by the so-called scientific teaching of sex. The teaching of evolution with no reference to divine intervention was seen as a further sign of scientific dogmatism.

This case richly illustrates the interaction of actors and issues in the power setting of population policy. For the Catholic hierarchy, the issue was the proper role of the state in moral instruction. This was a battle that dated to the Juarez reforms in the nineteenth century and came to a head during the Revolution of 1910. The resolution had been a tacit agreement that the church would keep responsibility for matters of personal and family morality, whereas the state would take the lead in secular matters, including public education. Introducing sex education into school textbooks struck many religious leaders as a breach of this compact. For those on the right, the textbook caper was but another sign of the runaway centralization of power. The fact that the books were obligatory for all students and touched on the moral domain dramatically symbolized the encroachment of the state on private life. According to one report, the ultraconservative members of the Monterrey industrial group gave the antitextbook campaign their wholehearted backing as a counterstroke against federal power.[15] For Catholic parents of a traditionalist bent, the blend of biologism and moral permissiveness was symptomatic of a growing dehumanization of society and a decline in their control over the moral education of their children. In the end the textbook debate attracted discontents of various kinds. Although President Echeverria and the national teacher's union rose to the defense of this venture and branded the parents' group as reactionary, the vigor of their rejoinders suggested that damage had been done. The main effect on population programs was that the government had to cut back on some planned innovations in sex education and to tread more lightly in all sensitive areas of population policy.

Other issues raised by population policy include the moral and religious acceptability of contraception, the effects of birth control on the morality of women, changes in religious or ethnic composition resulting from birth control, the relationship between population and national defense, the impact of population size on budgetary allocations for states (India), and the links between family planning and out-migration of citizens (Philippines). The question of the morality of birth control arose in one form or another in all of the countries studied here. In Kenya the issue was not only the morality of birth control in itself but its effects on the morality of women. As is shown in Chapter 10, Kenyan opinion leaders decried the promiscuity and cultural breakdown allegedly wrought by the free availability of contraceptives.

The matter of religious or ethnic balances was the central political issue in Lebanon and also appeared in India, Kenya, and the Philippines. In India the debate revolved around the seemingly higher fertility of Muslims and the long-term implications of that differential for Hindus. Tribal rivalries and tensions also affected reactions to the family planning program in Kenya, particularly when rumors circulated that the government program was a Kikuyu scheme to hold down the numbers of other tribes. This study and others further suggest that resentment of the Christian majority and its government may condition attitudes toward family planning among Muslims in the Southern Philippines.[16] Finally, in three countries, Kenya, India, and the Philippines, critics of antinatalist policies seized on the issue of harmfulness to national defense. Kenya's family planning program was introduced at the peak of the Shifta disturbances on the Somalian border, a fortuity that caused some comment about the need for greater numbers. During the debate on the government's proposed population bill, a few legislators in the Philippines also argued for a larger population to augment military strength. One commented, "Our population of 37 million is too small. If we are invaded by Indonesia, we will be taken overnight. We should increase our population so that we can defend our country."[17] Similarly, Indian commentators have sometimes argued for even larger numbers as a bulwark against invasions by China. These examples suggest that domestic reactions to population policy depend on the bonds between population and other issues of national concern and that some of the most critical issues, such as confessional rivalries in Lebanon, have distinct and deep roots in the country's experience.

CONDITIONS

The third element in the political context of population policy is conditions in the operating environment. The country studies bring out two conditions with particular relevance for population policy in the developing countries: threat and uncertainty.

Threat

Threat is present when the environment is seen as a source of impending danger. For governments the most obvious categories of threat are armed insurrection within the country and warfare with another nation. The country cases suggest that domestic rebellion can propel a country toward population control while international conflicts weaken the impetus for implementation.

In Mexico and the Philippines internal threats to stability galvanized concern about population growth. The period during which the Population Act was being debated in the Philippines throbbed with unrest. Demonstrators regularly marched before Congress to protest social inequities, and one group burst into the lower house during a debate on the population bill to demand an accounting of misspent government funds. Legislators interpreted the incident as "the gathering fury of the populace" and the "violent revolution" to come.[16] Some portrayed such events as dramatic evidence of the need for population control. Dr. O. D. Corpuz, then secretary of education and chairman of the ad hoc Commission on Population, stated publicly that student violence arose immediately from the schools but was ultimately caused by the population explosion. Similarly, the 1968 student revolt in Mexico and the violence that followed provoked a severe sense of threat within the government. Some officials concluded that there was no solution in sight without measures to reduce the numbers of the young. The Mexican sense of threat was accentuated by land invasions in cities and the countryside, a disorder even more easily linked to population pressure.

If internal tensions can push a government toward policy formulation, external threats can sap its commitment to implementation. In Egypt the government's attention to family planning dropped precipitously after the 1967 war with Israel. As political leaders concentrated their efforts on military mobilization, concern with family planning moved to the background. According to a popular slogan of the time, "No voice should be raised over the voice of battle." Egypt's heavy engagement with military questions continued well into the 1970s. Meanwhile, the Supreme Council on Family Planning rarely met, and there was an administrative vacuum at the top of the family planning program.

Uncertainty

Few governments are willing to take on controversial policies, and few officials are willing to implement them in the face of great political uncertainty. Lebanon's reluctance even to touch the population question is an extreme example of policy avoidance and the hesitation of many African countries to go far in this field may reflect their precarious stability. In an unpredictable environment public officials react in much the same way toward implementation. Fearing damage from a tainted program if the political winds shift, they may bide their time or recede into a bureaucratic slowdown. Such fears seem common in sub-Saharan Africa:

> However, a fact of life in most of tropical continental Africa is the instability of governments and the ever present possibility of their replacement by a new regime... which may single out the policies of the previous regime as having been wrong or evil. This... makes officials, both in government and private organizations, reluctant to beome too fully committed to one policy or to be conspicuous in pushing the development of a programme. Where the programme may be contentious in terms of the society's value system, as family planning programmes still are in most African countries, the officials may hedge their bets by letting it be known that their enthusiasm is qualified or they may proceed faster with the paper work... than with the build-ups of clinics and personnel.[19]

Despite persistent efforts to garb family planning programs in the sterile neutrality of medicine officials know that these programs are coated with the soot of politics.

This chapter shows that the contemporory political setting can influence almost any aspect of population policy, from the initial awareness of a problem to the shape and vigor of the solution. It also suggests that this contemporary setting is vitally affected by the country's historical experience with population and allied issues. Since policy analysts have generally ignored the role of history, several ways in which careful study of the historical setting can illuminate the current policy environment might be worth noting.

First, history is essential in judging the momentum of a country's population policy. Mexico is a prime example of a nation whose policy thrust was emphatically pronatalist over a long period. With fifty years of public pronouncements and actions in favor of a larger national population, the government could not simply announce that, as of 1972, the engines would be reversed. And after thirty years of silence on the subject, Lebanon could not easily break free of its inertial forces even to mount a census. These studies suggest unequivocally that the policy momentum of the past is always a force to contend with in the present.

Second, historical analysis helps predict the current issue context of population policy. Thus family planning in Mexico quickly became tied to church–state relations and to the traditional pronatalism of the Institutional Revolutionary Party; in the Dominican Republic it raised the specter of Haitian inundation; and in Kenya it evoked images of neocolonialism, genocide, and foreign tampering with national values. History sheds light on four aspects of the issue context: (1) questions that are currently salient and will be publicly discussed, such as the question of Haitian immigration into the Dominican Republic; (2) questions that are currently salient but cannot be openly discussed, such as differential fertility across the confessional groups in Lebanon; (3) questions that are not currently salient but could become so with a shift in the political scene, such as the heavy American influence on the development of population programs in the Dominican Republic; and, (4) the charge on any single issue.[20]

Finally, history is useful in predicting or comprehending the cast of actors involved in all aspects of population policy. One can assume that the Minister of Health will be a key actor in implementing family planning programs, but what about figures from the sidelines who enter the scene at critical moments? In Indonesia Islamic leaders have been co-opted into support for the government's family planning program, but they could easily become opponents in the event of religious militance. As Thucydides noted in discussing the Peloponnesian War, history may be judged useful "by those inquirers who desire an exact knowledge of the past as an aid to the interpretation of the future, which in the course of human things must resemble if it does not reflect it."[21]

7   The penetration of culture

A central thesis of this project was that culture impinges on every aspect of population policy, from the initial awareness of population as an issue to client perceptions of the services offered. That thesis has already been noted and will continue to be explored throughout the book. The aim in this chapter is to define culture, delineate the main ways in which decision makers have approached culture in this field, and show its immediate influence on reproductive decisions.

Culture refers to the inherited lifeways of a society, the historically transmitted attitudes, values, beliefs, knowledge, symbols, and behaviors common to a certain group. Some theorists portray these inherited lifeways as derivative from adaptation to the material conditions of life, whereas others grant considerable autonomy to culture as a pattern of meanings.[1] Whatever the approach and definition, most scholars acknowledge that culture affects how people react to policy interventions, particularly those touching the most tender nerves of the body politic.

There are five broad approaches to culture in the policy domain. The first is to ignore it and move ahead with policies based on a priori "rational" criteria. This is the essential thrust of machine theory. In fact, although one might conclude otherwise from key policy documents, no country has totally ignored culture in designing and implementing population policies. All have made at least tacit concessions to religious beliefs, popular notions of health and illness, norms about reproduction and kinship, and other elements of culture.

A second and very common approach is to give culture no explicit mention but to take account of its influence in practice. At first, the Knowledge–Attitude–Practice (KAP) survey seems to be culture-free, but in practice it offers numerous opportunities for using culture in interpretation. Although the typical KAP questions were acultural in their wording, analysts did in fact use cultural interpretations to make sense of the data. The great advantage of this approach for adherents of machine theory is that it both maintains the guise of rationalism and leaves scope for realism.

A third mode of handling culture is to recognize it only as an obstacle. The literature on population policy and on development in general is laced with references to "cultural barriers" and the like. This was essentially the mode adopted by the Population Council in its 1966 report to the government of Kenya. After laying out the steps required for a standard family planning

106

program, the authors commented: "Traditional attitudes and values – although likely to change rapidly in the relatively near future – will probably be a hindrance to family planning in Kenya for some time."[2] As Ndeti and Ndeti comment, "The tone of this discussion. . .reveals that the acceptance of family planning is an *absolute* value, one for which all others in competition must be sacrificed."[3] In this view, the culture of Kenyans has relevance to population policy only because it stands in the way of progress.

A fourth approach is to accept culture as having value in its own right and to seek ways of fitting population programs within its frameworks. One of the clearest expressions of this approach comes from the Filipino anthropologist F. Landa Jocano:

It is not necessary to totally destroy the traditional lifeways of the people in order to accomodate new ideas and technology. Likewise, technology can be modified to fit into the existing pattern of the local culture without necessarily altering its scientific base. New ideas must incorporate some of the old or traditional ones in order to provide continuity to the educative process in change and to make the experience in innovation one of exploration and discovery, not of difficulty and frustration.[4]

Some proponents of this view argue that family planning programs must be woven into traditional authority structures and religions before they will be acceptable to people. Thus the Indonesian government, particularly in East Java and Bali, has taken steps to incorporate family planning matters into structures of decision making at the village level and to win over sometimes recalcitrant Islamic leaders in the community.[5]

Fifth, one can seek to change culture by promoting economic, social, or political development.[6] The essential argument of the population-and-development school is that cultural pressures for large families diminish and interest in birth control rises when people have a better life. If infant mortality declines and individuals have higher incomes and greater education, the argument goes, cultural supports for high fertility will be eroded by changes in the material conditions of existence. Although culture is sometimes not even mentioned in the more deterministic versions of this thesis, it is usually given implicit status as a mediator between socioeconomic change and individual fertility decisions.

In the field of population, the real polarity has been between those who take culture seriously in any way and those who ignore it. The second position was the dominant approach among family planning advocates, program designers, and donor agencies in the formative period of the 1960s. Protagonists of population policies typically regarded culture as a nuisance, an obstacle to modernization, and gave it minimal recognition. Typifying the prevailing mode of neglect was the KAP survey. This research package was used in dozens of societies to show not only that traditional culture was no barrier to birth control but also that people were ready for organized family planning services. Given the critical role of the KAP survey in legitimating family planning and its manifest attempt to bypass cultural analysis, it deserves a

careful critique. But first it will help to analyze the cultural context of reproduction and the value of children. With this background, we will be able to
contrast the purportedly culture-free approach of the KAP methodology with
the cultural realities of the countries under study, particularly Egypt. Later
chapters then take up the import of culture for key aspects of implementation.

MARRIAGE, KINSHIP, AND REPRODUCTION

The cultural bias of all the countries in this study was toward fertility and
against sterility. The traditional marriage blessing pronounced by the Akamba
elders in Kenya is: "May you have as many children as possible until their
excrement buries you up to the neck." The wedding ceremony of the Bontok
people in the Philippines includes prayers for the fertility of the couple as well
as their animals and crops.[7] In Lebanon pronatalist values are pervasive and
childless couples are pitied. Couples usually do not want all the children they
can beget, but the society pressures them to be fertile and sanctions those who
are not.

Norms on reproduction

Every society has norms about who should get married and when; at what age
childbearing should start and stop; at what intervals children should be born;
how many children and how many of each sex are ideal; and how detrimental it
is to fall short on one of the foregoing prescriptions. These cultural standards
may be sharply or vaguely focused and may differ in their binding power even
within the same country, but they are invariably present in some form.

In this project, the most complete information on reproductive norms comes
from the Egyptian study. Detailed interviews with 457 married couples in
three rural communities of the Nile delta help to explain why family planning
efforts in such areas usually failed.

A first and critical source of pronatalism was the expectation of universal
and early marriage for women. It was considered normal for women in these
communities to marry between the ages of sixteen and twenty. One major
reason was the strong demand for premarital chastity among women and the
disgrace that its violation brought upon an entire family. Villagers thought
that the longer their daughters waited to marry, the more likely they were to
lose their virginity. One husband explained, "Parents here are eager to get
their daughters married as soon as possible, even before they reach puberty.
They are afraid that their daughters might become sexually involved when
they go out to work with boys in the field."

Adding to the pressures for early marriage is the belief that a woman's most
important functions in life are to bear children and build a family. As one

father argued, such crucial tasks should not be postponed: "There is no value in keeping our daughter at home after she is fourteen or fifteen years old. She can serve best by building a family in someone else's home." A related belief is that "girls who marry early stay younger longer than girls who marry late." One of the wives put it this way: "A girl who marries early stays young and attractive always, even after her husband gets old. If she marries late, she will look like an old woman after bearing the first child. Her husband will leave her and look for a younger and more attractive girl to marry."

Women in these villages are expected not only to marry early but also to have children quickly. The young wife should ideally have her first child within a year of marriage, the second about two years later, and others at intervals of two or three years. There are enormous pressures on the bride to have her first baby as soon as possible and a strong stigma if she does not. The woman, her husband, her parents, and her in-laws are all anxious for proof of fertility and nervous about delay. One wife commented:

The bride must get pregnant right away. I stayed four months after marriage without getting pregnant. I was very worried. Everyone was anxious to find out whether I was pregnant or not. Every time I had my period my husband's family talked about me. They expected me to get pregnant on the night of the wedding and they kept hoping that my period would not come.

Another woman had a more harrowing experience:

I stayed three years after marriage before getting pregnant. It was horrible. I was very sad and very worried. My husband and his family were very restless. They took me for treatment to everyone that was recommended to us, even to the ones we believed would not be able to cure me. There was a lot of talk about me because the length of time I stayed without getting pregnant was too long.

With the wife's first pregnancy everyone rests easier. Her parents do not have to worry that she will be sent home or that her husband will take a second wife to produce an heir. Her husband can be assured about the family line and his parents can regard the wife as a mature member of the household. According to one wife:

My husband's family treated me differently after I had the first child. I felt settled and secure among them. I became one of them. They all called me "mother of Hassan."

The situation is less desperate after the first child, but the pressures remain. Parents feel that if their only child were to die they would again be childless and the wife would again be in jeopardy. "Of course it's important to have more than one child," said one woman. "Do you know what my husband did after our first two children died, one after the other? He went to his mother and asked her to find him another wife." In addition to this need for insurance, most mothers feel that their childbearing is incomplete until they have at least one son. If the first child is a girl, the pressures are strong to have a boy.

After two children, including at least one son, the ideal interval between births rises to three years. Parents believe that they should have their children while they are young, strong, and able to raise them. Mothers also hope that they will have grown sons to take care of them should they be widowed. In these villages women are expected to go on having children until, as some put it, "a woman's period ceases naturally." Although educated women are aware that steps could be taken to end childbearing, the majority seem to assume that nature must take its course.

Anthropological research in two areas of the Philippines showed reproductive norms generally similar to those in rural Egypt. For the Bontok of northern Luzon, fertility is considered essential to marriage and infertility a reason for its dissolution. Neither the husband nor the wife is blamed for the inability to produce children, but wives see childbearing as the test of a successful marriage. The society has fertility rites in which the spirits of ancestors are asked for the blessing of children. Among the Bontok, fertility is valued as part of the broader power of reproduction in all that is alive.

In the Cavite area near Manila the blessing of ancestors is less salient than the ridicule of contemporaries. If the woman fails to become pregnant soon after marriage, her husband is taunted about impotence or homosexuality. These remarks were heard in two communities: "What big sinfulness are you being punished for? Maybe you don't know how to take care of children, that's why you are not blessed with them." One gibe referred to the government's population program: "Very good in family planning. They are sure to be the best family planning couple!" In the face of such derision, women who do not become pregnant within a few months of marriage lose no time in seeking help, whether from the Virgin of Salambao or the local herb doctor.

Sex preferences

Augmenting the pressures for continued reproduction in many countries is a strong partiality toward male children.[8] Sons are valued for their perpetuation of the family name, their contributions to the family economy, their responsibilities in caring for aged parents, their vital role in religious ceremonies, and for other reasons as well.

In Egypt the higher status of male children is reinforced by various Islamic laws and traditions. Under Shari'a law, the son is obligated to provide for his indigent parents as well as for any unmarried sisters. If a sister marries and has children, the son has numerous obligations as a maternal uncle. So great is the desire for male offspring that many couples continue to have children until a son appears. A member of the Family Planning Bureau in one of the governorates saw the implications for his program:

Having sons is regarded as better than having daughters. This belief lies behind the numerous births a family has, for they want sons and if they get daughters they will just try again and again until they get the number of sons they want. I know families who had nine daughters before they got a son.

In a study of city dwellers in Alexandria, Marzouk found much the same pattern.[9] Among respondents expressing a desire for more children, the main reason was the wish for a son.

THE VALUE OF CHILDREN

Why is the thrust of these cultures toward large families? Is the preference for many children just an irrational remnant of traditionalism, or is it rooted in the family's current economic and social needs? There is now a substantial literature on the value of children to their parents, much of it dealing with the child's contribution to the household economy.[10] Although a review of this literature is beyond the scope of this book, a few studies will be noted as background to the findings from the present research.

Economic contributions

According to the prevailing theory of family planning in the 1960s, a large family is an economic detriment to the parents. A manual on posters for family planning summarizes the conventional wisdom of the time:

A careful assessment of the present situation reveals that the economic value of children is much less than the public may think, and that it is declining rapidly. The moment a villager aspires to a level of life for himself and his children that is above a threadbare-barefoot-illiterate existence, the economic value of children plunges.[11]

This simplistic assertion, which is based more on faith than on data, stands in sharp contrast to the results of careful research. The most famous counter-example is Mahmood Mamdani's follow-up study on the family planning program in the Khanna region of India.[12] Anxious to understand why a large birth-control campaign in that region failed so dismally, Mamdani sought the views of the intended clients. His main conclusion was that birth control makes little sense in circumstances in which large families do pay. Even young children can bring grass and water for the cattle, graze them, deliver meals and tea to adults in the fields, and help in other ways. Further, "when a couple grows too old to work, their only shelter is among their children, and parents have a socially approved claim on the resources of their children."[13] And in addition to their economic value, children are often essential to physical security. In the absence of an effective police force and with factional violence a real possibility, there is strength in numbers. The fewer able-bodied males in the house, the more attractive a target a household is and the greater the danger of harm under attack.

Several of the country studies produced findings supporting Mamdani's basic thesis. In the Egyptian villages mentioned earlier, the economic value of children was the main reason cited by parents for having large families. In addition to performing a variety of jobs at home, children could earn cash elsewhere. In an economy in which cotton is the main cash crop, the income children bring home from their work may be the only source of cash between cotton harvests. Those without such income may have to sell their vegetables, eggs, and other food products to buy tea, sugar, kerosene, and oil.

In areas in which farming is not mechanized, children were often essential during the cotton harvests. With seasonal hands both expensive and hard to find, small landholders are often left with no alternative but their own or borrowed children. And for some aspects of cotton picking, children are essential. Weeding, plucking worm-infested leaves, and harvesting the cotton itself are all delicate operations requiring small workers who can move quickly without damaging the valuable plants. In fact, the government's agricultural-cooperative society requires farmers to use children for gathering infested leaves, and the society supervises this work in the fields. Children are like-wise necessary for the mutual arrangements developed by the farmers. One farmer explained: "Of course, unless one has children to lend to others when they need help, no one will lend him his children when he asks for help." Parents in these villages are well aware of the economic liabilities of their offspring, but they still find their economic contribution to be greater than their costs.

In the Dominican Republic children can be an important source of income even in cities. They may become shoeshine boys, newspaper vendors, beggars, domestic helpers, car attendants, or salespersons of lottery tickets. Even though each child may earn only a few cents a day, the pooled income can spell the difference between survival and starvation.

Another income-generating device in the Dominican Republic involves placing children in the homes of others. Under this arrangement, the child helps with household chores in return for room and board, a small salary, clothes, and medical care if necessary. Children are usually placed temporarily and then return home. In the interim, the small salary remittances help the mother maintain herself. And even after the child returns, the mother can expect gifts from the former employer, such as food and used clothing.

The point here is not that children are always and everywhere a net economic asset to their parents but that there are many situations, particularly in rural areas, where their economic value is substantial and sometimes irreplaceable. In these circumstances family planning programs premised on the notion that small families live better find themselves in trouble. Even parents who ideally would like only two or three children may conclude that they cannot afford a small family.

Other sources of value

The research brought out other ways in which children are of value to their parents. Foremost among these is parents' desire for old age security. In the Egyptian villages studied, the fear of being a widow without children, and especially without sons, is one of the strongest motives for women to produce more children than they might ideally desire. Unless the woman is sure that she has a good son to take care of her in her old age, she does not feel at ease. In the opinion of most respondents, the only way to be sure of having one good son is to have several sons. Also, with more than one son a mother can move around so that none will get tired of her.

For some respondents the main reason for having children is simply to enjoy them. The Bontok of Samoki village believe that children are necessary to complete the family and are meant to be enjoyed. A mother of five in that area commented: "It's natural for husband and wife to want children. They're the first fruit of our love. When my husband comes home, he is always happy even if he has problems because he is met by the children." A mother of three in the Indang region of Cavite expressed similar sentiments: "When children start to play their tricks, your anger fades away and you're happy." In Lebanon a large family is also important as a source of conviviality and amusement. In a society where most critical social interactions take place within closely knit family circles, children are, in the words of a Koranic saying, "the adornment of life." The view of many was epitomized in this remark by a Mexican woman: "My children are my greatest source of happiness, but also my greatest worry."

In many societies children are also a proof of the parents' sexual identity. In the Dominican Republic there is a widespread belief that the woman *has* children but the man *produces* them. To be the father of many children is a cherished symbol of virility; this is a potent source of opposition to birth control among men. In neighboring Haiti, men are likewise proud of their sexuality and expected to furnish visible proof of their masculinity. Although it is subject to much critical debate, the subject of Filipino machismo has received such extensive attention that it needs no further discussion here.[14] The research likewise makes much the same point for women. Taped discussions with poor women in Mexico brought out doubts about the effects of family planning on feminine identity. One woman said of her husband in this connection: "Then he'll say I'm no longer a woman."

Finally, children are often regarded as an expression of God's will and the divine confirmation of good moral behavior by the parents. Drawing on his observations of numerous Philippine villages, the anthropologist F. Landa Jocano writes:

Children are considered gifts of God, the grace derived from divine blessings, and the result of clean, honest living. Infants, for example, are considered to be "sweet, clean, spotless, and pure" little angels whose neglect brings about unbearable misfortune to the entire family.[15]

In Haiti children are seen as a sign of good fortune and a means of warding off evil spirits. For this reason many families try to keep a child in the home at all times. In addition to expressing supernatural meaning in themselves, children are also essential for religious ceremonies in some cultures. In the Bontok village of Samoki as well as in India they are particularly important in performing death rituals for their parents.

In summary, this research confirms previous evidence that the value of children to their parents depends heavily on the parents' circumstances. In situations in which children make direct contributions to the household economy, are the main source of old age security, are crucial in establishing a parent's sexual identity, or have deep religious meaning, parents are likely to be ambivalent about or even hostile to birth control, if they have thought about it at all. In situations in which parents receive few economic benefits from another child, an employer or the state provides adequate social security, women are employed outside the home, and the traditional hold of religion has weakened, the premium on large families is often much lower. The evidence at hand supports no simple or sovereign view about the value of children but argues instead for careful attention to sociocultural and economic contexts. And this attention is precisely what the KAP survey has lacked.

THE KAP SURVEY: CULTURE-FREE MARKET RESEARCH

The guiding theory behind family planning programs paid little heed to the cultural context of reproduction. When culture was mentioned at all, it was usually as an obstacle to family planning that would eventually be surmounted. The overriding message was that whatever their culture, individuals of reproductive age are interested in birth control and would like their governments to provide them with family planning services. As the Population Council proclaimed in its 1966 annual report:

It is often argued that in the traditional societies people are not really ready for or interested in family planning. The experience of the Council is that people are amazingly ready and that the difficulty lies in the failure of governmental personnel to realize the fact.[16]

The empirical basis for this optimism was the KAP survey.

The KAP study is a household survey in which respondents, usually women, are asked about their knowledge, attitudes, and practices on matters related to fertility. In addition to items on marriage, pregnancy history, and the like, KAP surveys typically included questions such as these:

Now we want to ask about families and their welfare. For example, in your case, do you want to have any (more) children?

(IF MORE) How many more do you want to have?

Now suppose that you could start your married life all over again and choose to have just the number of children that you would want by the time you were 45 years old. How many children would you want to have?

Many couples do something to delay or prevent a pregnancy, so that they can have just the number of children that they want, and have them when they want them. How do you feel about this? Would you say that you approve, disapprove, or feel uncertain about this?[17]

The practical intent of the KAP method was to avoid the entire field of anthropology. Rather than have an ethnographer spend months or years studying culture in a few villages, the survey could go straight to a country's motivational essence in a few weeks. If it is women who have babies, why not ask them how they feel about it and not bother with the larger culture? Whatever their kin networks, whatever their religion, whatever their household economy, if women say they want fewer children than they are likely to have without birth control, they will be prime candidates for a family planning program. Or so it was thought.

In many countries the method did not work, and the reasons had much to do with the cultural setting of reproductive decisions. Although half or more of the respondents seemed to favor birth control when asked in the KAP survey, when services were made available "program administrators are usually satisfied if 10 percent of the eligible population accept in the first year, and they are extremely pleased with a rate of 20 percent."[18] And in some countries acceptance was well below 10 percent in the first year and later.

This drastic shortfall between the promise and the results of the KAP survey prompted a thorough criticism of the entire approach, even by early practitioners.[19] Some attacked the method on ideological grounds, but more objected to its theoretical assumptions and research techniques. Although a full critique of the KAP survey would require a book in itself, here we can note the main weaknesses. These can be grouped under the headings of assumptions, measurement, and interpretation.

Assumptions

The foremost assumption behind the KAP survey was that reproductive decisions are an individual matter and largely controlled by women. Some see in that assumption an ideological bias against social or economic change. Mahmood Mamdani writes:

If population control is to be a substitute for fundamental social change, then the theorist must look at the population "problem" *independently* of other aspects of social relations. It also follows that he must look at motivations as individual motivation, independent of the individual's social existence.[20]

Although there may be some truth to such assertions, they are far too simple. A KAP survey might be done in a socialist country, such as Cuba (which makes extensive use of consumer surveys), to assess interest in family planning *after* social changes have been introduced. More to the point is the failure of this individualistic methodology to recognize the realities of even the immediate household in many societies. The Nigerian sociologist F. Olu Okediji argues that in Africa

the opinion of an elder carries more weight than that of a young mother and also the opinion of a husband carries more weight than that of his wife or wives. It will be recalled that most KAP surveys in tropical Africa usually solicit information from wives and not from husbands; and this procedure is not in consonance with patterns of authority in traditional African societies.[21]

The KAP survey further assumed that individuals regard themselves as crucial actors in determining their family size. That may have been an accurate assumption for some individuals in some societies, but in others a deep-seated fatalism prevails. Speaking of her own country, the Egyptian anthropologist Laila El Hamamsy writes:

The Egyptian, like other Moslem peasants, sees all nature and all that happens to it and to himself as willed by the creator, or God. He will plant his seeds, irrigate, use pesticides, and rotate his crops knowing from experience and example that nature will respond better when thus maintained, but he believes that the eventual result of all this effort will, in reality, be what God wills.[22]

It would be as mistaken to attribute universal fatalism to peasant cultures as it would to assume universal feelings of personal control. That problem is itself deserving of research. When KAP-like studies have made an effort to measure the degree of perceived efficacy, or at least have permitted respondents to give their own answers to questions about family size, the results have cast doubt on the presumption of individual efficacy. In a study of factors affecting fertility in Egypt, Hanna Rizk reported that over 40 percent of his respondents did not answer a question about ideal family size on the grounds that it was meaningless. For them, "God alone determines the number of children a wife might have."[23] A survey conducted in Kenya found, to the author's consternation, that 35 percent of the respondents answered questions about ideal family size with "as many as God wills."[24] Referring to a previous KAP study, the writer commented: "Heisel's field assistants were more successful than mine in discouraging this type of answer; less than 10 percent of his respondents gave such a reply but nearly 35 percent of mine did so."[25] Instead of treating answers about God's will as valid information both investigators handled this situation by arbitrarily assigning to such respondents a value of twelve children. In neither case was the calculus for quantifying God's will made explicit.

A third assumption was that respondents had thought enough about fertility matters in a sufficiently explicit way to have crystallized their opinions about them. Yet the literature on opinion research had long warned about the dangers of measuring opinions when there were none. In the typical KAP study, responses such as "don't know" or "never thought about it" were considered unacceptable, and interviewers were instructed to press for a substantive reply. When nonsubstantive answers were allowed, large numbers of respondents opted for them.[26] A Turkish survey specifically showed that about half the women interviewed said that they had never thought about the number of children they wanted to have.[27] It is hard to escape the conclusion that a significant proportion of those reported as being in favor of family planning had in fact never thought about the matter in the terms proposed by the interview.

Finally, the typical KAP study assumed that stated attitudes are valid predictors of future behavior. For instance, in discussing the results of a Tunisian survey Morsa commented that "a substantial core of Tunisian couples are concerned with the size of their families and offer good prospects for action in the experiment now underway."[28] Such extrapolation of intention to behavior is contradicted by mainstream theory and research on attitudes. Well before the heyday of the KAP survey social psychologists had noted the perils in such inferences, and the point was regularly made in courses on opinion research.[29] Yet analysts threw caution to the winds as they sought empirical grounding for a priori optimism about family planning.

Measurement

Faulty assumptions combined with slipshod methodology to produce a host of measurement problems in the KAP survey. Lest one think that the KAP survey of the past is being judged unfairly by the standards of the present, it should be emphasized that the methodological criteria used here were well known and widely taught in the 1950s and 1960s.[30] One of the best single studies of this genre, that conducted by Hill, Stycos, and Back, was published in 1959, as was a fine methodological monograph by Back and Stycos.[31] The problem was not a lack of knowledge about methodology but a lack of will to apply that knowledge when the cost might be muddy data or deferred action.

The following are the main limitations of the typical KAP survey:

1. *Poor understanding of the survey.* The kind of structured data gathering involved in a household survey may be foreign to many individuals, especially in rural areas.[32] In the typical study the interviewer would arrive unannounced, locate the respondent (usually the wife), give a quick explanation of the research, ask structured questions about the most sensitive aspects of the person's life, and leave after an hour or so. For persons who have no idea of what a household survey is supposed to be, who are not accustomed to sharing their most intimate thoughts with total strangers, and who have had no experience in compressing their feelings into the response categories in a KAP

questionnaire, this fleeting encounter is not likely to evoke confidence in the interviewer or considered expressions of one's true feelings. Consequently the data may be valid for some items, invalid for others, and mixed for still others. And without careful methodological checking, which was usually absent, one never knows which responses have what degree of validity.

2. *Semantic confusion*. Even among those who understood the survey method and who had crystallized opinions about the matters addressed, there was ample scope for confusion. In the case of questions about ideal family size, does the ideal in question refer to the number of children one might want to have in a world free of social and cultural constraints, or does it refer to one's real circumstances? Careful research in three Egyptian villages shows that these are quite distinct notions. Respondents there, as in many KAP surveys, generally reported an ideal family size of three or four living children. But the researchers also asked how many more children, beyond those already born, the respondents wanted to have. The results showed that, as a group, respondents then had an average of 3.8 living children. The number expressed as wanted (present family size plus the number of additional children desired) came to an average of 4.4 children. The data thus present a paradox: People had a mean of 3.8 children; they said their ideal was 3.6; and yet they wanted to have 4.4 children.

The Egyptian study suggests several possible explanations, all of which relate to the cultural context of reproduction. One is that couples want more children than their stated ideal to compensate for high infant mortality. Hence they bear surplus children to assure the survival of the desired number, including at least one son. Another possibility has to do with sex preferences. To have at least one surviving son it is safest to have two, and to have two sons it is often necessary to bear four or five children. A third reason is that couples may want more than the stated ideal number of children to meet their economic needs, and particularly the demands of cotton-based agriculture. Although the data from this study were much richer than those from the usual KAP study, they still cannot provide an explanation. But they do suggest the conclusion, heretical in the KAP orthodoxy, that people sometimes have more children than they consider ideal in the abstract.

3. *Response bias*. There is now, and was in the 1960s, an enormous literature showing that certain kinds of questions and certain forms of wording are highly susceptible to bias. Two well-known varieties of bias are acquiescence, or "yea saying" (answering positively regardless of the content of the question), and social desirability (giving the answer that seems most acceptable, regardless of one's true opinions). These and other kinds of response bias are most likely to occur when the matter under discussion is highly delicate or the respondent has no opinion on the subject at the time of the interview.

Although few studies made a serious effort to control for or investigate response sets, there is enough evidence to suggest that the problem is real. In one study that did explore this question in the research itself, Laing concluded, on the basis of data from the Philippines, that "It is apparent that a powerful 'yea-saying' bias affects the responses to these items. Clearly, then, none of the percentages for these items can be accepted as completely accurate reflections of actual approval [of contraception] among these respondents."[33] In examining numerous KAP surveys conducted in Africa, Molnos found many signs of social desirability. She notes, for instance, that many surveys ask respondents whether they want to learn more about family planning and related matters. She argues that the many affirmative replies must be seen "against the background of a general eagerness to learn more about any new thing that is so characteristic of rapidly changing East Africa. In other words, the stated interest cannot be taken as a specific indicator of positive attitudes toward birth planning and much less as a predictor of positive action."[34]

Some of the questions used in KAP surveys tend to lead the respondent toward a positive answer. Many of these surveys contained items such as the following: "Nowadays some married couples do something to keep from becoming pregnant too often or having too many children (more than they want). Generally speaking, do you approve or disapprove of their doing this kind of thing?" Marino comments:

Given the use of phrases like "too often," "too many," or "more than they want" as explicit cues to the respondent, we may well marvel not at the fact that a majority approve of "this kind of thing," but that anyone could possibly disapprove. Moreover, since the specific action of "something" is never defined for the respondent, each person may define it as he wishes.[35]

By the usual canons of survey research such items should be ruled out on the grounds that they suggest answers, but in the KAP survey even experienced researchers suspended conventional methodological rigor.

4. *Error from interviewers.* It is well known that interviewers can influence the volume and content of responses.[36] The chances of interviewer-generated bias usually rise when staff members have operational as well as data-gathering responsibilities and when the study directors make it clear that there are right answers. Although reports on interviewer performance are rare, the available evidence suggests cause for concern about bias from that source. In his study in the Philippines, Laing did give explicit attention to interviewer effects and came up with this conclusion:

In the Dumaguete study, there is all the more reason to expect interviewer effects to be important. . .During the training period, an attempt was made to mitigate them by stressing the problems of population growth and the economic problems of raising too many children. This instruction seems to have had the latent dysfunction of instilling in them a sort of missionary zeal and a feeling that they were expected to promote family planning. They were also aware that the clinic staff was planning to hire fieldworkers for the motivational campaign and that they would be likely candidates. It became evident that at least two of the interviewers were reporting excessively high motivation for family planning among their respondents, despite pleas to the contrary from the research director.[37]

Laing also reports data suggesting large variations among interviewers in the distribution of responses to attitude items. Given the quick and dirty character of many KAP surveys, there is reason to suspect these and worse interviewer effects, including some fabricated interviews.

5. *Falsification by respondents.* Any survey is open to distortion from lying, but the chance of distortion mounts when the questions mean little in themselves and deal with matters of considerable delicacy. Because few KAP surveys introduced even the normal checks for falsification, it is hard to know how much lying took place in these interviews. In one case where the truth was checked by anthropological observation, the results were not encouraging.

As part of his dissertation research John Marshall lived with his wife in an Indian village.[38] During his residence there, the village was visited by the local family planning program. Fieldworkers carried out an informational campaign and then, to gauge their success, conducted the equivalent of a KAP survey. Because the Marshalls had collected information on most of the same questions by means of observation and informal questioning of residents, they could compare the results of the survey with their own findings. The discrepancies were striking, particularly on contraceptive knowledge and practice. One question probed family planning methods. Although every man in the village at least knew of the vasectomy operation, over half of the answers to the question about knowledge were negative. Two other questions concerned past and present contraceptive use:

The tabulated survey data indicated that modern contraceptive techniques had been adopted at some point by twelve of the villagers and, in fact, twelve villagers had adopted some contraceptive method. But rather than the ten Thakurs, one Brahman, and one Jyogi described in the survey, it was five Thakurs, five Chamars, one Bhangi and a Jyogi, half of whom were more than sixty years old; the correspondence between the actual contraceptive users and those reported in the survey was...accidental.[39]

Marshall also found errors of omission. Five of the eight men who had had vasectomies were interviewed in the study, but none reported this fact during the interview. Marshall concluded: "In short, the accuracy of the formal family planning survey suffered from an overly structured format, unintentional and intentional recording errors of the interviewers, and the deliberate and inadvertent distortions in the villagers' responses."[40]

6. *Doubtful validity.* The real test of the KAP survey was whether stated (or imputed) intentions would predict the actual adoption of family planning. The greatest single indictment of this method is that when family planning services were introduced in areas reported to have a high demand, acceptance was typically low. To date, no systematic crossnational study has been completed on the relationship between interest as determined by the KAP survey and subsequent acceptance of family planning. The few existing studies pre-

sent a mixed picture. The best evidence of validity comes from a careful longitudinal study on Taiwan. In this analysis Hermalin and his associates did find a significant association between stated desire for children and later contraceptive usage, as well as additional fertility.[41] Using data from Kenya and Venezuela, Kar and Talbot found notable differences between the results from the two countries. As they put it, "Contraceptive intention is an important determinant of contraceptive use, but other psychosocial variables also have direct effects on contraceptive use independent of contraceptive intention."[42] Moreover, in Venezuela social support and husband–wife communication seemed to have a greater influence on family planning acceptance than stated intentions. A study in the Philippines, on the other hand, found only a low correlation between various attitudinal measures and adoption of family planning.[43] And a study in India found no difference between contraceptive users and nonusers in responses to the usual KAP questions.[44]

The most reasonable conclusion that can be drawn is that the validity of KAP data is questionable overall but differs greatly by situation. The respectable correlations found in Taiwan may reflect the favorable developmental conditions in that country. People who are literate and have decent incomes are more likely to understand the survey, to have crystallized their opinions, and thus to show a reasonable association between stated interest and subsequent behavior. Among poor and illiterate populations the survey itself and its specific content may be so poorly understood that there is no basis for predictive validity. And casting the strongest doubt of all on KAP data is the poor performance of family planning programs in many areas considered ready for these services on the basis of KAP data.

Interpretation

The final weaknesses concern the interpretation of KAP data. The most glaring problem has been massive overinterpretation. The report of the Population Council to the government of Kenya provides a clear example. Although no KAP survey had been done in Kenya at the time of the report, its authors offered these encouraging conclusions on the basis of surveys done elsewhere:

Studies in other developing countries have almost invariably shown that family planning is little practised by most of the people. However, contrary to common official opinion, the majority of the population in those countries has stated that more information would be welcome, and that they would like to limit the size of their families and to space intervals between the births of their children.[45]

This statement misleads in suggesting that the "majority of the population" in any country had made such statements. Samples were used in every case. Thus "the majority" was never contacted, and these samples typically had distinct urban biases. Furthermore, the authors misrepresent the real data when they say that "the majority would like to limit the size of their families and to space intervals between the births of their children." In fact, that assertion is a composite inference from questions about wanting more children, ideal family size, and the like.

A second problem in interpretation has to do with setting survey data in their social context. These data never interpret themselves; they must always be understood in the light of some analytic framework, however simple. This is true whether the study is done in the United States, Zimbabwe, or Bangladesh. And the more narrow the questioning process, the greater the need for the analyst to import assumptions and hypotheses from outside the study to give the data meaning.

In a controlled investigation of the process by which KAP data are actually interpreted, John Ratcliffe found ample evidence of analyst bias. When given sets of KAP data on Bangladesh to analyze, "culture-naive Westerners" and Bengalis approached their task in very different ways.[46] The westerners seemed to prefer a culture-free, straightforward approach to analysis. The Bengalis, by contrast, gave fewer responses and relied more on context-dependent explanations, such as "rural populations cannot afford" and "rural remarriage is essential to division of labor." The point here is that, even with supposedly hard data, Bengali interpreters introduced socioeconomic and cultural assumptions from outside the study to make sense of the findings. Ratcliffe argues that persons unfamiliar with a culture may fundamentally misinterpret data or miss important leads if they disregard the social setting. If the cultural context is ignored in the survey instrument, contextual interpretation will be bootlegged into the research during analysis. One way or another, contextual interpretations must be made if the data are to have any meaning.

In summary, this chapter demonstrates the importance of cultural contexts for reproductive decisions and the high costs of ignoring those contexts in the KAP survey. Data from the country studies illustrate the strong pressures for high fertility, particularly in rural areas. Expectations about universal and early marriage, rapid and repeated pregnancy, and having a safe number of sons all press couples toward large families, even toward larger families than they think might be ideal in the abstract. These pressures are reinforced by the economic contributions of children, parents' desire for old-age security, the desire to enjoy children, and other sources of value in children. These complexities of culture stand in sharp contrast to the conceptual and methodological simplicity of the KAP survey. Inattention to cultural contexts, among other reasons, led to faulty assumptions, measurement error, and overinterpretation of data. And paradoxically, in a method designed to circumvent cultural analysis, assumptions about the culture seemed necessary to make sense of the data from individuals.

Part III

Program implementation

8   Organizational settings: the ambivalence of bureaucracy

Social policies do not emerge fully embodied from governments. Typically they begin as broadly phrased executive orders or laws, and sometimes as congeries of loosely joined and conflicting goals that must be left vague in the interests of political harmony.[1] Far from being preordained by the inner logic and technical requisites of a given policy, the implementation structure itself often requires continuing negotiation. And once a government settles on an organizational arrangement, the resulting structure becomes an independent influence on the implementation activities of each constituent agency. The whole is not only more than the sum of its parts, but it also shapes the form and operating possibilities of each part. Competition and conflict among agencies working in the same domain can hobble implementation in the field, whereas effective coordination and strong leadership can mobilize the talents and resources of diverse executing bodies.

The present cases bring out two ways in which the bureaucratic context affects the implementation of population programs. The first effect occurs through relationships among the various agencies and levels of government involved. In Egypt and the Philippines interactions between a central population unit and other implementing bodies became a significant obstacle to program success. In Indonesia, on the other hand, effective coordination by the government's central family planning board has been a prime contributor to that country's apparent success in family planning.[2] Second, implementation can be influenced by internal characteristics of single agencies. In the Philippines vertical authority structures emphasizing decision making at the top reduced the scope for initiative among field implementers, whereas in Egypt the instability of senior officials removed much of the impetus for action. The country analyses further show that bureaucratic contexts are closely tied to the political and cultural environment. National or regional politics often affect which agencies receive what proportion of the action, and cultural norms commonly influence both organizational structure and the behavior of officials.

INTERAGENCY RELATIONS

The first major way in which the bureaucratic context impinges on implementation is through the relationships among organizations active in the same domain. There is no case on record of a national family planning program

125

operating with complete autonomy from other agencies. The most frequent model is one in which a coordinating agency tries to unify the activities of other government organizations, usually including the Ministry of Health, and sometimes private bodies as well. Even when other arrangements are present they invariably entail joint administration, concurrence, control, funding authorization, or other forms of interaction among several organizations. These studies show that the patterns of such relationships can have a potent influence on implementation.

Coordination

The bureaucratic structure adopted for the family planning programs in Egypt, Mexico, the Philippines, and the Dominican Republic relied heavily on a central coordinating body. In Egypt it was the Supreme Council for Family Planning. In the Philippines it was the Commission on Population (POPCOM), in Mexico the National Population Commission, and in the Dominican Republic the National Council on Population and the Family. These agencies' shared feature was their task of coordinating the efforts of the various actors on the national family planning scene. By the dictates of organizational rationalism that notion has immediate legitimacy, for nothing could be more obvious than the need to direct diverse activities in the same area toward a common end. As Caiden and Wildavsky point out in their discussion of planning,

> coordination is one of the golden words of our time. We cannot think offhand of any way in which the word is used that implies disapproval. No one wishes his children to be described as uncoordinated. Policies should be coordinated; they should not run every which way. Many of the world's ills are attributed to a lack of coordination in government. Yet, so far as we know, there has never been a serious effort to analyze the term.[3]

But closer analysis reveals that coordination is often a euphemism for power and, at the extreme, for coercion:

> Coordination means getting what you do not have. It means creating unity in a city that is not unified. It means the ability to enforce agreements on employers when you are unable to do so. It means compelling federal agencies and their component parts to act in a desired manner at the right time, when achieving this purpose is precisely what you cannot do...Achieving coordination, again, means getting your own way.[4]

At the far limits of power, coordination becomes coercion. When a commission on population threatens to shut down one of the agencies it coordinates unless that agency comes up with more family planning accepters, consensus gives way to compulsion.

The Philippines. At the time of this study the family planning program in the Philippines seemed to have the most complex organizational structure of any comparable program in the world. The basic structure called for a coordinating body, POPCOM, to direct, fund, and sometimes stimulate the activities of forty-three public and private agencies. The strategy was for POPCOM to obtain funds from the central government and international donors and then work out suitable agreements with these agencies. The task of orchestrating this array of organizations was complex and fraught with bureaucratic politics. And it was complicated by centralization, avoidance of initiative, and other intraagency factors.

POPCOM's difficulties with multiple-agency integration came to a head in 1974 when it proposed a new programmatic concept: the Total Integrated Development Approach (TIDA). Fresh from the World Population Conference at Bucharest, POPCOM's new executive director, Rafael Esmundo, sought concrete ways of integrating population and development. TIDA was the answer. Its basic approach was to set family planning programs in the context of individual and community needs. To do that, each provincial government was to set up a Provincial Population Office (PPO) to coordinate all population activities at that level. "Representatives and workers of the various agencies serving the rural areas will meet periodically in council to inform one another of what each is doing, and coordinate their efforts with one another."[5] Deconcentration of decision making was to be accompanied by some decentralization of funding to the provinces. And to promote harmony between population and development, PPO staff would in effect become coordinators of development for their regions.

If such coordination was not enough to cause trouble, POPCOM also hired almost four thousand full-time outreach workers (FTOW). They were to provide direct motivation of users and serve as local-level (*barangay*) supply points for contraceptives. In August, 1976, Esmundo stated:

We are employing 3,800 outreach workers with the hope that by 1977 there will be 5,420 whose task will be promoting family planning as an integral part of total development... These outreach workers will be the responsibility of the national government until such time when the local government is ready to finance its own program. When this time comes, the structure becomes property of the local government.[6]

Although Esmundo proclaimed his intention of remaining a coordinator and being only a short-term employer, others saw POPCOM's role in a less favorable light.

The battle was joined when POPCOM tried to apply TIDA to the Department of Health (DOH). If the plan were to work, PPO officials would need some operating authority over health officials in the provinces, and that was precisely what the DOH rejected. DOH officials protested that POPCOM's main job was budget allocation and that it had no line authority whatsoever over implementing agencies. Further, they said that POPCOM knew little about health work and should learn from more experienced agencies before it tried to displace them. And they criticized the hiring of full-time outreach workers on the grounds that they would duplicate the efforts of DOH workers in the provinces. In short, TIDA was perceived by DOH as a thinly veiled power grab that would create confusion, waste money, and break established lines of authority. These comments from DOH officials convey the sentiments in that agency.

POPCOM asked us to submit reports to them – we refused. We are not under POPCOM, we have our own central office to whom we owe our responsibility. POPCOM *asked* for our report not *requested*. Till now we submit our reports direct to Manila. And besides we have enough reports already. [Regional-level respondent]

We observe that POPCOM is appearing as an implementing body because they are hiring their own trainers and personnel for training, and they also try to have their own fieldworkers to supervise family planning activities of the [DOH] health personnel. So now we had a certain conflict with POPCOM – it goes down and inspects records without even notifying the health personnel of the [Provincial Health Office] or the DOH field representatives, resulting in confusion – which is the authoritative office – POPCOM or DOH? [Regional-level respondent][7]

DOH fears were fully confirmed when POPCOM used its funding leverage to force the dismissal of DOH family planning motivators. These and related frictions between POPCOM and the implementing agencies were partly responsible for Esmundo's dismissal as executive director in late 1976. Coordination had become control, and it was treated as such.

Egypt. Like the Philippines, Egypt chose a program design involving the coordination of activities in existing agencies by a new superagency, the Executive Family Planning Board. In theory, the board was not only to supervise the separate family planning work of the Ministry of Health and the Ministry of Social Affairs but also to promote cooperation between the two agencies. In practice, the result was confusion about who was to do what and competition in the field.

One immediate problem was a confusion and diffusion of line authority. On paper, medical personnel belonged to the Ministry of Health and social workers to the Ministry of Social Affairs, but when they worked on family planning both were nominally under the Executive Family Planning Board. In their haste to begin the family planning program, the designers of this arrangement failed to answer questions such as these: Who was responsible if a physician performed his health duties in the morning but neglected his family planning assignment in the afternoon? Who would decide on promotions, rewards, punishments, and transfers for the implementers? Were the two ministries to consult each other on the performance of their respective staff members who were theoretically working together, would they leave such matters to the board, or would they simply go on as before? For years there was no answer to such questions and no structure for obtaining answers. The result was disenchantment on all sides. A senior health official complained of "a confusion among the implementers as to what constitutes the responsibilities of the Ministry of Health and those of the Family Planning Board." Relations between the board and the Ministry of Social Affairs were no better, and those between the two implementing ministries were virtually nonexistent. Even a top official of the Executive Family Planning Board acknowledged the coordination gap.

Mexico. Mexico also opted for a complex coordinating structure that involved multiple agencies and different levels of government. The National Population Council (CONAPO) was headed by the secretary of the interior and had representatives from the secretariats of public relations, finance, labor, education, agrarian reform, and health, as well as the presidency. Although CONAPO had strong legal authority, substantial political influence, a large budget, and a sizeable staff, it had to work through other agencies to implement family planning. The two most crucial were the Ministry of Health, which was responsible for the Program on Maternal and Child Health, and the Mexican Institute of Social Security. CONAPO's powers of coordination were greater with the first than with the second, because the Institute of Social Security had independent financing and a semicaptive population made up of participants in the social security system.

Coordination of the family planning program under the Ministry of Health was complicated. In addition to CONAPO, this effort was coordinated at the national level by the Interministerial Commission on Maternal and Child Health and Family Planning. This body had representatives from the Secretariat of Health, Social Security, Social Security of the Workers of the State (a separate organization for public employees) and from other organizations, including private agencies. Then, as the program moved to the local level, it had to pass through Coordinated Services, an entity linking federal and state governments. Given the politics within the states, this set of filters created numerous opportunities for influence along the way. As noted in the report by Leñero,

when the central orders pass through the sieve of Coordinated Services, they are sometimes neutralized or given a different orientation by the local government, even when the budget comes from the federal government...

When they descend to this concrete executive level, the duplication of orders and the differing weight put on them frequently reach crisis proportions, and the effective realization of the family planning program of the Ministry of Health is often defeated.

The difficulties created by these vertical transactions were augmented by competition among the implementing agencies, public and private. In 1976 the authors of the Mexican report concluded that the coordinating role of CONAPO was largely symbolic.

Standing in sharp contrast to these cases of multiagency coordination is the experience of the Indonesian family planning program. As in the countries just cited, Indonesia relies on a central body, the National Family Planning Coordinating Board (BKKBN). This body works closely with public and private agencies, including the Ministry of Health, the Ministry of Religion, the Ministry of Home Affairs, which is responsible for regional government, and the provinces and other units of regional government. By all accounts the BKKBN has been successful not only in coordinating the efforts of the implementing agencies but also in promoting family planning in other ways. One reason for this success, according to Donald Snodgrass, is its effective use of operational decentralization:

Component programs are drawn up by the provincial governments and by cooperating central government departments and other agencies (including some private voluntary bodies), all following guidelines specified by the BKKBN. Once these programs are approved by the BKKBN and funded by it, sometimes with additional support from the implementing agency's own funds, their implementation becomes the responsibility of the implementing body or regional administration. However, these implementers must frequently report to the BKKBN, which continually readjusts its program guide-lines and budgeting decisions on the basis of what it is learning about program implementation. While adhering to the administrative centralization required by the government, therefore, the BKKBN has managed to achieve a considerable degree of *operational decentralization*.[8]

More recent research on the Indonesian program also brings out the importance of top-level commitment that is transmitted to key officials in the regional government, of respect for local cultures and informal leaders, and of continued rather than one-time efforts to overcome obstacles to implementation.[9] The Indonesian experience strongly suggests that even a complex organizational form can be used to good effect if commitment, resources, cultural adaptation, and other facilitating conditions are present.

Competition

If the intention behind coordinating bodies is to promote harmonious action toward common goals, the net result is sometimes discordant action toward disparate goals. The experience of Egypt and especially the Philippines shows how seemingly rational structures of coordination can set the stage for destructive interagency competition.

The source of competition in the Philippines was the unhappy combination of many agencies, scarce resources, and quantitative performance targets. Pressed by AID and anxious on its own account to show tangible results, POPCOM told the agencies under its funding umbrella that their annual budgets, and quite possibly their institutional survival, would depend on a good showing with performance statistics. These agencies were not slow to grasp the implications of this situation, and they set out in quest of accepters. Given the limited number of persons interested in birth control and the geographical overlap of the implementing organizations, client grabbing and other forms of competition were almost inevitable. The resulting situation was best described by two administrators:

There is acceptor-grabbing and sometimes they claim that they are the better agency to implement family planning and this boils down to their motivation of getting more funds. Each agency would like to get as much funding (as possible). They feel that family planning is where the money is and this is the root of all evil. [National-level administrator, Family Planning Organization of the Philippines]

There is interagency competition. One agency motivates. Another follows. The credit system is upset, i.e., who gets the credit of the motivation. [Regional-level respondent, Department of Health][10]

A specific case of competition involved working relations between stationary and mobile clinics. The mobile clinic system was set up by a religious group known as Iglesia ni Kristo (INK). In their vehicles, INK workers visited the barrios to dispense pills and insert IUDs and then moved on. Given the national program's stress on results, INK claimed credit for all accepters using its services, even those who had originally been contacted by local agencies. But when clients experienced side effects from pills or wanted to have an IUD removed, the mobile units were nowhere to be found. Quite understandably, staff members from the stationary clinics were unenthusiastic about backing up services from INK, especially when they might receive no official credit for their efforts.

Attempts to control such competition by introducing agency zoning caused their own problems. In one area, midwives under pressure to meet quotas went to the local market to find new accepters. But they found that many of the women who responded to their efforts were from the wrong zones. A doctor commented:

During Thursdays (market day) our midwives are in the market because they are trying to convince people but their acceptors are not from Clarin and Tubigon. So if these people accept family planning, we have to send a letter so that they will be transferred to their own family planning clinic in their own town. Our midwives go everywhere just to meet the quota. But this is a waste of time because we will have to refer the acceptors to their own towns.[11]

Competition was also observed at high levels in Manila. Heading the list of institutional rivalries was that between the Commission on Population, the governments's official population agency, and the Population Center Foundation (PCF), a private group under the tutelage of Imelda Marcos. In a development described by respondents as "highly anomalous," the PCF managed to obtain substantial amounts of funds from POPCOM and then used them to support private family planning organizations, a responsibility nominally assigned to POPCOM. The main reason for this unaccustomed leverage was that PCF was created and supported by the powerful First Lady. To make matters worse for POPCOM, its offices were assigned to the luxurious new building erected for PCF in a complex under the wing of Mrs. Marcos. Hence PCF, which during the period of this study was headed by a former director of POPCOM, was at once the latter's dependent and landlord. Differences in bureaucratic interests were apparently reinforced by distinctions in background and style. Speaking of a clique in PCF, one POPCOM official remarked:

Elite sila, kami masa [they are elite, we are of the masses]. If you do not speak English the way they speak, if you do not dress up the way they do, if you do not have your hair cut by Bujiwara, or if you do not have your dresses made by Auggie Cordero, of if you do not have a Manansala or Hernando Ocampo [famous painters] or whatever in your room, *hindi ka class* [you do not have class].[12]

From such trifles large divergencies grew.

Competition was likewise evident in Egypt, particularly in the field. The main reason for it was a compensation system requiring division of piecework incentives among participating staff. The program's contraceptive mainstay, the pill, was sold at first for ten piasters (about fifteen U.S. cents) per cycle, and later for five piasters. The proceeds were to be divided so that 50 percent went to the physicians, 25 percent to the social workers, and 25 percent to the rest of the staff. The social workers naturally complained that the doctors were getting more than they deserved, and the doctors retorted that the social workers were being overpaid, because they did nothing. The resulting antagonisms did little to enhance working relations in the field.

INTRAAGENCY BEHAVIOR

Other conditions impeding and supporting implementation arise from within the executing agencies. Intraagency conditions such as formalization and centralization are influenced by the larger cultural and bureaucratic environment and themselves affect interagency relations, but they have their own internal dynamics as well.

The population program in the Philippines shows the interplay of culture, organizational structure, and management styles. Aside from normal bureaucratic rivalries, one of the cardinal barriers in implementing POPCOM's policy of crossagency integration was the high degree of centralization within the executing agencies. The strongly authoritarian tradition of the Filipino bureaucracy supported a top-down, chain-of-command approach in which agency heads made decisions on all but the smallest details. Low-level officials responded by taking little initiative and by waiting for orders from above.[13] Fearing reprimands for excessive discretion and receiving no reward for independent action, implementers generally handled their problems by referring them up the hierarchy. The shifting of decision making to the top and the avoidance of responsibility at the bottom were reinforced by a plethora of rules, regulations, and formal procedures. Several administrators noted these tendencies and their effects on implementation:

They [implementing agencies] always wait for orders from the top because they fear they are liable to misinterpret their own policies. [Regional-level respondent, POPCOM]

There is a need to establish [regional] priority in training, but even if there is a priority, if the order is from higher-ups, we have to comply. [Regional-level respondent, Department of Health][14]

When POPCOM tried to introduce its integrated development approach (TIDA), the horizontal integration required in the provinces collided with deeply entrenched structures of vertical authority.

Within centralized bureaucracies, vertical ties are strengthened by personalistic relations between superiors and subordinates. Employees show strong loyalties to their superiors and unity often derives from common bonds with a single leader.[15] The leader is expected to reciprocate by attending to the welfare of his or her subordinates. As a consequence, interpersonal relations in bureaucracies become "structured along segments which define for their members the in-group and the out-group."[16] Superiors feel most comfortable working with subordinates whom they trust and to whom they are bound through particularistic ties. When they leave, they commonly take along a coterie of loyal followers, who acquire positions in the superior's new office. When the first executive director of POPCOM left the organization to head PCF, key individuals in POPCOM's planning division, a unit apparently favored by the executive director, resigned from POPCOM and followed him to PCF. The result was a serious gap in POPCOM operations at a time when the organization was heavily involved in developing new programs.[17]

POPCOM's efforts to integrate the many population agencies also tripped over intraagency formalism and preferences for protocol. Given strong tendencies toward centralism and narrow vertical loyalties, integration would have been difficult in the best of circumstances. But it was further impeded by a bureaucratic formalism rooted in other aspects of national culture. One such element is "the proclivity of the Filipino to avoid face-to-face problem solving situations, and their preference...for referring to formal rules and procedures (as well as authority) in resolving personal differences."[18] Rules and procedures become a structural mechanism for preventing interpersonal frictions and also acquire symbolic value in their own right. Violations of agency protocol are thus a triple offense, for they involve not only an infraction of rules but also an affront to the leader owning those rules and a breach of in-group solidarity among the leader's followers. Relations between POPCOM and its implementing agencies showed the effects of these sensitivities:

I have a particular experience with the regional POPCOM office. They asked us for a report on family planning implementation. They just sent their driver to pick it up without any letter...Personally, it would have been better if they sent a formal communication on what they really wanted the report to include or the purpose of the report. [Regional-level administrator, Department of Social Services and Development]

POPCOM is not aware of the structure of DOH [Department of Health]. They do not pass through the channels in correct level; they omit protocol. There is even a threatening posture taken by field members of POPCOM. They are telling DOH people that if they are not given what they ask for they will be reported to the Office of the President. [National-level respondent, Department of Health][19]

If centralization, personalization, and formalism were obstacles to implementation in the Philippines, sheer instability was a problem in Egypt. When the government's de facto commitment to family planning weakened after the 1967 war with Israel, the key agencies in family planning became wobbly platforms for implementation. The frequent rotation of top officials in the Supreme Council for Family Planning and the Ministry of Health left the program with no administrative thrust. Even in the best of situations the complex arrangements used for delivering family planning services would have led to difficulties, but with no central direction the program fell into lethargy and drift. This was a case in which the larger political environment directly affected the intraagency ability to provide leadership, which in turn influenced the success of interagency coordination.

In short, the bureaucratic context for population policy plays a crucial role in determining whether the policy as designed moves from the drawing board to the field and in shaping the specific directions and problems of implementation. Bureaucratic structures installed to promote coordination may instead generate competition or chaos, and, as in Lebanon, informal relations between government agencies and private bodies may facilitate implementation even without an official policy. The success of the family planning program in Indonesia further suggests that even complex coordinating structures can work well when other favorable conditions are present. Finally, the experience of the Philippines underscores the importance of such intraagency factors as centralization and formalism, whereas that of Egypt shows the need for stability of commitment and continuity of key personnel in implementing organizations.

9   The commitment of implementers

Other than client interest, nothing seems more basic to the successful implementation of population policies than the commitment of implementers. Governments may have the most logical policy imaginable, the policy may pass cost/benefit analyses with honors, and it may have a bureaucratic structure that would do honor to Max Weber, but if those responsible for carrying it out are unwilling or unable to do so, little will happen. Conversely, when key officials are throughly committed to implementation there may be action without an articulated policy. Such was the case in Lebanon, where public officials helped the private family planning program even though the government had no explicit population policy.

Commitment is an evanescent compound of belief, feeling, capacity, and the will to act. It manifests itself when officials have administrative discretion – they can act or not act, and they can act in this way rather than that. The true test of commitment is not whether implementers execute a policy when their superiors force them to, but whether they carry out a policy when they have the option of not doing so. Some degree of commitment is present when a nurse with responsibilities for family planning and three other health activities works on family planning when she might realistically spend all her time on the other tasks. Commitment is absent if she has the responsibility and the opportunity to provide family planning services but spends no time on that task.

The commitment of implementers to carry out a program is often situation specific. Far from being determined by the force of bureaucratic authority or compelled by the inner logic of a given policy, commitment varies widely with the conditions in which implementers find themselves. These conditions differ greatly across bureaucratic levels and over time. The environment of a chief executive is obviously different from that of a village-level implementer, and the situation for both may change dramatically from one time to another. A country or community may be hostile to family planning when the program begins, indifferent two years later, and favorable after five years. The point to be emphasized is that the commitment to execute a policy depends on the interactions between implementers and critical actors and elements in the program's environment.

The question of commitment is particularly salient for three sets of family planning implementers: the top leadership, including the country's chief executive, ministers, and senior program officials; middle management, such as clinic directors and district health officers; and field implementers, especially the doctors, nurses, social workers, and midwives assigned to local family planning posts. Each class of officials operates in a distinct environment with its own cast of influential persons, set of cultural characteristics, and currents of expectations. And what happens at one level vitally affects both the scope for action and the degree of commitment at others. Commitment, in other words, arises from both vertical and horizontal transactions. These varying sources of commitment can be illuminated first by describing some broad differences across hierarchical levels and then by focusing on the most critical group, the field implementers.

DIFFERENCES ACROSS LEVELS

The main difference between top- and middle-level officials is that the former move in a national and international environment whereas the latter must mediate between national–international and local settings. The main difference between both of these and field implementers is that the former are more closely linked to the program bureaucracy whereas the latter must deal with the communities in which they work. But the greatest contrast is between the national administrators and their world and the locally oriented fieldworkers.

In this study, top officials of government family planning programs were almost always well educated and had received foreign training at the expense of international donors, particularly the Population Council. They were often cosmopolitan, technocratic, and acclimatized to the values of the capital city. They might disagree with donor representatives about how fast and how far family planning should be pushed, but they typically shared their vision of modernization and planned development. They readily accepted the notion of a comprehensive family planning program designed in the capital city, and they were confident of their ability to carry it out under government auspices. Despite sporadic complaints about pushy foreigners, in training and in outlook they were often more like their expatriate advisers than their national counterparts at the middle and local levels. Hence they designed family planning programs based mainly on assumptions and models from the capital city and the donor community. When they evaluated these programs they were more concerned with statistical results showing the operation of the delivery system than with the sensitivities of local clients and communities. For field implementers the situation was the reverse of this; middle-level administrators were, as usual, in the middle.

The clearest evidence of differences between national and middle-level administrators comes from the Philippine study. Both groups were more like each other than like the field implementers in their judgments about the country's population problem, but they diverged on various questions of implementation. National administrators were more concerned with meeting quantitative targets and less worried about the costs of pushing too hard than were regional administrators. On the sensitive matter of sterilization, 91 percent of the national administrators interviewed felt that this method should be actively promoted, as compared with 65 percent of the regional and 58 percent of the municipal administrators. The Philippine report comments:

National administrators...realize the potential of sterilization as an effective, low-cost method which would generate less side-effects problems. RPAs [regional–provincial administrators] and municipal administrators are more concerned with immediate local problems of implementing existing programs than with innovations. They realize the difficulty of dealing with husbands and the barriers to the acceptance of vasectomy.

Similar differences appeared on the questions of whether pills and condoms should be distributed door to door in the community and whether family planning should be promoted before a couple has one child. Regional and local implementers had serious reservations about community distribution and saw grave risks in promoting birth control before a couple has demonstrated its fertility. On this second point three local implementers commented:

Child-bearing is the main reason for matrimony, so let them have their first-born child. [Doctor]

What if they won't be able to have children and they will be using family planning first. [Social worker]

Have a child first so that the vices of the man will be eliminated at once with the coming of the first-born child. [Social worker]

Such views were generally shared by regional and provincial administrators, whereas top officials overwhelmingly recommended contraception before couples had a child.

The Mexican study revealed comparable differences between top and middle officials. Shortly after the family planning program was launched in 1973, the Mexican Institute for Social Studies (IMES) conducted a survey of 181 officials from all three levels of administration. The results showed that, as in the Philippines, national administrators were more convinced of the existence of population problem, more committed to the idea of birth control as a solution, more taken up with meeting numerical quotas, and less concerned about the medical risks and moral liabilities of specific family planning methods than were middle-level officials. Even more revealing were the attitudes of middle managers, in this case clinic directors, toward birth-control methods. Thirteen percent of the directors were opposed to birth control in any form. Although a majority were favorably disposed toward the IUD, 37 percent said they would not recommend the condom, 38 percent would not recommend vasectomy, and 50 percent would not recommend female sterilization. The commitment of these middle-level implementers was also diluted by their various other responsibilities in the health clinics and by the widespread practice of double employment. With salaries low and official clinic hours running only until 2:00 or 3:00 P.M., many directors maintained after-hours private practices. The net result was not overt protest against family planning but surface compliance without deep commitment.

In Egypt, both middle- and top-level commitment to family planning was unstable, but for different reasons. As already noted, commitment among senior administrators fluctuated as a result of the wars with Israel and their aftereffects. The main damper on middle-level enthusiasm was a shift in the government's compensation system. In the beginning health supervisors in the governorates were given salary supplements for taking on the added work of family planning. When these were cut off, many supervisors suddenly lost interest in birth control. The government did maintain small bonuses for clinic directors, but these were regarded as a pittance. Hence many directors saw family planning as at best a burden and at worst a pain.

Data for Kenya suggest that commitment was strongest among field implementers, mixed among middle officials, and weakest among top-level officials. When asked who were the greatest obstacles to program implementation, local family planning workers mentioned such national figures as politicians and religious leaders. When asked to identify those who helped them most, over half mentioned chiefs, subchiefs, district officers, and other middle-level officials. These officials seemed quite aware of top-level ambivalence toward family planning. Thus they were unwilling to make a complete commitment to implementation, but they did provide considerable backing to local implementers.

FIELD IMPLEMENTERS AND THEIR ENVIRONMENTS

The most critical staff members for implementing a family planning program are those in direct contact with clients. Without the support of their immediate superiors and, to a lesser extent, the national government, the efforts of local implementers may be in vain. But even with the strongest commitment at the top and middle levels, not much will happen if local staff members are unwilling or unable to deliver the requisite services. The environments in which they operate and the conflicts generated by incompatibilities among those environments thus deserve close attention.

Family planning programs have often treated field implementers more as gears to be moved than as agents to be motivated. Following the machine theory of implementation, programs have concentrated on sending orders, setting standards, collecting reports, and correcting errors. Training courses have been held, but more in the spirit of casting metal into its proper shape than of inspiring human beings through internalized commitments. The assumption has been that if employees are clearly instructed, carefully checked, and stringently regulated, they will carry out programs in the manner intended. How they feel about their jobs or themselves on those jobs, how they are regarded by significant others, and whether they experience conflicts between their personal values and their organizational obligations should make no difference for implementation.

The view of implementers suggested by the country studies bears no resemblance to this gearbox model of implementation. The picture emerging is one of human beings whose feelings, preferences, ambivalences, and conflicts make an enormous difference in how they use the discretion available to them. In line with recent discussions of "street-level bureaucrats," this image moves away from unilinear notions of bureaucratic conformity and toward an emphasis on multiple demands in the work setting.[1] Specifically, the country studies highlight the importance of three sometimes incompatible sources of pressure; the organization, in this case the family planning program; the community, with its norms and expectations; and the implementer, with his or her own values, beliefs, and self-definitions. The conflicts and tensions created by crosspressures from these sources, and especially the ways in which they are handled, have a powerful impact on implementation.

The organizational environment: signals from above

The first source of signals to the field implementer is the family planning program, which may consist of several environments that transmit inconsistent signals about what should be done. One message may come from the national family planning program, another from the central office of the implementer's employing agency, such as the Ministry of Health, and still another from middle managers.

The population program in the Philippines showed unmistakeable evidence of mixed signals to implementers from the national level alone. The government's official policy was to give clients free choice in the selection of family planning methods through the cafeteria system. But in practice the Commission on Population (POPCOM), under pressure from the Agency for International Development, had the de facto policy of promoting those methods considered to be more effective, including sterilization, the pill, and the IUD. POPCOM made its preferences known to the agencies it funded, which passed them along to their family planning services. A private agency sent the following written reminder to its clinics:

Discourage condom acceptors and encourage more IUDs and pills. The clinic is evaluated on the method accepted by the clients. There will be no more supply of condom: so convince your condom acceptors to shift to pills and IUDs.

Please motivate mothers to methods with high effectiveness like the pills and IUDs. I noted that condom is the method being used by the majority of your acceptors. Don't sacrifice the good methods to condom.

Most of the mothers who become pregnant are using condom. It is high time to make these mothers realize that condom is not an effective method.[2]

One reason that this agency might have obeyed POPCOM was that clinics were being closed for poor performance. The dilemma for the implementers was that the government had one policy for public consumption and another for private implementation. Some considered this duality to be unprofessional and even immoral.

Egypt showed evidence of mixed signals across bureaucratic levels. From the beginning the pill, followed by the IUD, was the method preferred by national administrators. But the director of health in one of the governorates, although he was enthusiastic about family planning, opposed both the pill and the IUD. He stated: "These pills have hormones, and of course, side effects... All the conferences I attended rejected the pill and urged scientists to develop new contraceptive methods." He also regarded the IUD as dangerous on medical grounds. His recommendation was the condom, a method not ranked high by local implementers, particularly because their financial incentives came mainly from the pill.

But the most acute personal and moral dilemmas arose in India during the Emergency of 1975–7. Although the government never gave formal approval to the use of coercion, Sanjay Gandhi and his associates capitalized on the political situation to force sterilization on unwilling people. Karan Singh, minister of health from 1973 through March 1977, defended the actions of his ministry but acknowledged that there were extraofficial signals from above:

At no time was it the policy of the Ministry of Health or of the government that coercion should be used in the implementation of the programme. In fact several times I spoke personally with the concerned Ministers in various states urging them to ensure that coercion is not indulged in...

It must, however, be admitted that an extra-constitutional centre of power and authority was operating at that time, and it was this phenomenom that was responsible for the unfortunate manner in which the programme was implemented in some states, causing anger and revulsion in the public mind.[3]

Some government workers were apparently told unofficially that their careers would depend on results with sterilization, and they acted accordingly. One indication of their effectiveness is that in the last year of the Emergency eight million sterilizations were performed.

The community environment: signals from the side

A second source of signals for field implementers is the communities in which they live and work. Many of the local staff members interviewed in this study came from the area where they worked, were socialized into its attitudes and beliefs, valued the good opinion of their friends and neighbors, and hesitated to violate community norms about proper behavior. Yet family planning programs often required them to act in ways that were ill-understood, disapproved of, and even feared by local residents.

The best information on interactions between implementers and communities comes from the Philippines. There a powerful deterrent to motivating for certain family planning methods was the implementers' fear of blame or reprisals for adverse effects. Fieldworkers in the outlying areas were particularly wary of sterilization for this reason. A nurse remarked:

We have not met a client who has undergone a vasectomy so we do not know the real side effects. Vasectomy has not yet been performed here. What if there will be some side effects and we will be blamed for them?

The anthropological study in Cavite also tapped these sentiments about vasectomy:

That's stupidity! Getting operated, getting tied, whatever is being tied inside. Huh, you think you know more than God Almighty. [Husband]

This is my only pleasure and you would cut it. [Husband]

The case for vasectomy was not helped by the lack of a local term for this operation – the closest equivalent was the word for "castration." In this climate most implementers were understandably wary of pressing for male sterilization, and some wanted nothing to do with this method.

Client hostility toward family planning also strongly depressed implementer enthusiasm. In the Philippines, field personnel were continually faced with questions, challenges, and taunts about the physical safety of birth-control methods. Several implementers gave graphic descriptions of the problems they confronted:

There are many people who are resisting the program because they have heard that the women practicing birth control methods get sick and the cause is the method. Others follow superstitious beliefs and listen to the old people. It is forbidden to tamper with the body, and the use of birth control methods causes this [side effects]. [Midwife]

In one barrio a woman gave birth to triplets and she had been taking pills before. That was twisted all over the barrio: Look at that woman who took pills, she had three children at once! It is hard to explain to each person; you can explain it only face to face. [Nurse]

The couples do not practice family planning; they think it will harm them. They listen to the rumors about family planning – IUD causes bleeding, causes TB, makes the woman weak. They get scared with these talks. If I try to explain to them – they say, "Have you tried this method? You are still unmarried, what do you know about this?" [Social worker]

Fieldworkers in the Philippines reported particular difficulties with the *pilosopo*, a "wise guy" who argues for the sake of arguing. In many communities the *pilosopo* challenged the gospel of family planning, citing the value of children, the danger of side effects, and a belief in divine providence:

The people are "pilosopo." They will engage you in an argument to make you angry. They say it is good to have so many children so that you can make them work as servants. They regard themselves wiser than you are if you explain something. [Motivator]

The men are "pilosopo"; they reason it is good to have so many children to provide work in the farm and to have them work as helpers [domestics]. They also say it is good to have many children because it is given to them by God. [Social worker]

We sometimes encounter "pilosopo" clients. They argue that it is the will of God, yet these are the people who understand [the concept of] family planning but argue for the sake of arguing. [Social worker]

Implementers also reported harassment from husbands, some of whom were *pilosopo* and others simply contrary.

And the husbands also insult me. They say, "It is the will of God that I have many children. They are given to me so I receive them." [Social worker]

The husbands are not cooperative. They think the more children they have, the better off they are. Children become maids or help in the farm. [Motivator]

Uncooperative husbands are not sold to family planning. They think their wives will enter family planning so that they will enter the prostitution business. [Midwife]

The Dominican study noted other kinds of antagonism. A nurse at a rural clinic reported this incident:

When the family planning promoter gave a talk about family planning, they accused her of being a prostitute. The parents of the girls who went to the talk threatened her and said they were going to hit her, all because she spoke about sex education. If I were to speak in the capital about everything I was taught – they would kill me.

Other sources of opposition included older people who wanted many grand-children; religious leaders, who often preached against family planning; mid-wives, who spread and confirmed rumors about the dangers of contraceptives; and traditional medical practitioners, such as herb doctors, who were suspicious of competing remedies offered at health clinics (see Chapter 10).

Thus even the best-trained and most highly motivated implementers ran up against barriers in the local community. Over time, the perception that one's goods are not wanted can diminish or deplete the motivation to implement. For staff members who are poorly trained, who have little idea of what the family planning program is about, and who have more important goals than birth control, the impulse to counter local norms will be faint.

The personal environment: signals from within

The machine theory of implementation portrays implementers as executors of orders from above. With adequate training, clear instructions, and tight supervision, staff members will perform their assigned tasks and thus move the product through the delivery system. How they feel about themselves, their jobs, the community, family planning, or specific family planning methods should make little difference to the well-functioning bureaucratic machine.

This research suggests that the human side of organizations makes an enormous difference in the implementation of family planning programs. The country studies do not negate the importance of information, and in fact they underscore its salience. Implementation was weak in several countries precisely because implementers did not know what they were supposed to be doing. But more often the slippage arose not from implementer ignorance or faulty instructions but from attitudes, beliefs, and self-definitions. The result was a set of signals from within that was mixed at the point of origin and often incompatible with the messages from above.

Knowledge. Classical organization theory is perfectly justified in emphasizing the importance of knowledge and of training to promote that knowledge. This study provides clear evidence that some field implementers did not understand the policies they were expected to implement and were at times plainly misinformed. In their interviews with field staff, the Egyptian team found that only 65 percent of the social workers and 72 percent of the physicians were aware of the population policy they were ostensibly carrying out. The director of a health department in one of the governorates confessed his ignorance but blamed it on the higher-ups:

I didn't receive any clear-cut specification of the policy either as to what the program was expected to achieve or the way in which they wanted it to be implemented. The only important aspect, I was told, was the distribution of contraceptives.

Physicians in the Egyptian program also received little training in the correct use of contraceptives and in the detection and treatment of side effects. Social workers appeared even less well informed about family planning.

Fieldworkers in the Dominican Republic also seemed ill-instructed about family planning. A top official in the country's private family planning organization made this statement to the research team:

The nurses who are in charge of the rural clinics are aides, not university level nurses; . . . Given the teaching conditions in this country, you know that an eighth-grade student does not have a very good preparation. I believe that this is the reason many girls cannot assimilate better the teaching that they receive at the School for Nurses' Aides . . .

During the study the researchers observed a nurse giving a client an envelope of birth control pills. She told the woman to take them after dinner and then added: "If you forget to take your pill one night, take two together the next day." Another user was told that she should not take the pills whole but should "chew them together with yucca or banana and then have some milk or tea."

The anthropological study in the Philippines found similar evidence of misinformation. A nurse reported: "With the pill it is really possible to have cancer because the ovaries become rotten – just that I don't know how it happens." In Kenya several fieldworkers lamented their own inadequate training:

– Sometimes we encounter problems which we just cannot solve. As such times I feel ashamed that the client will think of me as being insufficiently trained for the job.

– I have no adequate knowledge in this field.

Such feelings of incompetence, and the lack of training from which they flow, are not likely to inspire confidence among clients who are themselves ambivalent about birth control.

Attitudes. Machine theory is right about the importance of information and training, but it overlooks the role of employee attitudes and feelings. Yet the country studies provide unmistakable evidence that such attitudes and feelings bear directly on the implementer's willingness to implement. Particularly important are attitudes toward the job itself, toward family planning, toward specific methods of birth control, and toward clients and the community.

The job. Some of the difficulties observed with implementer motivation grew out of generally poor job conditions. In Egypt family planning responsibilities were assigned to doctors, nurses, and social workers who already had full schedules (by their standards). To compensate for the extra work, middle-level administrators were given bonuses amounting to about 30 percent of their base salaries, an incentive they considered inadequate. The only extra compensation for fieldworkers was a portion of the incentive earned from the sale of pills and the insertion of IUDs. But even that created ill feelings, as doctors received twice or more than twice the amount given to other implementers. Moreover, some of the doctors assigned to rural areas were recent graduates serving out a two-year assignment in public health. Many saw work in rural clinics as an ordeal to be tolerated until they could begin medical practice in the city. The decrement in morale was compounded when doctors from urban areas found themselves among people whom they did not understand or much appreciate.

Poor job conditions also sapped implementer motivation in the Philippines. The problem there was not only low salaries but also delays in payment:

Incentives and salaries are perennial problems. We are not adequate in our needs. How can we implement with interest and sincerity? It is as if we are being abandoned and neglected when we deserve to receive sufficient compensation. [Doctor]

In 1974 I wasn't paid my salary for four months. This is the problem of most motivators. [Motivator]

Incentives come late and are too small. How can we live with 115 pesos a month. . . How can you expect these motivators to work hard? [Doctor]

Filipino implementers cited transportation problems as a specific source of job frustration:

We cannot afford to go to the barrios frequently because we do not have transportation allowance and if we will go there, we have to spend from our pockets with our salary being small. [Midwife]

Transportation is hard. You have to walk in mountainous areas. Guihal-o and Salvación are the only places reached by bus, all the rest are hilly. You have to pass rivers which are sometimes flooded. You really have to walk to reach these places. [Midwife]

The meaning of such comments was not that the implementers disliked traveling to remote areas but that it was unfair to be given quotas involving those areas without adequate travel funds.

In the Dominican Republic, nurses in particular seemed upset about low salaries, overloaded schedules, and scant help from medical doctors:

– Here the biggest problem is the lack of staff. For us nurses there are days when our two hands aren't enough and our heads are ready to explode.

– I think the clinic is overloaded with work and we don't have any stimulation nor material to work with and to do the examinations. CONAPOFA should give us better pay for our services and give us better working conditions if it wants to keep the people here.

The result, according to the Dominican report, is "an attitude of little involvement, and little faith, not in the philosophy and objectives of the program, but in its implementation." That comment applies more generally to the countries observed in this study.

Family planning. In most of these countries significant numbers of family planning implementers did not believe in a population problem or in the family planning program. Interviews in Haiti brought out that general tendency but also showed marked differences in support across organizational levels. Overall, 61 percent of the respondents favored family planning, 29 percent did not, and another 10 percent were rated as indifferent. Favorability was greatest among administrators, clinic directors, and medical doctors; mixed for nurses and medical aides; and low for "contact personnel," such as receptionists and secretaries. In this last category only 30 percent expressed support for the program, yet they were often the first workers to meet new clients.

In the Philippines there was a wide gap between national administrators and field implementers in the perceived sense of a population problem. Survey data showed that, whereas 71 percent of the national administrators saw that population problem as "quite serious" for the country as a whole, only 29 percent of the municipal administrators came to the same conclusion for their own areas. Field implementers claimed that land was still available for farming, that people were resourceful about obtaining food, and that their areas were not as crowded as Manila.

The strongest opposition to family planning came from clinic staff in the Dominican Republic. One nurse cited the grave dangers of birth control:

All these things that they are using – the methods make them sick and they are destroying the women. I think it is preferable to have the children God wants than to live with so many side effects and even look for something worse.

Another nurse saw a conflict between the program and her religious beliefs:

I like the program, but the only thing that made me afraid was that I am religious and I was afraid that God was going to call me to account.

Overall, the Dominican study found great ambivalence toward family planning among the implementers surveyed. Most saw the logic of birth control and the need for convenient methods, but many thought the program clashed with other key values in Dominican society.

Family planning strategies and methods. Fieldworkers also had mixed reactions to the birth-control strategies and methods used in family planning programs. Implementers in most countries were personally opposed to sterilization and abortion. In Egypt, 91 percent of the social workers interviewed and 83 percent of the physicians opposed the legalization of abortion. Their reasons included religious objections, particularly the view that abortion violates Islamic law; moral objections, including the feeling that abortion leads to promiscuity; and pragmatic considerations, such as dangers to women from the operation. Over two-thirds of the Egyptian implementers also opposed sterilization because it is against the Islamic religion, is not compatible with Middle Eastern values, it removes the possibility of more offspring if existing children should die, and it has harmful psychological effects. In the Philippines 86 percent of the municipal implementers also opposed abortion, for much the same reasons heard in Egypt. Local staff members were also far less enthusiastic about sterilization than were national administrators, who urged diffusion of this method.

National and local implementers in the Philippines also disagreed over the commercial distribution of condoms. About 60 percent of the municipal workers felt that making condoms available in variety (*sari-sari*) stores would foster immorality:

If contraceptives will be sold in the sari-sari stores the morality will become cheap because even the young children will recognize the condoms; there will be no respect for sex, it will become very cheap. [Doctor]

I don't approve of the commercial sale because then anybody can buy it. I am talking about the young people. One way to leave open to them an invitation to promiscuous behavior. [Social worker]

Local workers also opposed the commercial distribution of pills, especially to the unmarried. Their judgments about both pills and condoms seemed to reflect not only their own moral values but also their concern about their image in the community. Some plainly did not want to be associated with a program their neighbors regarded as immoral.

The countries studies also uncovered implementer doubts about birth-control methods dispensed from clinics. Field staff in the Dominican Republic often seemed more like their clients than like national administrators in their attitudes toward the pill and the IUD. For example:

I don't think it's good that women use birth control and then, five years later, quit using it and have another child. Now one very good method is rhythm; you don't have to take anything, but you do have to know how to use it. . . The IUD produces cancer and bleeding, and the woman can become pregnant and have a child with the IUD stuck in some parts of its body; you can't tell that to the people, because you just can't and it wouldn't be wise to. [Nurse]

The device [IUD] at some point is supposed to cause something – an ulcer – I don't know! Because just think, they're giving the women something that is alien to her organism. . . Personally, I would only use the rhythm method. [Nurse]

Family planning workers in the Philippines, especially in rural areas, showed similar reservations. When asked whether she would use any of the methods she was promoting, a rural motivator commented: "No. I'm afraid something might happen to me."

Clients and the community. If implementers are affected by the community's attitude toward themselves, they are also influenced by their attitudes toward the community. When they regard clients as friends and neighbors who, whatever their education, deserve the best treatment possible, they are inclined to show them respect and to take their concerns seriously. But if they see the community as hostile or alien and their clients as mulish and backward, they may react accordingly.

The import of implementer attitudes toward clients was most clear in Mexico. There one category of implementers was medical students assigned to rural areas for a field internship (*pasantes*). Many came from universities in which they had acquired the standard Marxist notions of underdevelopment. Most were also from middle-class backgrounds and had little understanding of rural people. Like their counterparts in Egypt, they saw this assignment as an unwelcome detour on the road to professional success in the cities. The result, according to one clinic manager, was an attitude of revolutionary paternalism:

Often the *pasantes* tell us that we are the slaves of the capitalist countries, or that we should let the people have however many children they want, that it is their problem. . . The problem is that when a woman goes to the center because she already has four children and [the *pasante*] tells her to come when she has eight, they take away her enthusiasm and harm the program.

Some implementers in the Philippines also felt that backward clients should be told rather than asked what method of family planning was best for them. And in India during the Emergency, government officials married expedience to paternalism as they rounded up hundreds of illiterate and lower-caste men for sterilization, presumably on the grounds that it was good for them.

IMPLEMENTERS' RESPONSES

Field implementers may thus find themselves caught between the incompatible demands of self, community, and organization. The signals from these sources are sometimes consistent, but more often they are not. Commonly, what program administrators want, such as productivity, does not square with the implementer's own notions of proper behavior or those of the surrounding community. The question, then, is how implementers deal with these inconsistencies.

One way to approach this problem is to treat the conflicting signals as a case of attitudinal imbalance. Social psychologists have long argued that human beings seek balance among interdependent attitudes in the same psychic domain, such as one's job.[4] When a family planning motivator has positive attitudes toward herself, her employer, and her friends and neighbors, but these three sources send out different signals about how family planning should be carried out, she experiences attitudinal imbalance. Balance theory argues that, under these conditions, the individual is under pressure to resolve the imbalance. This can be done by changing one or more of the attitudes, by raising the tolerance for imbalance, by compartmentalizing one's life so that the inconsistencies are less evident, and in other ways. Applied to the present case, the literature on balance and consistency suggests several generic ways in which field implementers can handle conflicting signals in the job setting.[5] These range from compliance with the demands of the organization to withdrawal from it.

Compliance

For many implementers the easiest way to resolve inconsistent expectations is to follow the signals from above. This response is most likely when the family planning program sets and enforces specific performance targets, when fieldworkers are strongly identified with the employing organization, when options for employment elsewhere are few, and when fieldworkers are not natives of the community in which they are assigned to work. If the employing organization is itself disorganized or ineffective, the implementer can more easily strike a balance that favors self or community. This is much harder to do when the bureaucracy works well and particularly when promotions, salary increases, and other rewards depend on the attainment of quotas. Similarly, implementers may deflect a program's demand if they have good opportunities for employment elsewhere, but such is not usually the case with family planning workers. And implementers have more difficulty ignoring community expectations if they are from the area or plan to live there for a long time than if they are on a two- or three-year rotational assignment.

The country studies show two kinds of compliance with organizational demands. The first is *simple conformity*. In this mode, implementers resolve the problem of mixed signals by accepting both the ends and the means specified by their superiors in the program. Thus, despite some of their own reservations and signs of opposition in the community, many implementers in the

Philippines complied with instructions to motivate for the so-called more effective methods of family planning. And in so doing they did not resort to deception, coercion, or other violations of accepted procedures in their organizations. By meeting the production targets set by their superiors they could satisfy the bureaucracy, and by avoiding flagrant violations of procedure they could maintain their self-image as professionals. Even so, as these quotations make clear, some felt it necessary to rationalize their actions:

Clients have the right to choose the methods they want but there are clients who can't choose for themselves. They are ambivalent, especially the illiterates, they can't decide. They depend on the worker so we have to decide for them. [Social worker]

Since the client does not have the training to make him capable of determining what is best for him, we can help him by emphasizing the more effective methods. He should enjoy this privilege of being helped by those who know more about family planning. [Motivator]

The pills or IUD are the ones which are effective. It is necessary that methods be effective; we are out to help decrease birth rates. [Doctor]

These and other implementers who complied with the program's demands obviously saw an inconsistency between promoting the "more effective" methods and their obligations to clients, but they resolved it by citing some higher principle supporting the stance of the program.

A second type of compliance is *overconformity* to pressure from above. Here the implementer abandons the letter of the law to conform with the superior's intention. The most extreme case arose in India during the Emergency. Although the government never officially approved the use of coercion, word circulated among family planning implementers that results were the order of the day. The Indian report states:

Taking advantage of the special immunities and powers under the emergency, the bureaucracy went beyond the official policy framework and implemented the programme virtually as a compulsory programme...While officially, the government appeared to be slowing down with regard to mass sterilization camps, actually the bureaucracy was forcing it on the helpless, ordinary rural folk.

The main extraofficial source of pressure for results on sterilization was the five-point program of Sanjay Gandhi, the prime minister's son. One of these points was rapid action on family planning.

Covert resistance

Another way of handling incompatible pressures is through covert resistance. Here the implementer seems to be doing the job but in fact either does as little as possible or subverts the program unobtrusively. In so doing, the individual satisfies the organization by appearing to meet its demands and responds to self or community by means of clandestine nonconformity. The country studies bring out five main kinds of covert resistance: minimalism, selective implementation, administrative abuses, mistreatment of clients, and programmatic subversion.

Minimalism involves doing as little as possible on the job. It is one of the most potent weapons available to the implementer, and one that was often seen in family planning programs. In Egypt fieldworkers often failed to appear at clinics at the assigned times, did not maintain the proper records on clients, did not follow up on dropouts, and otherwise did not exert themselves. A community study showed that only 13 percent of the families said they had been visited by the social worker assigned to that area, despite this person's presence there for seven years. Only 5 percent reported being visited by a motivator who had been in the community for three years and was supposed to make regular home visits. A family planning official gave further evidence of minimalism among nurses:

The program calls on nursing assistants to advocate family planning services. And who are these assistants? They are girls who are dissatisfied with their circumstances. The only commitment to the program is to collect their pay at the end of the month.

An even more specific example came from the Dominican Republic:

In a rural clinic. . . the nurse in charge of it has set up a small beauty salon in one of the bathrooms of the clinic where she attends the clientele commercially. The researchers who performed the interview had to wait for the nurse to conclude her duties as hairdresser before beginning.

Field implementers may likewise resolve value conflicts by means of *selective implementation*. When some but not all parts of the job are offensive to self or significant others, the individual can carry out only the acceptable elements. A clear case arose with sterilization in the Philippines. This method, which was strongly urged by the national program, was often disapproved of by the implementers and by the communities in which they worked. The simplest tactic was not to motivate for that method at all, but because there were performance targets for sterilization that choice was difficult. A compromise practiced by over half of those interviewed was to motivate for sterilization only after a couple had four children. This stratagem satisfied the implementer's fear of backlash from sterilizations among those with fewer than four children and respected community norms about family size. As a doctor put it: "I think that permanent limitation should be thought of only after the fourth child because an average family should have at least four. This is the average size for a family."

Implementer resistance is also reflected in *administrative abuses* such as falsification of records or violations of procedures to raise earnings from incentives. Pecuniary abuses are most likely when both the base salary and the intrinsic motivation of implementers are low and the program tries to compensate them with piecework incentives. Such was the case in Egypt, where abuses seemed rampant:

It is reported that some clinics have forced their patients to buy a cycle of pills if they wanted other kinds of medical attention. Another practice was to sell cycles of pills to commercial pharmacies at 5 piasters a cycle, when the market value was two or three times as high...In the early days of the program, incentive payments were made to anyone who could recruit a new user to the clinic, and to women who kept an IUD for six months or more. This too led to abuses, such as: recruiters and users splitting the take on incentives; roving teams that visited several clinics, having the loop removed in one and reinserted in another. Sometimes with the active connivance of the clinic staff.[6]

Moreover, according to the Egyptian study, to increase their earnings doctors were recommending that women have their IUDs changed every year, even though such replacements were not necessary. Falsification of records, especially overreporting of accepters, was also observed in Egypt and assumed to exist in other countries.

A fourth kind of covert resistance is *mistreatment of clients*. Locked into a frustrating job or faced with taunts and jibes from the community, fieldworkers can strike back at the weakest actors on the scene – the clients. The typical form of mistreatment involved rude, contemptuous, disrespectful, or indifferent service, as in this account from the Philippines:

What became obvious was that people worry about the rumors they hear about certain forms of contraception...Instead of explaining, however, the motivators tended to be defensive when confronted with this type of situation. On more than one occasion, one reacted rudely, abruptly cutting off the conversation of anyone who disagreed with them or brought up the subject of rumors.

In more extreme situations implementers can vent their frustrations or act out their prejudices by using force against weak and resented groups. According to reports from India, Hindu fieldworkers capitalized on the Emergency of 1975–7 to force vasectomy on disadvantaged Muslims. Similarly, in 1976 Haitian women working for the State Sugar Council in the Dominican Republic were reportedly conscripted for "voluntary" sterilization, sometimes by sheer force and sometimes under the threat of deportation to Haiti.

Finally, fieldworkers can show covert resistance through programmatic subversion. This takes place when, through their actions or their inaction, implementers undermine a program's credibility, political support, organizational underpinnings, or other resources vital to execution. With family planning programs, perhaps the most damaging form of subversion is rumors about the harmful effects of birth-control methods. This research uncovered no instances of deliberate rumor mongering by implementers, but some did spread misinformation about side effects, unintentionally or half-intentionally. And there was even stronger evidence of subversion by failure to counteract rumors started by others. The Egyptian study noted that implementers "made little or no effort to solicit the community's support for the program, to promote individual adoption of contraceptive use, or to refute widespread rumors and misconceptions about family planning and contraceptive methods." When clients hear rumors and see that fieldworkers do little to combat them, they may well conclude that the allegations are true.

Withdrawal

A third broad way of reconciling mixed signals from program, self, and community is to withdraw from the family planning program. For employees who lack other job alternatives or whose assignment to the program fulfills an inescapable service requirement, the easiest form of withdrawal is absenteeism. Thus although Egyptian clinics were supposed to provide family planning services for three afternoons a week, in many the staff members who were responsible simply did not appear. In fact, 60 percent of the Egyptian physicians interviewed in this study said that they set aside no special hours for family planning. Similarly, the Mexican report had this to say about student doctors assigned to family planning clinics:

The medical student *pasantes* in general have feelings of insecurity which are reflected in their unstable attitude while working in social service. When they perform their service in rural towns with access to the city their degree of absenteeism is quite high. An ambivalent attitude persists throughout their period of social service. On the one hand, many of them feel that they can take the initiative in community development – some of them in a revolutionary spirit. But on the other hand there is a more frequent sensation of impotence, isolation, frustration, or more or less imposed obligation, because they feel that their work does not correspond to what they would like to be doing in this initial stage of their career.

The ultimate form of disengagement is resignation from the program. Given the tight job market in most developing countries and the low transferability of skills from family planning to other sectors, this is not a realistic option for most implementers. Hence there was little talk of resignation, though one Filipino doctor did raise the possibility:

I am thinking of family planning. Why is it like this? I know that those with big families should practice family planning, but there must be other methods – effective methods without having to suffer all of these side effects. I no longer want to be a family planning physician. I must want to have my private practice. I feel so guilty. I can only avoid this by resigning from family planning.

Short of resignation, disaffected implementers can request a transfer to other parts of the system where job conditions are less stressful.

Psychological theory suggests another kind of response to conflicting job expectations: aggression against the program. Civil servants who object to coercion or production targets might, for example, organize themselves and call a strike against their employers. The more alienated might destroy supplies or even the clinics themselves. It may be significant that the country studies brought out no instances of such aggression. Although there was ample evidence of frustration among implementers, in no case did they mount protests, strikes, or other direct hostility against their employers. Perhaps the conflicts at stake were not strong enough to prompt such extreme responses, but a more likely explanation is that the implementers simply did not have the power or the inclination to take on the government. In several countries participation in strikes or similar actions would have landed them in jail, and in most it would have put their present jobs and prospects for advancement in serious jeopardy. Although psychologists might speak of fight and flight as the archetypal responses to stress, in countries with authoritarian governments and limited job markets implementers might have to confine their fighting to indirect rather than frontal attacks.

To recapitulate, field implementers are often caught between the incompatible expectations of the bureaucracy, the community, and themselves. Contrary to the assumptions of machine theory, they do not always resolve these conflicts and ambivalences in favor of the family planning program. Some do comply with the demands of their superiors, and sometimes they overidentify with those demands, but even there they may have to rationalize their actions to themselves. A second way of resolving attitudinal imbalance is to engage in covert resistance, including minimal performance on the job, selective implementation, administrative abuses, mistreatment of clients, and quiet subversion of the program. Another route is withdrawal, whether in the limited form of absenteeism or the ultimate form of resignation. Although psychological theory suggests aggression against the program as a fourth means of handling job stress, that did not seem to be a realistic option for the implementers studied in this research.

10   The sway of opinion leaders

Standing between programs and clients are intermediaries who define the meaning, appraise the worth, and interpret the consequences of family planning for individual users. The most crucial intermediaries are the client's spouse, relatives, friends, and neighbors.[1] The next most important are trusted sources with specialized roles in the community, especially traditional practitioners of medicine and religious leaders. Herbalists, midwives, mullahs, and parish priests may have little else in common, but they are often the gatekeepers for family planning programs in rural communities. Their leverage derives not from their expertise on birth control, which they may scorn, but from their salience on matters of health and morality. The atmosphere for family planning is also affected by persons with regional and national influence, including journalists, party leaders, elected officials, and intellectuals. This chapter is concerned with the second and third groups, who will be called opinion leaders. The discussion focuses first on local leaders, then on national leaders, and finally on interactions between the two.

LOCAL LEADERS

In Egypt and Mexico midwives played a crucial role in shaping client responses to family planning programs. In rural Egypt the traditional midwife (*daya*) is a prominent local figure, particularly for women. Not only does she handle most deliveries of children, she also helps with female circumcisions, wedding preparations, and even with the deflowering of brides. Her centrality to social, cultural, and health functions bestows on the *daya* an aura of trust and respect in the community.

Unfortunately for the family planning program, the Egyptian Ministry of Health decided that these midwives did not have enough medical training to work in the health system officially. This rejection, coupled with the obvious threat of birth control to their economic interests, did not endear the family planning program to the *daya*. As one physician pointed out:

The *daya* plays a serious role in hindering the [family planning] program, as she is believed and trusted by the inhabitants. Therefore she plays a dangerous role in propagating the negative effects of the pills and, as she is one of them, the women believe her more than they do the physician.[2]

Several midwives themselves stated their opposition to family planning:

154

–Frankly, I want people to have children every day. Supposing a woman does not want to prevent pregnancy, what do I gain by going and telling her to practice birth control?[3]

–Family planning means that children are numerous and people should practice birth control to be able to bring up the children they already have. I heard about all this from the day the pills were brought into the village. [She laughed.] You family planning people have taken the bread from our mouths.[4]

Not only did family planning steal the *daya*'s bread, but it violated her image in the community. Beyond delivering babies, one of her most valued services was to help with problems of infertility. If the wife did not become pregnant very soon after marriage, the *daya* was called in for advice. As one *daya* put it:

If a woman wants to become pregnant she comes to me and I will help her; if I cannot, I advise her to go to the doctor. But if she has many children and wants to stop procreating, she would not possibly come to me. Is it conceivable that she would come to me and that I tell her to control pregnancy? Certainly not.[5]

The midwives hit back at the family planning program where it was most vulnerable – in the area of client understanding and interest. By spreading rumors about the adverse effects of birth control methods, they created doubts about the safety of family planning. Their efforts took on double force when they tied into client guilt, anxieties, and fears. In places where infant mortality is high, as in rural Egypt, mothers not only worry about the health of their live children but are susceptible to rumors about causes of their sickness and death. One *daya* told a woman with a sick child, "You are to blame for the child's illness. After he was born, you started to take those pills and I warn you that they may cause the child to die." The mother's response was, "If this is so then I shall stop the pills."[6]

Midwives also exploited client ignorance about specific contraceptive methods. Some told women that the pill and the IUD did not work and were dangerous to their health. A physician commented:

In the area there are 2 or 3 *dayas* and they have absolute control over the women of the village since they are called upon for delivery. They are responsible for the women not continuing with the pill, since they tell them that the pill causes hemorrhage, general weakness, headache and what is most serious of all that it causes sterility and cancer.

By virtue of her command over vital services and the trust the community placed in her, the *daya* was a formidable influence on family planning in Eygpt. So long as she considered the program to be a threat to her self-definition and her economic interests and so long as the government treated has as a nonentity, the *daya* had ample reason to sabotage the program.

Traditional midwives were also influential in rural Mexico. Their power derived from their prestige in the community, their contact with women before, during, and after birth, their reputation as experts on female ailments, and the fact that they were often the only health expert in rural areas. According to the Mexican study, of the more than two million births in Mexico in 1970 only 25 percent occurred in hospitals or other health institutions. The rest took place at home, and of these the majority were attended by midwives. These health practitioners often proved to be irreplaceable, not only because they delivered babies at home but also because they could take charge of the household and children after the delivery.

In Mexico as in Egypt, there was a barrier of distrust between midwives and the medical establishment. The government was reluctant to incorporate midwives into the health system for several reasons: their low level of schooling; the fact that they worked part-time, which made it difficult to fit them into the health bureaucracy; their own resistance to work that impeded the goals of their occupation; and, above all, opposition by the medical profession to their lack of formal credentials. The Mexican study does not spell out the specific impact of midwives on the family planning program, but it hints that their response was less than enthusiastic.

A second group of local gatekeepers for family planning was the religious leaders. In Egypt there was a marked gap between the official teachings of Al-Azhar, the country's center for Koranic interpretation, and the behavior of rural religious leaders. Although Al-Azhar had given its support to the family planning program, the message was obviously not internalized by local leaders. According to a physician posted in a rural clinic:

Some *Sheiks* have said in the Friday sermon that family planning is sinful and against the Muslim religion. There are some *Imams* here who advocate family planning, but their words do not carry much weight since they have as many as nine children. The people are not convinced by them very much.

Another physician lamented his own lack of ability to counter the influence of religious leaders:

The religious leaders here do not approve of family planning and, since the rural areas are geared more to the religious leaders' opinions and pronunciations, it is very difficult to convince the people. One word from the local *Sheik* equals ten words from me and, therefore, I am in a weak position trying to make them understand the concept of family planning, since the religious leaders themselves are not convinced.

A similar pattern of opposition from local Islamic leaders has been found in Bangladesh, Indonesia, Nigeria, and elsewhere in Africa.[7]

Why this break between religious teachings in the capital city and that in the villages? One reason has to do with the personal origins of the rural imams. Many come from the communities they serve and are chosen more for their popularity than their erudition. Some may not even be aware of the position taken by Al-Azhar and may share the beliefs and biases of their fellow villagers about birth control. A member of the Executive Family Planning Bureau in one of the governorates summed up the situation:

The family planning program also utilizes the *Imams* of mosques to advocate the program. But, I tell you, who are these *Imams*? In this governorate alone, there are 370 government mosques, 100 government-subsidized mosques, and 300 privately-sponsored mosques, *but the registered Imams number only 85*. The rest of the *Imams* are men chosen from the community, and the only thing these men are required to know is how to call for prayer. Now, can you imagine such *Imams* being advocators of family planning!

With this tension between official and de facto teaching, clients were understandably confused about the true message of Islam on family planning. One woman remarked:

The *Sheik* in the Mosque has been telling us, "How dare you try and decide how many children you will have. What if God turns around and takes away those that you already have."

Local religious leaders in Egypt thus played on religious fears much in the same way that *dayas* played on anxieties about health. Just as medical rationalism did little to counteract the dangers rumored by the *dayas*, so the official prouncements of Al-Azhar had little impact on the negative messages from the *imam*. With the potent forces of health and religion fighting it in rural areas, it is not surprising that client response for family planning was weak in those regions.

In the five provinces studied in the Philippines, all of the local influentials identified as opponents of family planning were priests. Significantly, however, when asked about who obstructed their work, two-thirds of the municipal implementers could not name any specific individuals. The Philippine study strongly suggests that program implementation is not much affected one way or the other by the usual opinion leaders.

The clergymen who did speak out against family planning cited diverse objections. One saw it as a violation of the Biblical mandate to populate the earth:

Family planning is diabolic! God said, "Go and multiply and fill the earth." He said to Abraham, "Look at the sky and count the stars. Can you count them?" Abraham said, "No." And God continued: "I want you to procreate children as many as the stars in the sky and as many as the sand in the seashore."

Another said that the population problem was not as serious as Filipinos were being led to believe:

Though there are areas where population is a problem, should birth control be the solution when we are convinced that there are many areas in the country which are underdeveloped, with good arable lands for agriculture?

Other critics saw ulterior political motives in the government's promotion of family planning, including the expansion of American capitalism, the government's need for foreign exchange, and the desire to undercut popular movements against the existing political structure.

Some priests also denounced the family planning program's stress on materialism and its harmful effects on sexual norms, marriage, and the family:

– The government is only aiming at the materialistic view of things, on the easy life, the leisure of people.

– Sexual deviations like homosexuality, and premarital sex are being propagandized through moves like selling condoms in the sari-sari stores. Now, people have no *delicadeza* nor sexual ethics.

The Philippine study was not able to determine the impact of such views on the behavior of clients. But from all indications, clerical opponents were few and were not the main reference group for client opinions on family planning. Compared to the imams in rural Egypt, their impact seemed weak, as did that of the opinion leaders who supported the program.

Seemingly more powerful were the voodoo leaders (*houngans*) in Haiti. The *houngan*, who is often a healer of both natural and supernatural illnesses, holds considerable sway over his followers. According to the Haitian study, these leaders do not overtly oppose the family planning program or discuss birth control during the various voodoo ceremonies. Still, because the *houngan* is a prominent and respected community figure, people do consult him about whether they should trust and visit the family planning clinics. Hence

when a family planning center has recently been established, especially in the countryside, the employees who are responsible for its operations always include within their activities schedule a visit to the local *houngan*. . . to obtain his cooperation or, at least, to assure his neutrality. Cooperation is possible, and, in certain cases, it is effective. By using his influence among the population, the *houngan* can assist officials in operating their family planning centers by convincing persons who ask his advice on the subject to accept family planning services. . . In fact, *houngans* in rural areas where family planning clinics are in operation receive special attention from the officials in charge of clinics.[8]

In one case observed by the researchers, the *houngan* served as the community representative responsible for visiting families and motivating them for family planning. The Haitian study does not provide enough information to indicate how often *houngans* were coopted into the program and how often they used their influence to undercut it. Whatever the case, they had the resources for substantial impact.

NATIONAL LEADERS

National leaders often write the script and set the stage for local skirmishes and debates. Statements by a prominent physician that the pill causes cancer may be picked up by the national media and transmitted to persons with regional and local influence and then may move into various informal channels. Thus expressions by national leaders rarely reach local clients in unmediated form, but they do provide the raw material for mediated communications.

The two countries whose national leaders were most outspoken about family planning were Kenya and Mexico. To explore their influence in Kenya, the research team there interviewed 170 opinion leaders, including prominent religious, business, civic, university, union, and ethnic-group figures. When asked if Kenya had a population problem, almost two-thirds replied "yes." The specific problems mentioned most often were land shortages, unemployment and rapid population growth. This same sample suggested four main kinds of solutions: family planning services and education; redistribution of land; generation of new employment; and greater agricultural production. When queried about the specific meaning of family planning, over half of the respondents defined it as the spacing of births. A director of social services replied, "Family planning is the spacing of children with no limit to the number."

Confirming the notion that family planning means spacing were responses to a question about what constitutes a large family. Among the 135 respondents who answered that question, 36 percent mentioned six or seven children, 19 percent mentioned eight or nine, and 22 percent mentioned ten or eleven. Interestingly, only 8 percent thought five or fewer children made up a large family, whereas 12 percent cited twelve or more. The concept of the two-child family had obviously not arrived in this group. A farmer commented: "There is nothing like a large family. Because the more children you have, the more respected you are." A religious leader said that his own family had eight children, but that they were planned because they were spaced three years apart. In defining family planning as spacing, these opinion leaders affirmed traditional African values on childbearing. Such practices as polygamy, postpartum abstinence, and separate houses for husbands and wives had long been used in Africa to permit a reasonable interval between births. What was not congenial to traditional culture was the notion of interventions made simply to limit the number of children.

Kenyan leaders were also asked what complaints they had heard about family planning from people they knew. The most common complaint concerned the negative effects of contraceptives:

– It is mainly fear of side effects. Others fear you can be sterile and others think they would be outcasts if they use family planning. [Nutritionist]

– Fear of side effects, bad treatment of personnel at clinics – who go so far as advertising that so and so is in the family planning group. [Trade union leader]

A second major complaint or concern was that the family planning program had a corrupting effect on Kenyan morality. When asked specifically whether modern contraceptives harmed people's morality, over two-thirds of the sample replied "yes." The most commonly cited effect was damage to the morality of women:

– Yes. Single girls and school girls indulge in sex with "sugar-daddies" in return for material aid because the girls know they cannot get pregnant. [Nutritionist]

– They have made it easier for pre-marital sex to be undertaken without fear. It removes the sense of guilt and, therefore, has changed the nature of our younger generation's moral approach. It is no longer something you relate to you and your God but to you and your body. [Magazine editor]

– Yes, now women can move loosely, some leaving their husbands shrunk cold in their houses. They do all the nonsense because they are sure the contraceptives will hide them. Unmarried girls are in fact worse. They feel that sexual intercourse is a normal and common link with men. This is morally damaging. [Provincial officer]

– Yes. It encourages prostitution at all levels. Also, unfaithfulness and I know of such cases where families have separated due to such things. It also encourages promiscuity. [Unidentified opinion leader]

Others complained that the family planning program was staffed with too many divorced or single women of dubious virtue. Significantly, the sole focus of the comments on moral deterioration was women; no comment was made about the morals of men.

National opinion leaders in Mexico, particularly members of the Catholic hierarchy, sometimes had a direct impact on the country's family planning program, but more often their influence was oblique. The Mexican study conducted detailed research into the role of various cultural agents: priests and other religious leaders; politicians; intellectuals, writers, journalists and other media figures; professors and university students; and prominent medical doctors. The most general finding was that these people were simply not very well informed about the family planning program and thus had little direct impact on its course. At the same time, this group as a whole shaped the climate in which implementation took place, including the issue context that was of relevance to administrators.

The most conspicuous and formidable influentials in Mexico were the religious leaders. During the family planning program's first year of operations, religious-based opposition broke out in several parts of the country, including Monterrey, Guadalajara, and Puebla. At one point rumors spread that the government was using vaccinations against smallpox, polio, and typhoid to sterilize young Mexican girls. The rumor became so strong that parents kept their children home from school and used loudspeakers to warn neighbors about the threat of sterilization. Although no one could document that this rumor was started by religious leaders, the government did speak of "fanatical reactionary sectors" of religious inspiration as its source.[9] From all indications, the rumor began in Puerto Rico, where an archbishop spoke out against sterilization, gathered momentum in Yucatan peninsula, and then rapidly spread across Mexico. Along the way it undoubtedly received a boost from Catholic groups opposed to birth control, and perhaps from an occasional bishop, but there is no evidence that the rumors themselves were propagated by the church hierarchy. A similar situation, but one in which church leaders were more directly involved, arose when the government incorporated sex education into the country's official school textbooks (see Chapter 6). But these confrontations were sporadic and had no lasting effect on program implementation. By 1976 most religious leaders either were silent about the family planning program or spoke about "responsible parenthood" in broad terms.

Leaders of the Institutional Revolutionary Party (PRI) were enthusiastic backers of the program, at least after 1972. Partly through the party's efforts, a subprogram was set up for the Confederation of Mexican Workers, an important member of PRI. By June 1976, this subprogram had run 93 courses and seminars for workers and 150 meetings on family planning. The other political parties had little to say about the program, although the main opposition party (PAN) was known to be opposed.

Newspaper writers, editorialists, and other media figures seemed ambivalent at first but ultimately came to support the program. Media personalities organized round tables to publicize family planning, and most articles in the press, including editorials, were favorable to the government's initiatives. Business leaders were divided, but on balance they were well disposed toward the program. Some saw government's intervention in this area as yet another infringement on individual liberty, but most considered the effort to be worthwhile. And to demonstrate its support, the banking system installed a subprogram within its own social security operation.

In short, the Mexican study underscores the significance of public opinion and specifically the effect of opinion leaders in legitimating a controversial social policy such as family planning. The report contrasts this viewpoint with the narrow focus of Knowledge–Attitude–Practice (KAP) research:

The acceptability of programs and methods is not a question which touches only the women users who attend the clinics, as the KAP studies erroneously asserted. Instead, it is a social question, since the consistency and permanence of the use of birth control methods depend to a great degree on the acceptability they come to have for the community through its institutional agents and representatives.

No client is an island standing apart from community and society. The disposition to accept and continue with family planning is most immediately affected by kin, clan, and community, but it is also touched by the broader currents of belief and opinion in the society.

LOCAL–NATIONAL LINKS

We can now summarize some of the specific links between local and national leaders and between both of these groups and the clients of family planning.

First, national leaders can make family planning an issue, or more of an issue than it would have been without their attention. For example, they can signal to the country and to their counterparts that the topic is in need of discussion. Local leaders may then pick up the issue and transmit the concerns, sometimes in garbled form, to their local constituents.

Second, national leaders may raise fears or start rumors that are taken up by local leaders and spread to clients. Statements by prominent medical figures that the pill causes cancer, or by major religious authorities that birth control is immoral, can play into the prejudices of local leaders and be used for their own purposes.

Third, local leaders can provide national leaders with grist for controversy or for support. Parish priests in the Philippines told their bishops about the implementation strategies actually being adopted, which differed from those proclaimed as official policy. With this bottom-up communication, the church hierarchy could then criticize the government for its execution of the program.

Fourth, both local and national leaders may give voice to client fears, doubts, and apprehensions about family planning, thereby legitimizing debate at all levels and confirming the validity of client concerns. In Kenya national and local leaders articulated client anxieties about the side effects of contraceptives. In this way they provided adversaries with grounds for criticism and the media with material for commentaries. The resulting public debate then worked its way back to the client population, often through the very leaders who had set it in motion. A clergyman who encouraged his bishop to speak out against family planning might later find editorials in the national press supporting his own and the bishop's opposition. With this ammunition he might feel fortified in his efforts to challenge the local program.

Thus opinion leaders can affect client attitudes at all levels of the society – national, regional, and local. Local leaders usually have the greatest influence, mainly because they are known, trusted, and close to the clients. This research suggests that midwives and local religious leaders are particularly important influences on family planning programs, although their significance varies by country. National leaders may also have a crucial impact on the climate for implementation, but their impact is usually mediated through local contacts. Finally, there are often three-way interactions among clients, local leaders, and national leaders, many of which are roundabout but still potent in their impact. In the end client attitudes toward population programs must be understood in the total context of a society, with all of its crosscurrents and interdependencies of opinions, rather than in the narrow setting of personal preferences.

11   The significance of clients

The clients of a service delivery program can speed, slow, stop, or redirect implementation. At one extreme they may simply accept the services offered and use them as intended. They may also accept the services but either not use them at all or not use them as intended. Mamdani gives an example of this possibility from the Khanna region of India. Reflecting on the work of the foreigners who had come to install a family planning program, one of the residents tried to explain why many villagers had accepted the contraceptive tablets offered but had never used them:

> But they were so nice, you know. And they came from distant lands to be with us. Couldn't we even do this much for them? Just take a few tablets? Ah! even the gods would have been angry with us. All they wanted was that we accept the tablets. I lost nothing and probably received their prayers. And they, they must have gotten some promotion.[1]

Client influence can be even more insidious. When seeking certain valuable services, such as food stamps or free methadone, clients may enter false eligibility claims or otherwise deceive the implementers.[2] They may also bribe administrators to secure more than their allotted share of benefits or to avert certain punishments, such as prosecution for welfare fraud.[3] Disaffected users of program services, such as women suffering severe side effects from IUDs, can sabotage the entire program by starting, spreading, or confirming rumors about the dangers of participation.

Further along the scale of activism, dissatisfied clients may mobilize political resources to obtain more or better service or to remove administrative abuses. Frustrated by the total paralysis of the local housing agency, residents of squatter settlements in Cali, Colombia, picketed municipal offices to demand housing services.[4] Welfare-rights organizations in the United States have likewise campaigned for speedier and less demeaning procedures for handling client requests. And finally, disgruntled clients may use the ballot box or other political means to bring down an entire government associated with abuses in service programs. Such reactions are rare, but the response of Indian citizens to the compulsory sterilization programs carried out under Indira Gandhi's Emergency is a case in point. Thus, far from being passive receptacles for the services delivered, clients can accept or reject the items offered, demand that services be provided in greater quantity or in a different manner, bargain with or suborn the implementers, lobby to change the implementation system, or even bring on the collapse of an offending government.

In the family planning programs under study, the most common client reactions were: disinterest in program services; initial acceptance followed by subsequent discontinuation; subversion of the program by rumors; and, in a minority of the cases, full acceptance and use of the service provided. Clients had the greatest impact on family planning programs by simply not accepting the services offered and by failing to continue with family planning once a method was tried. To understand how clients reacted to these programs it is necessary first to consider how the programs treated the clients.

PROGRAM TREATMENT OF CLIENTS

Client reactions to service-delivery programs depend on a variety of conditions, among them initial interest in the services, accessibility and convenience, and the perceptions generated by the services and the entire program in the surrounding community. But judging from these and other studies, one of the most powerful predictors of client response is the manner in which clients are treated by the program itself. Contrary to the assumptions of machine theory, which pays more heed to the flow of services than to the feelings of recipients, clients are affected by the who and how as well as by the what of service delivery. A program that shows respect for clients, helps them to understand the nature, risks, and benefits of services, and assists them in dealing with any adverse effects will elicit favorable reactions. A program that coerces, dupes, manipulates, degrades, or injures clients will cause them to respond negatively.

Aspects of treatment

A program's treatment of its clients can be scaled along four interlocking dimensions. The first is *coercion versus freedom*. Coercion takes place when a program forces individuals to do something they do not want to do or normally would not do or to refrain from something that they normally would do. The most obvious case of coercion in population policy is India's use of compulsory sterilization following the Emergency of 1975. Freedom is present when a program increases either the capacity or the opportunity for individuals to act in ways that they desire. A family planning program increases capacity when it gives clients new knowledge about means of carrying out their desire to limit fertility. It increases opportunity when it provides the means for those interested in controlling their fertility to do so.[5]

A second dimension is *paternalism versus respect for individual autonomy*. A program is paternalistic when implementers try to provide for client needs according to the implementers' rather than the clients' definition of those needs. The most common form of paternalism in family planning programs is the assumption that poor clients are ignorant about their own and the country's needs, and that the doctor knows best. If clients are poorly informed, it is up to the implementer to make the choices about the best methods of family planning. As a national-level administrator in the Philippines put it:

My conviction is that if you are really serious about the costs of population, you should not promote the less effective methods...There are times when somebody has to decide for people. If you are going to allow every individual to put up reasons for a decision you are going to take, nothing will be accomplished.

The opposite of paternalism is respect for individual autonomy, or allowing clients to participate in a program on the basis of their own definition of their needs. The anthropological study in the Philippines provides an example of respect in this statement from a midwife at a rural health unit in the Bontok region:

My relationship with the clients is one built on confidence and sincerity. I try to make them feel at ease by pointing to myself as an example of a successful pill user. For an example of an IUD user, I point to the nurse, as an example of a healthy acceptor. I also tell the clients frankly the possible negative side effects of the different methods if the clients don't come back for regular checkups, or if they don't follow instructions.

In general, staff members at this clinic showed considerable respect for client autonomy in their motivational activities.

Third, service-delivery programs differ in *truth telling versus deception*. The essential question is whether implementers give clients an accurate picture of the services offered, including the risks, or misrepresent that picture. The most common forms of deception in family planning programs involve withholding information about the deleterious side effects of family planning methods, with the implicit promise that these methods are safe, and giving false assurances when questions are raised openly about such risks. Moral philosophers would quickly point out that there is a difference between the withholding of information and outright lying, and indeed there is, but for present purposes it is enough to note truth telling and deception as polarities in the treatment of clients.

Finally, programs can be scaled on *active promotion versus disregard of client welfare*. "Welfare" is always an elusive concept, but here the word refers mainly to the health and well being of service recipients. Although proponents of family planning regularly argue that the mere provision of the means to control fertility is itself a form of welfare, the present concern is with the secondary effects of those services. Specifically, family planning programs differ sharply in the extent to which they provide physical examinations before birth-control methods are issued and medical backup thereafter. Some programs take pains to ensure that the most suitable and least risky method available is provided to clients and that users have full access to medical services in case of difficulties. Others simply dispense methods of birth control with no direct provision for medical support.

A human-relations approach to organizations would suggest that client reactions to a service-delivery program would be most positive and adoption of services most lasting when the program's treatment of clients leans toward freedom rather than coercion, respect for autonomy rather than paternalism, truth telling rather than deception, and promotion rather than disregard for client welfare. A machine theory approach would probably disregard these matters, for concern about the human side of implementation is not part of its paradigm.

Specific forms of treatment

These four dimensions of treatment help shed light on three critical points of contact between family planning programs and their clients: the initial motivation to accept the services offered; the explanation of family planning methods; and medical support for complications or side effects. The country studies suggest that these three kinds of interaction or the lack thereof have a powerful impact on client response to the program.

Motivation. Despite the euphoric predictions of demand generated by Knowledge–Attitude–Practice (KAP) surveys, most people in the countries under study had to be motivated to accept family planning services. For those already interested in birth control, motivation might mean nothing more than informing clients about the methods available and telling them where they could be obtained. More often, however, motivation meant stirring an initial interest, overcoming fears about family planning methods, and encouraging the adoption of the particular method preferred by the implementer. In carrying out such activities field implementers could use methods approaching the positive or the negative end of the dimensions just outlined or many points in between.

Observations in the Bontok region of the Philippines bring out a case blending freedom, respect for autonomy, truth telling, and the promotion of welfare. Implementers from the rural health unit felt that women in the community needed and probably wanted family planning but would be worried about accepting services seen as new and risky. Hence rather than launching a crash marketing program the staff members opted for a gradual approach built on respect and understanding. A nurse commented:

The showing of respect for one's dignity is very important, especially here in Bontok. Clients find family planning procedures to be something totally new to their cultural background. It sometimes goes against the very teachings which are inculcated all their lives.

To bridge the gap between tradition and family planning, this nurse tried to show her clients that because there had been a drop in infant deaths large families were no longer necessary. But she did not overstate the case and stayed within the bounds of her own sincerity. As she pointed out, "If they feel that you are not sincere, they won't even bother to come and ask information regarding family planning."

In rural Egypt freedom and autonomy were carried to an extreme when the family planning program provided essentially no motivation. Women interested in contraception were left to pick up pills on their own from the nearest clinic with little explanation and less follow-up. Such inattention created the potential for rumors, fears, and attributions of evil to birth control.

Further removed from a humane approach were appeals based on fear. Some clients in the Philippines were told that if they did not limit the number of their children they would breed delinquents, run into trouble with the government, or experience other misfortune:

Because you have many children, you won't have time to check your children, you cannot discipline them. They will be a menace to society; they will become juvenile delinquents. [Motivator]

I inform them about the Presidential Decree on tax exemptions. I tell them that after four children tax is levied. Then they get apprehensive because of taxes. [Motivator]

More extreme approaches were seen in India when the government pressured civil servants to undergo sterilization or lose access to public housing and other benefits. And at the outer limit, motivation disappeared entirely when government agents rounded up beggars, Muslims, and loiterers for involuntary vasectomies.

Explanation of methods. Humane treatment waned rapidly as implementers shifted from broad motivation to the explanation of specific methods of birth control. Pressures for quantitative results, the lure of financial incentives, poor training, paternalistic attitudes and general expedience worked against freedom and truthfulness. The first corner cut was failure to mention all available methods. In Egypt, although 90 percent of the implementers interviewed advocated free choice and multiple methods, most recommended only the pill and, to a lesser extent, the IUD. Their preference was undoubtedly influenced by piecework incentives for each pill cycle distributed or IUD inserted. Similarly, in the Philippines when Manila-based program administrators were asked if they followed the official cafeteria approach or promoted the more effective methods, twenty-one of the twenty-two respondents mentioned the latter. The other respondent gave no reply. As one administrator commented: "It is well known that though the policy is cafeteria, strategies give more thrust to the more effective methods because the goal is to reduce the birth rate."

The second corner cut was failure to disclose potential side effects. In Egypt pill cycles were dispensed to clients with no mention at all of potential hazards. Most fieldworkers interviewed in Kenya thought that clients received enough information about side effects, yet when pressed they made comments such as these:

– We preach to them about the importance of family planning and only tell them about the minor effects, e.g., nausea; otherwise we don't tell them of the major side effects for fear of losing them.

– If they are told of the side effects the patients may not come back. Instead we give them appointments for check-ups.

Kenyan workers also used the injectable drug Depo Provera without explaining that it was still in the experimental stage. In fact, some of the implementers themselves were not aware of this fact. Field practice in the Philippines was more mixed, with some staff members giving reasonable explanations of potential side effects and others withholding this information. The information gap left during these explanations was often filled later by client fears, rumors, and cultural explanations of health and illness.

Medical support. A critical test of a program's concern for client welfare is the presence of ancillary medical care. Does the family planning program require a medical examination before women are given pills or have an IUD inserted? Does the program monitor for side effects among users or does it just wait to hear about them? When side effects or complications do occur, are medical remedies available locally and is there access to a hospital for serious cases? How do program staff members react to clients who report such vague symptoms as feelings of weakness or disorientation?

Among the four countries covered by the major studies, the Philippines had the best medical support for family planning and Egypt the worst. Clinics in the Philippines were generally well staffed and their personnel well trained. Still, some implementers failed to recommend the available services when such action could work against attaining their quotas. A mother of three complained, "They are happy when we request for IUD insertion, but are against our request for it to be removed." A further problem in the Philippines was that clients who suffered complications had to advance their own funds to cover hospitalization costs. These individuals would submit vouchers to the government and then wait several months for reimbursement, which might be only partial. A regional administrator described the resulting predicament for the client:

We have two or three [cases wherein] the patient was hospitalized and spent a big sum of money. We have a scheme for reimbursement but it is limited to 500 pesos. There are some patients who are really indigent and have difficulty securing the money.

Whatever the problems in the Philippines, at least there were some facilities for medical backup. In Egypt these were often lacking:

In many family planning clinics physicians do not see the clients themselves, except in cases of IUD insertions or in the treatment or serious side effects. Otherwise the client is most likely to be handed the pill by the nurse (when available), a nursing assistant, or even sometimes, by a member of the clerical or custodial staff.

Some clients in Egypt specifically complained about the poor treatment they received from medical personnel.

Client welfare can also be jeopardized when family planning services squeeze out other health services. Critics in several countries complained that the family planning component was so well financed and supplied that other services in the same unit suffered. A hospital director in the Dominican Republic lamented:

Here the only things not lacking are contraceptives. . . I have sent many letters reporting a shortage of supplies, and the only thing they ever send are pills, condoms, and other contraceptives!

Staff members at a rural health unit in the Philippines also bemoaned the frequent shortages of medicines for respiratory and gastrointestinal infections while supplies for birth control were limitless. The authors of the anthropological study comment:

No one in the RHU [Rural Health Unit] expressed any problem about family planning supplies. Different contraceptives notably pills in packets, condoms, and IUDs decorated the personnel's small, three-foot-tall Christmas tree, giving the impression of abundance as far as supplies are concerned.

And at that clinic contraceptives were sometimes dispensed when they were not wanted. One woman came to get vitamins for her baby and walked out with a pack of condoms. In the Philippines and in several other countries one has the sense that administrators tried to use generous incentives and abundant supplies to increase the proportion of scarce staff time spent on family planning.

CLIENT RESPONSE TO PROGRAMS

Client response to programs in the countries under study was less than overwhelming. Statistics and informed opinion suggest that as of 1976 only about 20 percent of the eligible couples in those countries availed themselves of family planning services.[6] Many others accepted at some point but dropped out after a brief period of time. Even when allowances are made for regions not reached by the official programs, the average response was low. The question, then, is why a large majority of the intended clients either failed to make use of family planning services at all or defected from the program after trying one or more methods.

An adequate answer would have to consider several interlocking explanations: weakness of demand, availability of services, poor understanding or misunderstanding on the part of clients, actual experience with the program, the effect of rumors, and community pressures working against acceptance of services among those interested. Neither this study nor any other has been able to explore all these factors simultaneously. But what we can do is note sources of disaffection that arose close to the programs themselves, particularly direct experience with family planning methods and the role of culture in shaping client perceptions about participation.

Client reactions to family planning programs are conditioned by the interplay of their own background, experience with the program, and the immediate cultural setting. Personal background establishes the parameters of meaning for a program. People who are illiterate and extremely poor, who have had no exposure to modern medicine, and who are unaccustomed to dealing with bureaucracy are prone to misunderstand family planning services from the outset. Their experience with the program can work either to counteract or to accentuate such misunderstandings. When implementers try to explain family planning in terms meaningful to the clients, encourage them to articulate their concerns and fears, and generally adopt a supportive posture, the program may overcome its initial liabilities. When, however, field staff adopt the demeanor of officialdom, talk down to clients, use terms that clients do not understand, fail to listen when problems are raised, dismiss client fears as ignorant or irrational, and try to finish their business as soon as possible, initial doubts may be compounded by actual contact.

If uncertainties remain or increase after exposure to the program, clients naturally turn to trusted sources of information, such as friends, relatives, the local midwife, or the parish priest. And these sources will, more likely than not, pass on traditional understandings that countervene the program's intent and reinforce the client's starting doubts. The Egyptian report comments:

Given the failure of the national program to provide adequate information to contraceptive users or to establish communication with the community at large, those desiring information or advice on contraceptive use are often forced to rely on relatives, friends, and neighbors as sources of information. A study conducted by the [Social Research Center of the American University of Cairo] showed that, for each of the contraceptive methods under consideration, these individuals constituted the major source of information about the method and its use.

The effects of interactions among client background, program experience, and cultural setting are particularly clear in two areas: reactions to specific methods of birth limitation and broader reactions to family planning programs. The country studies show that such interactions affect not only the willingness of clients to adopt and stay with given methods but also larger reactions vital to the success of a family planning program.

Reactions to family planning methods

To judge from the country studies, the greatest single obstacle to continued use of family planning services was adverse experience with the methods adopted. Some negative reactions, such as intermittent bleeding, were plainly physical and directly attributable to the methods. Others, including nausea, hypertension, and weight loss, were in the gray area between the physical and the psychological. Still other reactions were fears that derived not from the client's own experience with the method but from the observed or reported experiences of others. Cases in point are a woman's anxieties about having a baby born with an IUD in its scalp or a husband's worry, based on local hearsay, that the IUD scrapes the tip of the penis. And at the extreme of cultural fabrication are fears that the pill brings on epilepsy, that the IUD causes insanity, and that condoms slip off and enter the uterus. These fears can rarely be attributed to a single source. The meaning to a client of even the most gross physical symptom, such as bleeding, derives not only from its physical manifestations but from its significance in the larger culture and its interpretation by local reference groups. Bleeding is rarely just bleeding. It may be seen locally as the beginning of menstruation, a sign of imbalance between hot and cold rhythms, or a symptom of cancer.

The pill. In these countries the strongest fear evoked by the pill was cancer. Western studies suggesting the risk of cancer have found their way to the developing countries, and their spread is often helped along by the local media. In rural areas, stories about cancer and the pill are then passed along, often with embellishments, by midwives, healers, priests, and politicians. And such messages are often assimilated into local theories of gynecology. A nurse in the Philippines reported rumors that "pills do not dissolve and instead accumulate in the uterus and consequently cause cancer." This interpretation arose from indigenous notions of cancer being produced by a "rotting uterus."

Other complaints about the pill centered on less severe symptoms, including headaches, dizziness, nausea, and irritation. Clients also reported weight loss, weight gain, feelings of weakness, and a general sense of being run down. A client in the Philippines reported that after shifting from the IUD to the pill, "I began to experience vomiting, frequent headaches, dizziness, and I was easily irritated with everything. I noticed that I began to lose weight and I felt the same feelings as if I was pregnant again." Reactions to weight gain or loss hinged on local cultural interpretations. A Filipina considered weight gain a liability: "I tried pills at first, but I grew so stout that I had to discard it." By contrast, some women in Kenya favored the pill precisely because they thought it would make them grow fat. Other effects ascribed to the pill included both an increase and a decrease in the sexual urge, sterility, epilepsy, mental disorders, varicose veins, loss of hair, reduction in breast milk, and phlebitis. And for some the problem was not any specific symptom but a general unease about tampering with the body's natural rhythms.

The IUD. The most common side effect from the IUD was bleeding. A Kenyan implementer noted "a lot of excessive bleeding causing anemia in certain mothers who tend to preach against it." Also frequent were reports about damage to the penis during intercourse. The Philippine anthropological study contained these accounts by clients:

As days went by I felt something tickling my tip. I thought it was just hair pulled out until this time it really hurt me. I had to tell my wife to have the IUD removed. [Husband, thirty years old]

My husband scolded me thinking that I was doing "something" with myself down there. The next time we "slept together," he again complained. This time he explained that he gets scraped and loses interest each time we come into contact. The next time we tried it he withdrew as if in pain because the IUD did scratch him. [Wife, thirty-five years old]

There were also fears and rumors about the effects of the string attached to the IUD. The most picturesque story came from the Cavite region near Manila:

An IUD user and her husband got hooked into each other during sexual intercourse; they had to be taken to the hospital one on top of the other.[7]

In this Christian country the biblical norm of "two in one flesh" had obviously been taken literally.

The mysterious appearance and poorly understood operation of the IUD gave rise to rumors about its wanderings. Many clients in the Dominican Republic, Kenya, and the Philippines thought that once the IUD entered the body it had a visa to travel where it wished. An implementer in Kenya noted

a fear that it may get lost in the body – may even reach the brain or heart. To remove it would call for an operation. It forms a wound in the stomach.

Others feared that the coil would become lodged in the uterus, where it could cause cancer or be difficult to remove.

Clients also feared that the IUD would become hooked into a baby's scalp, ears, or other parts of the body. As this comment from the Philippines suggests, such fears were not entirely unfounded:

An IUD user had a stillbirth in the fifth month. I handled the delivery. The IUD was with the placenta. The woman was not fed up; she practiced family planning again. But the neighbors had big stories about it. They also said there was a woman who was airlifted to Cebu because she was bleeding . . . once they hear about an incident, they are afraid to use family planning methods. [Nurse]

Other complaints were that the IUD is unreliable in preventing pregnancy, falls out when women are working in the fields, produces vaginal ulcers or a change in menstrual flow, and in extreme cases, causes death from tubal pregnancy.

Condoms. One problem with condoms was that men hesitated to pick them up at family planning clinics filled with women. But the main difficulty with the

method itself was the widespread perception by women that the condom is
"vulgar" and used mainly with prostitutes. A Filipina remarked: "Goodness,
it's filthy...I'm not uncomfortable with it but I think it's vulgar." In Kenya a
field implementer reported that "women are afraid of them. They think it can
stick in the uterus. They think it is meant for prostitutes and not housewives."
In several countries men objected to the condom on the grounds that it inter-
feres with sexual pleasure. And in Kenya it ran up against cultural taboos
against males seeing their own semen. One implementer specifically noted "a
cultural belief that no man should see his semen." But overall the main
drawback to the condom was not any perceived medical side effect but a
general sense that the method is crude and distasteful.

Sterilization. Among the countries chosen for major studies, only the Philippines included sterilization in its national program. And there, as in other
countries, the greatest difficulties arose with vasectomy. A particular problem
in rural areas was the lack of an appropriate term for vasectomy in the local
languages and the consequent association of the procedure with castration. In
the Cavite region the local term for this operation is *kapon*, the same word used
to describe the castration of pigs and other animals. Because of this association, implementers hesitated to use the local word, but then their circumlocu-
tions raised doubts among clients about what was being promoted. Also creating
opposition to vasectomy were fears that it creates impotence and destroys
virility. Such perceptions were shared by both men and women. A mother of
eight in the Cavite region commented: "Once a man has an operation, it seems
that it makes him lose something. It will be said that he is not a 'he-man'
anymore." Fears about this operation were even stronger in the isolated Bontok
area of northern Luzon. According to the Philippine anthropological study,

rumors that the procedure has resulted in sexual disability are currently circulating
both in Samoki and the población. The prevalent sentiment about vasectomy has been
expressed by a client in the following statement: "Only crazy people will allow themselves to be castrated. What a way to die!"

Tubal ligation does not seem to raise comparable fears. In the Philippines it
is regarded as an inconvenient and somewhat risky operation, but one that
poses few threats to self-image or social definition.

Broad reactions

In addition to and sometimes in conjunction with their reactions to specific
methods, clients develop broad views of family planning programs and their
consequences. For example, they form attitudes about the net good or ill
wrought by birth-control methods and their side effects. Of particular relevance in agricultural areas are perceptions about whether family planning is
generally good for the user's health. In Egypt, local perceptions that the pill

and the IUD cause generalized weakness cast doubts on its value to rural families. As the Egyptian report puts it:

Since the methods in question are widely claimed to cause debility or weakness, further problems may be encountered in that such weakness, whether real or imagined, could interfere with the wife's ability to carry out her normal household activities and responsibilities. In rural areas, where wives are often involved in agricultural activities as well, this could led to a reduction in household income through her inability to carry out her work in the fields.

Husbands might understandably object to continuing with family planning under these circumstances. Similarly, the intermittent bleeding sometimes produced by the pill and the IUD may stir feelings that family planning is bad for marriage. In cultures where women do not distinguish between menstrual bleeding and that produced by contraceptives, taboos on intercourse may come into play whenever blood appears.

A second broad reaction involves blaming family planning for other evils in the user's life. Clients who have little education, many fears, and a poor understanding of physiology can easily blame birth control for any misfortune. A midwife in the Philippines remarked:

How can it [family planning] be successful when you are operating against the bad rumors spreading around? People read in the newspapers that family planning is bad because it is cancerous. They have only a sore throat and they blame it on family planning.

A doctor in the same country complained that a woman in his area even blamed the IUD for a case of diarrhea.

While some of this blaming was mere scapegoating, much of it seemed to be an indirect result of poor explanation and poor medical care. Fears about cancer among pill users in the Dominican Republic could be traced in part to the unavailability of the Pap smear test for detecting cancer. One client recounted her own experience:

I went to get a Pap Smear, but they said they wouldn't give it to me because they only give it to women older than 30, since before that you don't get cancer.

In the Dominican Republic and elsewhere, failure to give medical examinations before dispensing birth control, coupled with failure to provide tests later, confirmed client fears that they must be suffering from serious illness, usually cancer.

Even when support services were available, programs were hampered by female resistance to physical examinations by male doctors. A woman in the Philippines put the matter succinctly: "I chose the pill because, as they say, you won't be examined too closely." A Mexican client commented: "If I don't even let my husband see me, I'm not about to go there [to the clinic, where the doctor examines all women]." In many countries husbands likewise objected to having their wives disrobe before other men. And in Islamic regions, such examinations are specifically prohibited by the Koran. The net effect was to deter women from approaching clinics requiring physical examinations, to foster a preference for methods requiring no examination, and to make women reluctant to return to clinics for periodic checkups. With the pill and the IUD this last reaction created situations in which clients who needed help with complications waited until the symptoms were truly serious. Then local savants cited their cases as proof that birth control was harmful to a woman's health.

A final broad reaction has to do with the perceived morality of family planning. Feelings that users of birth control are promiscuous or even prostitutes sometimes deter potential clients from entering a program and move accepters to drop out. For users such cultural norms may not be apparent until they become the subject of gossip in community. According to a woman in the Dominican Republic,

I have ten children and I am using family planning with the "little device" [IUD]; it worries me that there are some people who are saying that with family planning there are women who can now have two or three lovers and no one can prove that they aren't faithful to their spouses.

The Mexican report makes much the same point:

– My husband wouldn't think it was one bit funny if I did anything to avoid having children. I might become loose and go off with other men.

– Just think if the girls [adolescent daughters] found out I was doing something to prevent having a child. . . they might want to do it too so that they could "play around."

The Kenyan study likewise notes cultural and moral fears about family planning, including "being known to use any method is a fear of being named as a prostitute."

Risk aversity and family planning

After reading this account some might be tempted to dismiss the client reactions reported as ignorant and irrational. Family planning enthusiasts might agree that such responses exist but argue that they can be countered by better information and education. Indeed, such statements have been made by leading experts:

Many couples are afraid that the use of pills, IUD, injections, or other contraceptives for a long period of time will cause permanent damage to their health. These fears are based on rumors or reports that are very widespread among the population and which are firmly believed by many. Beliefs that cancer, sterility, damage to vital organs, bodily disfiguration, reduction of libido or bearing of deformed children can result from prolonged use of contraceptives prevent many thousands of persons from adopting family planning who are otherwise favorably disposed.

Until these fears are dispelled by wide diffusion of the truth, adoption of family planning will continue to be disappointing. The public must be helped to understand that the risk of ill effects is very low.[8]

In other words, if people had full information about family planning they would have no cause for concern.

This research suggests a different way of approaching risk avoidance among poor clients. For people close to the edges of survival, risks to health beyond those normally experienced may be intolerable. For people who live in near-subsistence conditions, and even for those who are better off, the present costs of illness may be so high that they simply cannot take chances with new hazards, such as those of birth control. When one's yearly earnings, not to mention one's life, can be wiped out by a bout with influenza, the inclination to experiment with pills, IUDs, and other ill-understood contraceptives is minimal. Indeed, the very poor may well assess the probability of harm from such experimentation at a higher level than is objectively the case. Whereas the statistical chances of serious complications from the IUD are perhaps 1 percent, a woman may react as if the were closer to 99 percent. And when, as in the Philippines, clients themselves must bear some or all the costs of medical problems, the pressure to play it safe will be doubly strong. Proponents of rationalism may judge such caution about birth control as misguided in the long run, but poor families often have no choice but to live in the short run. If that goes wrong there may be no long run.

In summary, a program's treatment of its clients and client reactions to the program are interconnected, but not in any simple or deterministic fashion. Programs that show respect for clients in their motivational activities and in the explanation of family planning methods and that provide adequate medical back-up for the services offered elicit client responses that are more positive than when little respect is shown or little medical support is provided. But no quantity of respect or medical support can stimulate initial demand when the objective and subjective interests of clients are served by large families, nor will such support necessarily neutralize other hostile forces, such as belligerent opinion leaders or disaffected midwives.

Clients, for their part, can directly affect implementation by the way in which they react to family planning. Clients' fears about side effects and complications condition their initial willingness to adopt a given method as well as their disposition to continue with that method. Clients can also have indirect effects on implementation through broad reactions to family planning programs, especially their perceptions of the net gains and losses for them in the program. Finally, the widely reported risk avoidance among poor clients might best be viewed not as ignorance or irrationality but as a reasonable response to an environment already laden with uncertainties and health risks. For those hovering at the edge of physical or economic disaster, the prospect of harm from unknown or ill-explained birth-control methods may simply be intolerable, whatever the actuarial facts of the matter.

Part IV

Conclusions

12   Implementation as transaction

Implementation has been the organizing concept of this book. Previous chapters explored the conditions under which population policies and programs are most and least likely to be carried out. I have argued that implementation hinges on the adequacy of the theory behind a program; the process of policy setting and program design; the interactions between a program and its political, cultural, and bureaucratic settings; the commitment of implementers at all levels; the reactions of opinion leaders; and the cooperation of clients. But the present study also suggests a larger view of implementation that both embodies and transcends these specific hypotheses.

MODELS OF IMPLEMENTATION

To date there have been three main approaches to implementation: the machine model, the games model, and the evolutionary model. The first is by far the most common and the most fully conceptualized; the other two are seen less often and remain skeletal in conceptualization.

The machine model, also known as planning and control, Theory X, or classical administrative theory, was summarized in Chapter 3. It assumes that a clearly formulated plan backed by legitimate decision-making authority contains the essential ingredients for its own implementation. With well-articulated goals and a detailed specification of the actions that are to take place, implementation requires only hierarchical authority, trained staff, and close supervision. More sophisticated versions of machine theory add monitoring and evaluation systems to chart progress and warn of slippage, but the guiding concept of implementation is the same.

The games model, best represented by the work of Eugene Bardach, swings from total rationality to virtual irrationality in implementation.[1] Bardach depicts implementation as "(1) a process of assembling the elements required to produce a particular programmatic outcome, and (2) the playing out of a number of loosely interrelated games whereby these elements are withheld from or delivered to the the program assembly process on particular terms."[2] The games include diversion of resources, deflection of goals, tokenism, territory, and "not our problem." The games model plays down plans and policies and plays up the power of bargaining and exchange. Although it offers a healthy corrective to the unreality of machine theory, its deep cynicism runs the risk of reducing program execution to poker playing and of

179

trivializing the moral commitment of implementers. It also misuses the metaphor of games, for in a true game the players know they are players and are aware of the rules of the game. In many programs, including those reviewed here, key players are not even aware that the game is being played.[3]

The evolutionary model, first proposed by Majone and Wildavsky, views policy in much the same way that biologists view embryonic tissue.[4] Just as the tissue of the fruit fly can develop into a wing, a leg, or an antenna according to the environmental influences impinging on it, so also does policy evolve in its own setting. Policy is significant not because it sets the exact course of implementation but because it shapes the potential for action. A population policy might give rise to a family planning program or an organized effort to curb foreign immigration, but it rarely leads to the construction of a steel mill. The more general the policy the less likely it is to be executed in any single way. Thus implementation is evolution in the sense that a policy's potential takes specific form through interaction with environmental conditions: "At each point we must cope with new circumstances that allow us to actualize different potentials in whatever policy ideas we are implementing."[5]

The evolutionary model has considerable potential, but has not yet been tested in the harsh environment of analysis. The idea that policy establishes the possibilities for implementation is useful, but it does not go very far toward explaining specific cases. With population policies the tough question is not whether they will be carried out differently in varying environments but how those environments bear on implementation. The model is also incomplete in its failure to recognize that implementation can change its own environment, as happened with family planning programs in several countries. Nor is it enough to point out that discretion is necessary and inevitable. That is true, but for analysis it is more important to know how discretion comes into play, why it is exercised in one way rather than another, and what difference it makes for the direction, speed, and outcomes of implementation. Finally, the very term "evolution" has a serious and perhaps fatal limitation for implementation analysis. However the definition is delimited, "evolution" carries connotations of human action being determined by impersonal forces in the environment. Majone and Wildavsky seem to reject that implication by emphasizing learning from experience and the conscious correction of errors during implementation. But the force of the term remains and may give the wrong message to implementers and their superiors.

The approach suggested here will be called the transactional model. The term "transaction" has its own semantic liabilities, particularly the implication of cold-hearted business exchanges, but it is closer to the model at hand than any other term.

Specifically, the *Oxford English Dictionary* lists three meanings of "transaction" that are relevant to the present view of implementation.[6] The first is the accomplishment of a result, as in the transaction of business. The notion of getting something done lies at the heart of implementation and is not captured by such synonyms as "interaction." Although molecules may be said to interact within an atom, the concept lacks the intentionality that is at the essence of implementation. A second meaning of "transaction" is the adjustment of a dispute between parties by mutual concession or compromise. Negotiation and other forms of dispute settlement are crucial to the transactional model, although they are not the only significant kinds of transactions. The third and perhaps the broadest meaning of "transaction" is a dealing with someone or something. Implementation can fruitfully be seen as a series of dealings between program representatives and others whose actions are necessary to attain the program's goals. Sometimes these dealings are interactive, as when government officials deliberately seek out the participation of religious leaders in promoting a family planning program. But in other circumstances the dealings can be one-sided. Such would be the case when policy planners try to adapt a family planning program to different cultural contexts on the basis of existing research rather than on the basis of direct contact with cultural leaders. In this case, the planners deal with varying cultural settings but in a unilateral and technocratic manner. In short, the concept of transaction implies deliberate action to achieve a result, conscious dealings between implementers and program environments, and, as a particularly critical kind of dealing, negotiation among parties with conflicting or otherwise diverging interests in implementation.

Applied to implementation, the transactional model begins with seven assumptions:

1. Policy is important in establishing the parameters and directions of action, but it never determines the exact course of implementation. The evolutionary model is basically correct in viewing policy as a potential to be actualized rather than a pattern to be unfolded. The machine model is misguided in assuming that a detailed specification of policies and programs will produce the intended outcomes during implementation. At the same time, implementation may take place without an explicit policy and in fact may be necessary to develop that policy. In several countries, family planning programs were carried out quietly and on an experimental basis precisely to show that they were feasible. Their successful implementation was then used as evidence of the need for an explicit national policy to support extension of the experiments.

2. Formal organization structures are significant but not deterministic in their impact. First, their simplicity or complexity affects the number of points at which key transactions take place. Other things being equal, the more complex the structure, the greater the number of decisions points and the greater the need for transactions at those points to promote action.[7] Second, the formal structure of implementation conditions the organizational routines involved. Family planning programs that work through the Ministry of Health

usually have to deal with routines associated with health care. These include the use of doctors, nurses, and similar personnel; medical care organized around clinics; and procedures designed to prevent harm to patients, such as medical examinations before contraceptives are dispensed. Family planning programs that employ social workers or teachers have to work with or around the routines of those professions and their respective bureaucracies. Third, where the organizational structure involves several bureaucracies with different routines and perspectives, there may be conflicts, tensions, or frictions among these units. Program managers may then have to spend large amounts of time transacting solutions to difficulties within the implementation system. In other words, formal structures are significant not only because of the de jure lines of authority and responsibility they establish but also because of the de facto problems created by the perceptions and behaviors of the people involved.

3. The program's environment is a critical locus for transactions affecting implementation. The essence of implementation in the transactional view lies in coping with environmental diversity, uncertainty, and hostility. The most common difference between programs that are carried out and those that fail is that the former link policy intentions to environmental realities whereas the latter proceed as if the environment were either invariant or irrelevant. The transactional model specifically assumes that program environments are (1) multiple; (2) shifting; and (3) difficult to predict in any detail before implementation takes place. The historical, political, cultural, and even bureaucratic settings for implementation often differ across geographic regions and by administrative level within regions. This research has uncovered great differences between program environments in the capital city, provincial or state capitals, and villages of the same country. In addition to their multiplicity, environments are in continual change, sometimes for reasons not directly related to the program, such as rising educational levels or incomes in the region, sometimes in direct response to the program's implementation. To cite but one example, the political environment in India was much different after the country took up compulsory sterilization in the mid-1970s than it had been before. Indeed, the implementation of the family planning program during the Emergency was a key factor in the downfall of Indira Gandhi's government in 1977. And the precise composition of the environment, particularly the political context, is often hard to know before some amount of implementation takes place. Programs that appear innocuous in the planning stages sometimes prove to be surprisingly divisive, whereas those assumed to be controversial are occasionally implemented without dissension.

4. Judged by its impact on implementation, the process of policy formulation and program design can be as important as the product. Process not only affects the product directly by defining who participates and how but also acts on the environments for implementation. If key figures from the power setting

are ignored or offended during policy setting, they may take their revenge later when their influence is stronger. If their support is solicited, they may be persuaded to be cooperative or at least neutral, even if they are not enthusiastic about the policy being implemented. One of the keys to the success of Indonesia's family planning program in rural Java was winning the neutrality and sometimes even the active assistance of local religious leaders. This was done mainly by consulting these leaders about the overall acceptability of family planning in their region and by showing them respect in other ways.

5. Implementer discretion is universal and inevitable. It is also the basis for the most critical transactions during implementation. Whatever the policy and whatever the formal structure of authority, implementers can advance or destroy a program. If they are suitably prepared and favorably motivated, they can mobilize the resources necessary to overcome seemingly insuperable obstacles; if they are dissatisfied with their jobs and unconvinced of the program's worth, they can sabotage a program even with the strictest system of controls. Indeed, more creative implementers can use bureaucratic regulations as one means of subversion, by working to rule or stalling action by referring procedural minutiae to their superiors for clearance.[8] Overall, discretion will be vitally influenced by such human considerations as the desire to maintain self-esteem and community respect. The machine theory of implementation breaks down precisely at those points at which implementers not only have discretion but also can use it with impunity. In the typical social program those points are many.

6. In human services programs, clients have a potent influence on the outcomes of implementation. Far from being receptacles into which services are dropped – an image not uncommon in machine theory – they, like the implementers, have substantial discretion. They can reject a service entirely, accept it but not use it, accept it and use only those parts that suit their interests, strike deals with implementers, organize others to accept the service, or mobilize opposition against the service or the entire program. Clients are above all human beings with their own hopes, fears, aspirations, and interests. How they react to a program depends not only on their objective need for the service but on their subjective reaction to it, the site in which it is offered (such as a family planning clinic), the implementers, the program as a whole, and the government. However much a woman may seem to need family planning in the abstract, if she feels that pills will give her cancer, that she may be sterilized without her knowledge at the local health clinic, or that the implementers will treat her rudely, she may not accept the services offered; if she does, she may discontinue their use after a brief period. As obvious as this point may seem, it was widely ignored in the design and execution of family planning programs in many countries. Perhaps the most critical transaction of all in family planning programs is that between the program and the client, for all others ultimately revolve around that nexus. If this transaction fails, the program will fail with it.

7. Implementation is inherently dynamic. Because of its transactional nature, implementation is usually an unstable and often precarious process. As political, social, and even physical environments change, different interactions take place between the program and those environments. One government may be enthusiastic about a program, whereas the next government may be decidedly unenthusiastic, if only to show the folly of its predecessor. And even the same government may differ in its commitment to a program over time. In 1973 the Suharto government in Indonesia was nominally in favor of family planning but did not back up its program with the full weight of the presidency. Around 1975 President Suharto himself delegated responsibility for family planning to the regional governments and made it clear that he wanted results. Even with little change in the formal implementation structure, the program, particularly in east Java and Bali, began to show improved results. Should family planning suddenly become an issue in the struggles between the Indonesian military and the Islamic parties, the situation could change yet again.

In Mexico the implementation of the government's family planning program was influenced by its association with the candidacy of Mario Moya Palencia and then by his defeat in the presidential contest. In the Philippines the Marcos government's turn to martial law was accompanied by a tougher stance on birth control. And in India the defining of population as an issue to be dealt with in the Emergency had a crucial impact on the implementation of that program then and later. Thus neither from an analytic or a practical standpoint can the implementation pattern observed at any given point in time be treated as stable. It is best viewed as a temporary equilibrium between the program and the environment, one that can change with a shift in either.

SUMMARY HYPOTHESES

The specific implications of the transactional approach can be illustrated by a series of hypotheses concerning population programs. These ideas can be grouped around the topics of this book, such as process, contexts, implementers, and clients. Each hypothesis suggests one or more conditions likely to promote or retard implementation. All should be assumed to begin with the phrase "other things being equal."

Process. Social programs are most likely to be implemented when key figures in the power setting participate in their formulation and design; when foreign influence is perceived by those concerned to be nonexistent or within acceptable limits; when programs are adapted to varying geographic, cultural, political, or social circumstances; and when the language of policy presentation is consonant with national values and does not raise divisive issues. Implementation is least likely when there is either no participation or inordinate participation by critical figures; when foreign influence is seen as excessive in itself or emblematic of broader harm, such as genocide; when the program is applied rigidly to diverse environments; and when the language of presentation either sets off controversy or fails to stir enough interest for action ("ho-hum – another educational reform").[9]

Several kinds of transactions are implied in these hypotheses. One is the dealing required to identify those who count at critical stages in the program's life. For that more is involved than scanning organization charts. Often the gatekeepers for implementation appear on no chart and can be identified only after careful study of specific situations. A second and very delicate transaction involves having critical figures participate in policy setting and program design to the point where they feel they have adequate influence but not to the point where they sabotage or paralyze the entire process. A third and also sensitive transaction is the assessment of acceptable levels of foreign influence. As used here, "foreign" may mean either from outside the country or, in local programs, from outside the region. In the United States, federal assistance to local schools is sometimes perceived in much the same way as American foreign aid is perceived in developing countries. Clearly, some programs, such as road building and hospital construction, have a higher tolerance for acceptable foreign influence than others, most notably population. But overall acceptability hinges on a variety of considerations, including the country's past and present relations with the donor, the delicacy of the issues raised by the program in question, and the state of international relations at the time.

Political context. Implementation also depends on the political actors, issues, and conditions in the country or region involved. The chances for successful implementation are greatest when the chief executive of the country, region, or agency is committed to the program's implementation; when relevant domestic interest groups back the program and mobilize support for its execution; when the program becomes linked to energizing issues; and when the operating environment is marked by low or medium threat and uncertainty. Implementation is least likely when the chief executive's support is necessary for action but weak or absent; when domestic interest groups either oppose the program or have no interest in it; when the effort raises either debilitating issues, such as genocide, or no interesting issues at all; and when the operating environment shows a high level of threat or uncertainty for the country, the political regime, or the implementers.

The central idea behind these hypotheses is that programs and their political environments are vitally interdependent. A program that fails to deal with its power setting runs the risk of irrelevance, opposition, or devastation. And even political support can be a mixed blessing. A program that represents the highest priority of a beloved political leader, embodies some of the country's deepest aspirations, and enjoys weekly publicity in the national press can fail because of its excessive popularity. With so many hopes loaded onto their shoulders, implementers may be frightened or ashamed to report problems, and for the same reason their superiors may want only good news. As a result, the normal possibilities for self-correction from within and for changes from without are eliminated.[10] Likewise, a program that generates no opposition may run aground when the hidden cost of such benignity is lack of interest.[11] Programs are most likely to be carried out when they evoke interest and even mild opposition but do not stir either violent antagonisms or extreme support. Achieving this balance is one of the most critical transactions in implementation.

Cultural context. Implementation further depends on the interplay between the program and its cultural setting. Some programs are more sensitive to cultural influences than others, and even the same program may be more sensitive in one region than another. A food-production program may be perceived in region A as simply a technical effort to help farmers produce more rice. But in region B it may be attacked as a covert step toward government control over rice production and in region C as an intrusion on the prerogatives of religious leaders.

A social program stands the best chance of implementation when it is seen as compatible with or even growing from the society's dominant traditions; when local interpreters of culture, such as religious leaders or traditional healers, support or at least do not oppose the effort; when it does not play into socioethnic conflicts or cleavages; and when experience in the culture engenders favorable attitudes toward the services offered. Socialization into the culture may inculcate attitudes or beliefs that predispose potential clients to accept or reject certain services, including family planning, injections, schooling, or loans. These predispositions are related to but not identical with the broader perception of compatibility between program and culture. As a result of their socialization, members of a certain ethnic group may favor the idea of spacing children but still reject a family planning program because of its foreign image or fears of domination by another ethnic group.

A program is least likely to be carried out when it is seen as dissonant with or damaging to the surrounding culture; when local interpreters of culture oppose the program; when the policy or its mode of execution accentuates internal divisions within a group or conflicts with other groups; and when experience in the culture leaves members with hostility, doubts, or ambivalence toward the services offered. Generally, programs have the best chance for implementation when there is a basic harmony between the program as implemented and the culture involved, but not so much harmony that clients and opinion leaders consider the effort dull, uninspired, and passé. A small amount of novelty and controversy may help to stir attention, but too much of either may create resistance and lead to rejection. Designing a program that fits its cultural setting is a transaction of the highest importance for implementation.

Bureaucratic context. Even programs that are sound in concept, shrewd in process, congruent with the culture, appealing to clients, and motivating for implementers can be impeded by bureaucracy. Outright competition, covert subversion, poor coordination, weak communication, and sheer incapacity can bring any social program to a halt. By the same token, effective transactions within and across implementing agencies can promote action and compensate for other liabilities in the system.

A program has the best chance of being carried out when there are a few rather than many agencies involved; when one organization has clear responsibility for the overall results; when relations among the participating agencies are marked by cooperation rather than competition; when the basic missions and perspectives of these organizations are reasonably compatible; and when the agencies assigned to deliver services already have or can soon develop the routines necessary to do so. The more numerous the agencies involved, the greater the need for crossagency communication and thus the greater the chances for misunderstanding and delay. Putting a single organization in charge helps implementation when that agency has the authority, the resources, and the skill necessary to coordinate the total set of participants. Otherwise, as seen with population programs in Egypt and the Philippines, single authority may become yet another source of competition and confusion. Harmonious relations are also more likely when the participating units have similar missions and outlooks on their work. As Gordon Chase has pointed out, a prison health program has a built-in potential for conflict when it requires close cooperation between guards, whose prime concern is security, and medical doctors, whose mission is the health of individuals.[12] The same is true of family planning programs that try to harness the efforts of doctors and nurses, whose main commitment is to health, to those of commercial distributors of contraceptives, whose guiding motive is profit. Finally, implementation depends on organizational routines, or standardized ways of solving problems and carrying out action. Barring a strong stimulus to change, most organizations will go on doing tomorrow what they are doing today, and in much the same ways.[13] If the requirements of a social program fit into the routines of the implementing organizations, the chances for success are good; if they do not, there often are problems.

A social program has the smallest likelihood of implementation when many rather than few agencies are involved; when no agency has primary responsibility for program outcomes; when one has this responsibility but lacks the will, skill, or resources to exercise it; when interagency relations are marked by competition rather than cooperation; when the basic missions and outlooks of these units are incompatible or in conflict; and when implementing bodies do not have and cannot develop the routines necessary to provide the requisite services.

Overall, the vital relationships within and among implementing agencies require active and typically personal transactions rather than paper coordination. Despite the impression often conveyed by organization charts, effective joint action is never created by drawing lines between boxes or by laying out the ideal apparatus for action in a policy manual. Effective working relations typically result from bargaining, cajoling, accommodation, threats, gestures of respect, and related transactions. Straight lines that link square boxes mean little if the underlying reality is a jumble, whereas effective working relations can be established by transactions among agencies with no formal connections whatever. In short, bureaucratic contexts favorable to implementation more often grow out of human interactions than hierarchical regulation.

Implementers. The individuals whose transactions are most directly related to the success of a social program are the implementers, particularly fieldworkers. It is they who can adapt a program's form and substance to the realities of a community or who can decide that such tailoring is too much work. It is they who can try to win over a religious leader or midwife or who can follow established procedures at the cost of political support. And it is they who can stir client interest with their patience, warmth, and respect or kill it with disinterest, paternalism, or disdain.

Implementation is most likely when implementers have the capacity to carry out the program, including an understanding of its purposes and methods; when they are favorably disposed toward their jobs, the program, and the specific methods used; when they have no alternative time commitments or they have such commitments with a clear demarcation of their program responsibilities; when their program responsibilities and the expectations of the community in which they work are compatible; and when there is reasonable congruence between their job responsibilities and their own self-definition, including, where relevant, their image of themselves as professionals. Implementation possibilities are smallest when implementers lack the intellectual ability or training needed to execute the program; when they are hostile to or ambivalent about their jobs, the program, or the methods used; when they have multiple responsibilities and the time allocated to the program is not clearly set aside; when the program is poorly understood or is the object of antagonism in the community; and when the program requires them to carry out actions violating their self-definition or image as professionals.

This research suggests several specific ways in which transactions by implementers can affect program success. First, employees who detest a program and who have several other tasks assigned to them can spend as much time as possible on those other tasks and as little as possible on the program. Health workers who dislike family planning and who have responsibilities for prenatal and postnatal care can concentrate on these latter tasks. In this way, they can strike a legitimate compromise between their own needs and the demands of the health bureaucracy. If their motivation to promote family planning is low, they can make only a minimal effort to interest clients in it or even subvert the program by passing along misinformation about side effects. Should the community object to some but not all of their family planning activities, they can play down those activities that are objectionable, such as motivating for sterilization. Such transactions are the stuff of implementation and the bane of machine theory.

Clients. Most important of all for the implementation of most social service programs are the clients. Programs are most likely to be carried out when there is initial client demand for the services or such demand can be created in a brief period; when clients are accessible to the program; when clients hold favorable attitudes toward the implementers, the program, or the point of service delivery, such as a health clinic; when the services delivered entail little or no risk of side effects and complications for users and those close to them, such as the spouse and children; when clients have an adequate understanding of the service itself and of any potential side effects or complications; when the program provides for back-up services to deal with any adverse effects that may materialize; when the conditions promoting initial acceptance remain constant over time; and when the service in question is not the subject of rumors, fears, or gossip in the user's community.

Programs are least likely to be implemented when there is little initial demand for the services offered and such demand cannot be created in a brief period; when clients are not accessible to the program; when clients have negative attitudes toward the implementers, the program, or the point of service delivery; when the service offered entails serious risks for the users and those close to them; when the clients have a poor understanding of the service itself and of its potential adverse effects; when the program fails to provide supporting care to handle side effects or complications from the service; when continuation with the service depends on personal or social conditions different from those at the time of acceptance; and when the service is highly susceptible to rumors, fears, or gossip in the community. The last two hypotheses are closely related. When a given service, such as contraception, is subject to rumors and the like, the factors leading to initial interest may be wiped out by forces working against continuation. A woman who became a pill accepter after assurances that there were no adverse effects may lose interest a few months later after she hears stories that the pill causes cancer, loss of hair, and irregular bleeding. Such reactions, in turn, will be most likely among women who have little initial understanding of their own physiology and who were given only cursory explanations of how the contraceptive pill operates. The transactions most vital to implementation are those between the programs and the clients. No amount of success on other fronts can compensate for the rejection of a program by its intended clients.

Implementation means transaction. To carry out a program, implementers must continually deal with tasks, environments, clients, and each other. The formalities of organization and the mechanics of administration are important as background, but the key to success is continual coping with contexts, personalities, alliances, and events. And crucial to such adaptation is the willingness to acknowledge and correct mistakes, to shift directions, and to learn from doing. Nothing is more vital to implementation than self-correction; nothing more lethal than blind perseveration. The spirit of transactional flexibility was well stated by Shakespeare's King Henry IV: "Presume not that I am the thing I was."

13   Programs versus people: toward an ethics of respect

> ...to reaffirm faith in fundamental human rights,
> in the dignity and worth of the human person...
> *Preamble to the Charter of the United Nations*
>
> The end cannot justify the means, for the simple
> and obvious reason that the means employed deter-
> mine the nature of the ends produced.
> Aldous Huxley, *Ends and Means*

The dominant approach to population control has been to treat it as an exercise in social engineering. With ends taken as obvious or given, the focus shifts to means. How can we deliver family planning services more efficiently? How can we stimulate demand? How can we use the media to promote the idea of a two-child family? And at the extreme, how well can coercion work in bringing down the birth rate? When this approach is used, the main constraint on means is effectiveness. Coercion is to be avoided not because it violates human rights but because it will bring down the government faster than it will lower fertility. Financial incentives for avoiding births are to be shunned not because they play on the vulnerability of the poor but because they are too expensive and too hard to control.

Although attention to means is important in any social program, the discussion cannot end or even begin there. Population programs raise inescapable questions of religion and morality. No religion and no ethical system is indifferent to marriage, family, health, illness, abortion, sterilization, or contraception. Nor are religions silent on such matters as coercion, manipulation, and truth telling. To treat population control as a value-free technical question is to skirt a host of fundamental moral issues.

This chapter makes a strong plea for explicit attention to the ethics of population control. Its basic thesis is that, whatever their specific inspirations and intentions, population programs must be guided by a respect for the dignity of human beings. The discussion begins with five guiding principles and then moves to specific recommendations about policies and programs. The analysis necessarily is preliminary and incomplete. But I hope that even this brief essay can highlight critical problems requiring ethical scrutiny and suggest a broad approach to the subject.

One qualification must be made. Every one of the recommendations offered here could be amply justified on the grounds of sound management.

191

Coercion could be ruled out because it is politically counterproductive; medical backup for contraceptive services could be recommended as a means of preventing rumors; and showing respect for clients could be encouraged as a means of increasing continuation rates. But the case for respect should not have to rest on the foundation of programmatic expedience; or then, if it were suddenly discovered that coercion, deception, and manipulation were the best means of population control, the argument for human dignity would collapse on its own premises. Efficiency and effectiveness are valid considerations for an ethics of public policy, but their moral significance derives not from themselves but from other values, such as social welfare and human liberty. Hence in this essay arguments for humane population programs will be made on explicitly ethical grounds.

FIVE ETHICAL PRINCIPLES

Any serious analysis of the ethics of population control must begin with moral principles applicable to the issues in that field. And when the geographic referent of the analysis is the entire world rather than a single society, one immediately confronts the question of derivation. Where is one to come up with principles that apply with equal force to dozens of nation states spanning diverse religions, political systems, and ethical traditions? Is it even meaningful to speak of universal principles in this context?

While the challenge of developing a cross-national ethics is daunting, the task is not hopeless. At its founding and on many subsequent occasions the United Nations has had to face that question and has responded with fairly consistent statements about human rights. In 1948 the UN General Assembly adopted the Universal Declaration of Human Rights, a statement laden with explicit ethical affirmations. Other declarations, including several directly related to population policy, have been approved over the years by the General Assembly and such bodies as the International Committee of Human Rights.[1] Although anyone familiar with the UN system knows the inevitable and often byzantine politics surrounding pronouncements on human rights, the underlying consensus on basic principles is striking. Their derivation may be shallow, their scope nebulous, and their enforcement precarious, but principles they are and principles they have been for over three decades. Just as it would be naive to treat them as the expression of a deep and universal commitment by governments, it would be cynical to dismiss them as manifestations of political expedience. Here five principles derived from UN declarations are put forth as of particular relevance to population policies and programs.

Freedom. No value has received greater attention in UN declarations than personal freedom. Article 3 of the Universal Declaration of Human Rights states: "Everyone has the right to life, liberty, and security of person." Article

12 of the same document is more specific: "No one shall be subjected to arbitrary interference with his privacy, family, home, or correspondence, nor to attacks upon his honor or reputation." Article 18 likewise establishes "the right to freedom of thought, conscience, and religion."

Beyond such broad endorsements of personal and political freedom, several UN documents make specific reference to reproductive freedom.[2] But the most forthright statement came with the World Population Plan of Action in 1974: "All couples and individuals have the basic right to decide freely and responsibly the number and spacing of their children and to have the information, education and means to do so;..."[3] This principle went farther than its predecessors in emphasizing not only the right to choose but also the means to act on one's choice. Freedom in this view is not only the absence of restraint on choice. It also involves creating the capacity to choose, particularly through information and education, and the opportunity to carry out reproductive decisions with the requisite means.

Welfare. Another prominent value in UN statements is welfare or well-being – the conditions necessary for a decent life. According to Article 25 of the Universal Declaration of Human Rights,

Everyone has the right to a standard of living adequate for the health and well-being of himself and his family, including food, clothing, housing, and medical care and necessary social services and the right to security in the event of unemployment, sickness, disability, widowhood, old age, or other lack of livelihood in circumstances beyond his control.[4]

The World Population Plan of Action specifically links national development and population policies to the goal of welfare: "The principal aim of social, economic and cultural development, of which population goals and policies are integral parts, is to improve levels of living and the quality of life of the people."[5] The same document puts strong emphasis on reducing mortality and improving health as aspects of human welfare:

The reduction of morbidity and mortality to the maximum feasible extent is a major goal of every human society. It should be achieved in conjunction with massive social and economic development. Where mortality and morbidity rates are very high, concentrated national and international efforts should be applied to reduce them as a matter of highest priority in the context of societal change.[6]

Other UN documents speak of the right to be free from hunger, the right to adequate food, and related aspects of welfare.

Distributive justice. The essence of distributive justice is fairness in the allocation of benefits and harms.[7] Although the justice theme is given less attention than either freedom or welfare in UN declarations on rights, it is particularly salient, though often implicit, in the World Population Plan of Action. The following was mentioned as a goal of development bearing on the context of reproductive decisions:

The promotion of social justice, social mobility and social development, particularly by means of a wide participation of the population in development and a more equitable distribution of income, land, social services and amenities.[8]

The plan of action likewise affirms the right of women to complete integration in the development process, particularly by means of equal access to education and equal participation in social, economic, cultural, and political life.[9] Considerations of justice also enter into UN prohibitions against discrimination by race, color, sex, language, and religion and into the plan of action's ban in principle against curtailing welfare benefits to reduce incentives for fertility.

National sovereignty. As the United Nations is an organization of sovereign states, it is not surprising that it has strongly endorsed national sovereignty in domestic population policy and foreign aid. The World Population Plan of Action is explicit on this point:

The formulation and implementation of population policies is the sovereign right of each nation. This right is to be exercised in accordance with national objectives and needs and without external interference, taking into account universal solidarity in order to improve the quality of life of the peoples of the world. The main responsibility for national population policies and programmes lies with national authorities.[10]

This statement is equivocal in defining population decisions as the "sovereign right of each nation" and then in giving national authorities only the "main responsibility" in that area. The plan of action also recommends that international cooperation play "a prominent role in accordance with the principles of the United Nations Charter." But despite some qualifications, national sovereignty receives strong endorsement in the plan of action and other UN declarations.

Truth telling. Although freedom, welfare, justice, and national sovereignty are explicitly affirmed in UN statements, the value of truth telling receives mainly implicit support. If information is a prerequisite of free choice, truth telling is a sine qua non of information. Lies, fabrications, distortions, and selective disclosures of the truth all undercut the possibility of free choice by removing the most critical means of evaluating alternatives. Failures in truth telling also violate justice when those denied information are the poor and weak of the society and those manipulating the truth are the rich and powerful.

Skeptics may say that five moral principles drawn from highly negotiated UN documents provide a rather shaky foundation for ethical guidelines. To some extent this is correct. Compared to such masterpieces as John Rawls's *A Theory of Justice*, the ethical reasoning in UN declarations is shallow and fragmentary.[11] UN principles are announced but rarely derived, and they offer little guidance on how to resolve conflicts and incompatibilities even among themselves. When freedom and justice clash, which should be given primacy? And what is the proper stance of other nations when a given country commits flagrant violations of human rights? Should national sovereignty reign supreme, or can liberty make some moral claims across national borders?

Yet for all their limitations, the principles endorsed by the UN serve better than any others in establishing a basis for cross-national discussions of population ethics. And on closer analysis they do not differ greatly from principles suggested elsewhere. For example, in a detailed study of ethics, population, and the American tradition, the Hastings Center identified four values related to U.S. population policies: freedom, justice, welfare, and security/survival.[12] Other relevant values cited were truth telling and beauty. The main differences between these and the set of principles presented here is that the UN documents, and specifically the World Population Plan of Action, do not emphasize survival. In debates about population policy, the survival theme has been closely identified with hard-line advocates of control and has thus become anathema to others. And the UN in general has preferred appeals to freedom over evocations of fear in making the case for family planning. But aside from differences over survival, the values cited by most other writers on population ethics are strikingly similar to those suggested by the United Nations. Although other formulations may be more complete or more elegant, UN statements have the great advantage of agreed-upon applicability across nations and cultures. And that is no small benefit in a field riven with debates about relativism.

ETHICAL GUIDELINES

The five values suggested by UN declarations can be treated as prima facie obligations in formulating population policies and in implementing population programs. None of these obligations is absolute, but all should be observed unless they are overruled by a higher principle. Together they suggest the following guidelines.

1. There should be no coercion in population programs. Debate has gone on for years over the moral acceptability of compulsion in population control, but until India's experience during the Emergency of 1975–7 most of the discussion was theoretical. That experience made the issue concrete and generated specific evidence about the empirical correlates of coercion.

The most obvious case against coercion is that it is a direct violation of individual freedom. Instead of helping individuals and couples to "decide freely and responsibly the number and spacing of their children," governments decide that certain individuals are to have no more children. In India's experiment with compulsory sterilization, violations of liberty were compounded by infractions of justice as the program was applied unequally by sex, caste, and class. Whatever the intentions of the government, the brunt of compulsion was borne by the poor, by men, by the lower castes or "scheduled" castes, and by Muslims.[13] The resort to coercion likewise damaged the welfare of the individuals affected and, when accompanied by deception or misleading explanations, violated truth telling.

The staunchest defenders of human rights would say that compulsory sterilization, forced abortion, and similar tactics are never justified as means of population control. Another group might argue that coercion may be justified under certain conditions, but only if it passes five strict tests.[14]

First, population growth must present a clear danger to the common welfare. Here one quickly comes back to theory and evidence. Few would deny that in India, rapidly increasing numbers do strain the country's ability to provide food, clothing, shelter, and other basic services to its people. But a related question is why India's population continues to swell. Several theories suggest that the deepest root of population growth may be the country's failure to bring the benefits of development to the rural poor. To hold these people responsible for rapid population growth and to punish them with coercion seems a classic case of blaming the victim. If the causes of population growth are complex and if government failure is one of those causes, it is not justifiable to adopt coercion for individuals without first increasing national efforts at development.

Second, serious and sustained efforts must have been made to create the developmental conditions favoring demand for family planning. It is not fair or even sensible to mount a tough campaign for population control when the government has not put forth comparable vigor on other aspects of development. In India before the Emergency, the government did increase its efforts for developmental change, but it did not implement a massive, effective land-reform program, nor did it take dramatic action to break the grip of rural elites and money lenders. At the very least, a government should take no more forceful action against high fertility than it does against its underlying causes.

Third, to justify coercion, noncoercive methods must have been tried and have failed. Specifically, voluntary family planning services must have been made available in most areas of the country and presented to potential users with reasonable skill. In one sense, India before the Emergency did try everything short of compulsion – voluntary clinics, public exhortation, mobile units, financial incentives, and mass vasectomy camps. Yet by 1975 basic family planning services were not available to large segments of the population, particularly in rural areas. And even when the services were available, clinic administration was often so insensitive that eligible clients stayed away. It would be a considerable exaggeration to say that before the Emergency voluntary family planning had been tried and had failed.

Fourth, a coercive program should have a reasonable chance of being carried out. If a country undertakes a coercive program and argues that it is a means of promoting the common good, the program must be likely to succeed for that argument to stand up. Otherwise the damage to liberty and justice will not be offset by the advantages for welfare.

Someone once said that any government that can mount a gargantuan apparatus of compulsion probably does not need it. Nations able to produce such a feat are usually in the middle to upper reaches of development and possess the social conditions fostering lower fertility. By contrast, India before the Emergency did not even have an adequate system of birth and death registration in some of its poorest areas. It is hard to imagine how a government that cannot manage vital statistics will be able to mount an effective enforcement system for coercion. Given the horrors that compulsion creates, expectations for implementer motivation would be dismal and the results for clients obvious. If a government cannot organize itself for activities perceived to be in the people's interest, it is unlikely to do so for programs that are roundly detested.

Fifth, for coercive action to be just it must be applied fairly to all individuals designated as eligible for such action. It is patently unjust for the scalpel to fall disproportionately on the poor, the illiterate, the untouchables, and on religious minorities. And yet that seems to be exactly what happened during India's experiments with coercion.[15] An earlier study by Robert Elder, Jr., showed that differential implementation occurred even with presumably voluntary sterilization programs.[16] Elder documents that, although the scheduled castes (formerly untouchables) made up only 29 percent of the population of the state of Uttar Pradesh, they accounted for 49 percent of the vasectomies. One reason was undoubtedly the use of financial incentives, which are typically more attractive to the poor. But there was also solid evidence that public officials under pressure to meet sterilization quotas used pressure and intimidation on the weak. Such is likely to be the case in most countries. Not only are the upper and middle classes in a better position to pay bribes and pull strings to defend their reproductive systems, they are also better armed through education and experience to take evasive action against the sterilizers. Frustrated by obstacles in the higher social strata, fieldworkers compensate for their losses with those less able to resist. Whatever the stated intentions of justice in implementation, injustice is likely to be the norm in practice. Hence on any of the five yardsticks cited here, the case for coercion is weak.

2. Enforced production targets and quotas should be ruled out in family planning programs. Targets and quotas have been used in different ways. Sometimes the numbers set down by administrators are only a rough guideline to the results expected and entail no sanctions if they are not met. Superficially, the risks of this approach seem minimal, although much depends on the behavior of the organizations involved. If implementers are told that they will not be punished for their failure to meet accepter targets, but promotions go exclusively to those who have achieved their targets, the potential for abuse exists. The likelihood of abuse rises with the rigor of the enforcement system. To date, the greatest abuses of clients and implementers have arisen from targets and quotas backed up by strong positive incentives for achieving results and strong penalties for shortfalls. When implementers run the risk of being fired from their jobs, forfeiting promotions, or losing income, they are sorely tempted to pressure clients, cut corners on explanations, and falsify reports.

The dangers were most evident in India, where public officials used many ethically dubious tactics to promote sterilization.[17] In the state of Uttar Pradesh, schoolteachers were ordered to be sterilized or lose a month's pay, and family planning workers not meeting their sterilization quotas had their salary withheld. In Madya Pradesh it was decided that irrigation water would be sold at subsidized rates only to villages that came up with specified numbers of sterilization accepters. Teachers in some areas were instructed to tell parents that children from large families would not be able to attend school unless one parent was sterilized. Unemployed day laborers were told by contractors that they would be hired only if they could show a sterilization certificate. These and other violations of personal liberty were the direct result of a quota system backed up by stringent enforcement. Less serious but still significant abuses occurred as a result of the accepter and method targets adopted in the Philippines.

The point is not that performance targets are intrinsically evil but that they are readily open to abuse. It is practically sensible and ethically defensible to expect a certain amount of work from employees and even to quantify that amount. But it is not legitimate to put those employees in a situation wherein they are expected or often tempted to violate the human rights of clients. Practices such as those described destroy meaningful freedom of choice for clients and commonly entail violations of justice as well. When the pressure applied is more effective with the poor, the illiterate, and the weak, there is no longer fairness in the distribution of harms. Further, quotas leading to violations of client rights by implementers typically involve infringement of implementer rights by administrators. When their employment options are few and their financial obligations heavy, fieldworkers who disagree with the system have little effective freedom of conscience. Hence from the standpoint of human rights the soundest practice is to avoid stringently enforced quotas and to seek other means of achieving results.[18]

3. Piecework incentives for implementers should be avoided. Several countries have tried to increase the productivity of fieldworkers by offering financial rewards for each unit delivered or produced. In Egypt, doctors, nurses, and social workers were paid a fixed amount for each pill cycle dispensed and each IUD inserted. In India, incentives were provided for the person undergoing sterilization, to the surgeon performing the operation, and sometimes to the motivator or finder. Similar schemes have been tried elsewhere.

Whatever their stated intentions and controls, piecework incentives encourage disregard for and often abuse of clients. The combination of quotas and financial incentives in India has led to the sterilization of very old and very young men, often without their knowledge of what was at stake. An extreme example concerned an eighty-year-old man who was reportedly vasectomized three times during a sterilization campaign.[19] The demographic effects may have been minimal, but the fees were tempting. The following cases were reported in Uttar Pradesh:

Hindu I is a poor man of lower caste. His age is eighty and his youngest living child is aged thirty-nine. On his way back from the market he sat down by the roadside to rest and shortly thereafter was accosted by an H.A. [Health Assistant] who told him if he would come for nasbandi [vasectomy] he would earn a great deal of money. Hindu I was not at all certain what this nasbandi was, but his total monthly salary when he worked was barely thirty rupees and the young man had promised him twenty-one rupees for one hour of his time one afternoon. Telling his relatives that he had found some simple labor, and that he would be back by evening he went off for vasectomy.[20]

Hindu IV: Young unmarried – Calcutta. Bablu Dey is a young unmarried man, aged nineteen. As he was getting onto a train in a suburb of Calcutta he was accosted by a man who promised him eighteen rupees if he would only come with him. Bablu had never imagined so much money for what seemed to be so little. He agreed. They got off the train at a stop outside Calcutta and went directly to a camp being held there on that day. The motivator listed Bablu as being thirty-three years old and the father of several children. Although what he had to go through was somewhat painful and humiliating, Bablu kept his end of the agreement. It was only afterwards, when he searched for the motivator and his promised reward and was told that the latter had departed, that he became alarmed.[21]

Financial incentives to implementers in Egypt led to the unnecessary insertion of IUDs, to poor and often no medical supervision of pill users, to padded reports on the number of accepters, and to other abuses. Moreover, in Egypt and elsewhere the monetization of service delivery seemed to beget an attitude that every unit of work deserved an equivalent unit of pay. In such an atmosphere the quest for quantity drives out concern for quality, often to the detriment of client welfare. In short, piecework incentives to implementers often infringe upon freedom of choice, distributive justice, welfare, and truth telling.

4. Implementers should not be required to carry out actions violating their consciences, their standards of professional ethics, or official population policy. The Philippine study brought out situations in which field staff were pressured by their superiors to engage in behaviors that they considered immoral and that directly contravened the government's announced population policy. Whereas the national policy was for freedom of choice in methods of birth control, the de facto policy in some organizations was to push sterilization, pills, and IUDs. Others in the Philippines had moral and prudential reservations about recommending sterilization to young people or those with fewer than four children, yet they were expected to meet quotas for that method. Although documentation is sparse, problems of professional ethics must have been acute for Indian surgeons participating in coercive or semicoercive sterilization campaigns. Under widely accepted standards of medical ethics, the first consideration in treatment is the welfare of the patient. Yet in the sterilization drive during the Emergency, doctors were expected to perform operations that often worked against patient welfare, as with vasectomies on the young, and mainly served the interests of the state.

Although this is not the place to draft a bill of rights for implementers, three suggestions can be made. First, governments and other program sponsors should not misrepresent the nature of their policies and services. If the truth is told in the first place, fieldworkers will not have to worry about the morality of deception. Second, program administrators should not put implementers in a position in which they are strongly tempted to violate accepted standards of professional ethics. Although the boundaries between organizational responsibility and professional probity are often unclear, cases such as those mentioned in the Indian sterilization campaign should not be permitted to arise. Third, if family planning programs observe the standards given here and implementers still find themselves in situations creating severe dilemmas of conscience, they should be permitted to transfer to other positions without loss of benefits or status. If transfers are not feasible, they should at least be given the freedom not to perform actions that they consider morally unacceptable. Those opposed to sterilization, for example, might be exempted from motivational activities in that area should they find them objectionable.

5. Clients should be given free choice among approved family planning methods. In line with the principle of freedom, clients should have a choice among methods of fertility control. They should not be pressured to adopt a method serving the program's convenience, nor should information about other approved methods be withheld from them. Under the principle of national sovereignty, governments are not required to offer all available methods of limiting births. They may decide that some methods, such as sterilization or abortion, are unacceptable for religious or cultural reasons, and that others, such as injections, should be restricted in the interests of medical safety. But when a government does approve several methods for inclusion in its program, clients should be able to choose among them.

6. Clients should receive accurate and intelligible explanations of the risks and advantages of available family planning methods. In order to exercise free choice on family planning, clients also need a reasonably clear idea of the risks and benefits of each method. The World Population Plan of Action specifically recommends that all countries

ensure that information about, and education in, family planning and other matters which affect fertility are based on valid and proven scientific knowledge, and include a full account of any risk that may be involved in the use or non-use of contraceptives.[22]

This research brought out evidence that fieldworkers sometimes oversell the benefits of certain methods and fail to mention hazardous side effects. One implementer admitted that she told women about the minor drawbacks of pills, such as temporary nausea, but mentioned nothing about more serious problems. Another fieldworker withheld information about side effects because "if the client is not educated, she only understands the bad side and not the good side." But the most extreme cases of nondisclosure arose in India, where some men were rounded up for sterilization with no idea that the operation would end their reproductive ability.

This recommendation argues for accurate and intelligible explanations but urges no one means of providing those explanations. It is certainly not necessary for a field implementer to read a packaged explanation of each method and then have the client sign a standard consent form. That would be carrying ethnocentrism to a ludicrous extreme. Instead, the aim should be to offer explanations that are meaningful to clients in their own cultural settings. These might be given by midwives who are known and trusted in the community, by other accepters who have been specially trained for that purpose, or by so-called barefoot doctors. The discussions need not take place in clinics, and those offering them need not wear white coats. The ethically significant points are that explanations be given, be accurate, and be understood.

7. Family planning programs should provide adequate medical services to deal with side effects and complications of birth-control methods. The principle of welfare argues strongly for support services to prevent, detect, and treat adverse effects of family planning methods. If the program is responsible for bringing on medical difficulties, it should help the client overcome those difficulties. Some have argued that, given a choice between expanding family planning services and providing medical support, the former should prevail. The rationale for expansion is that the dangers to women from available contraceptives are considerably less than those from pregnancy, even when no medical backup is available. This assertion may be true, but it does not justify eliminating support services. In many countries the choice is not between maximum expansion and minimal services, but between moderate expansion and reasonable services. From an ethical if not an actuarial standpoint, the case for helping clients with complications and side effects seems strong. And even on pragmatic grounds a failure to provide medical support breeds rumors and doubts about the safety of contraceptives.

Once again, medical backup need not come in the guise of modernity or the garb of the health professions. In Indonesia, preliminary monitoring for side effects and complications is often handled by family planning workers with no formal medical training. If there are minor problems, such as headaches or nausea from pills, they have instructions on what remedies to offer. If more serious problems develop, fieldworkers take the clients to the nearest medical center. Adequate care may not require elaborate facilities, but it does require a serious commitment to the welfare of every client. Whatever the statistics on risk in the aggregate, it seems callous and inhuman to tell a woman that she is better off with her complications than she would be if she had become pregnant. Those should not be her only options.

8. Family planning services should not run ahead of basic health care. In most countries, family planning programs are part of the national health system and compete with other parts of that system for staff, funds, and facilities. Within this context, family planning programs are sometimes given special attention while other services languish. Staff members providing these services have been paid more than their counterparts in the same clinic, have been hired with lower educational requirements, have had better facilities, and have enjoyed other advantages, such as foreign travel and special seminars in the capital city. Although there is nothing wrong with any of these benefits in themselves, they raise ethical questions when their intention or net effect is to divert scarce resources from other basic health services, such as preventive medicine or postnatal care. When, as was reported in this research, clinic directors request a variety of medical supplies and are sent only pills, IUDs, and condoms, commitment to overall health care seems tenuous. In the interest of welfare, family planning should be given fair but not preferential treatment within the full spectrum of health services. Although there may be short-term spurts and lags for any single area of service, the overall aim should be a running balance guided by the criterion of overall health care.

9. Family planning programs should help to treat sterility and subfecundity. In various regions, but particularly in West Africa, infertility is regarded as a serious population problem. Women who cannot have children are considered physically deficient and may be divorced for that reason alone. The principle of welfare argues for dealing with infertility and subfecundity in family planning programs and for devoting resources to this problem according to its severity in the region. The World Population Plan of Action also recommends such action on the grounds of freedom. Countries are urged to

ensure that family planning, medical and related social services aim not only at the prevention of unwanted pregnancies but also at the elimination of involuntary sterility and subfecundity in order that all couples may be permitted to achieve their desired number of children.[23]

The principle of truth telling leads in the same direction. If the stated purpose of a family planning program is to help people realize their desired family size, it is hard to see how it can justify working on only one side of the fertility equation. Although the practical difficulties of treating infertility are legion, the question should be taken seriously.

10. Donor agencies should avoid all forms of clandestine aid. Over the years donors have used various subterfuges to promote birth control in the developing countries. IUDs have been imported as Christmas tree ornaments, contraceptives as fungicides, and abortion kits as devices for taking tissue samples. More recently, several agencies have provided covert aid for abortion.[24]

Clandestine aid is ethically objectionable on two counts. First, it usually entails a direct violation of national sovereignty. The main reason such assistance is necessary is that countries do not want or are legally unable to accept monies or supplies for certain purposes. Where, as in the Philippines, abortion is both illegal and explicitly against the government's official population policy, no amount of maneuvering can legitimize overt aid for abortion services. Although there are many muddy situations, such as those in which contraception is banned by law but approved by the government, the case for any kind of clandestine assistance is unconvincing.

A second argument against clandestine aid is that it can damage welfare by jeopardizing open assistance for national development. The great bulk of economic assistance goes for activities other than population, including agriculture and nutrition, education, health, and electric power. Aid programs commonly try to advance welfare by finding better ways of producing rice and wheat, by increasing access to schools for the rural poor, and by similar means. To work well in promoting development, foreign aid requires mutual trust and collaboration between donors and recipients. Covert aid for population runs the great risk of polluting this environment and putting all foreign assistance under suspicion. And even in the population field, doubts about donor integrity can make a government wary about assistance for family planning or even demographic research. From the standpoint of welfare the costs of stealth can be high.

11. Donors should refrain from pressure tactics to obtain results or move money. This research brought out clear evidence of donor pressure for results and its effects on implementation. In the Philippines during the 1970s, the Agency for International Development (AID) threatened the government with reduced funding. Because AID was the major donor and the lifeline for several agencies, this threat could not be dismissed as bureaucratic bravado. Partly because of AID's insistence and partly for their own reasons, national administrators then demanded that agencies receiving government funds raise their productivity. Overall quotas as well as method quotas were established, and the message was sent out that scant results might mean closure. As this message moved down the line, implementers felt increasing pressure to promote sterilization, IUDs, and the pill. To meet their quotas, many began to skimp on explanation, to avoid discussion of side effects, and to put off clients who complained about complications. The net result was a rise in the number of accepters and a decline in the quality of client care. The main arguments against such practices are that they violate the client's right to freedom of choice and sacrifice welfare in the interest of productivity. It is reasonable for donors to indicate what they are willing to support and to expect a fair accounting of their funds, but pressures of this sort are ethically unjustifiable.

Another common practice is for donors to press applicants to take more money than they really want. The population field is full of stories about agencies and individuals who, when they asked for $10,000, were told: "Can't you take $100,000?" For donors who judge their success by the volume of funds disbursed, the temptation to move money is great indeed. And complex, expensive internal review procedures of the kind used by the World Bank often mean that small grants will not pass the agency's cost/benefit analysis even when they are all that the recipient really needs. Although due allowances must be made for such bureaucratic realities, donors should try to meet the needs of applicants and stay within their absorptive capacities.

Some will say that these guidelines are unrealistic and would probably put some donors out of business. If governments and donors respected clients, worked in the open, told the truth, and provided adequate medical support, how could they ever mount an effective family planning program? Good ethics is really bad business.

This argument was raised many times during the course of this project and can be rejected on its own terms. Its central premise is that rapid action on population control requires tactics violating freedom, justice, welfare, truth telling, and national sovereignty. If it comes to a choice, program effectiveness should outweigh conventional ethics, because effectiveness serves the higher goal of population control. But this study and the world's cumulative experience with family planning programs challenge the assertion that deception, manipulation, and strong-arm tactics are the most effective means of population control. Coercion has never been shown to work, and running roughshod over clients and implementers always seems to bring on a backlash. At the very least, the case for programmatic expedience should be made on empirical grounds rather than on the assumption that toughness always works.

In the end we must go beyond concerns about effectiveness to visions of human beings in a just society. Are people to be treated only as means to improve the well-being of their own or the next generation? Immanuel Kant held that humanity should always be treated as an end and never merely as a means. "But a man is not a thing, that is to say, something which can be used merely as a means, but must in all his actions be always considered an end in himself."[25] By this logic, people have an intrinsic dignity that cannot be sacrificed by treating them as instruments to achieve a lower or higher birth rate. Viewed as an end of development, even the most tattered beggar becomes a person to be served rather than a tool to be exploited in meeting production quotas. Limits may have to be set and social incentives changed, but the notion of the person as an end must remain. And even in pragmatic terms, means based on force and fraud will not yield a society based on truth and justice. A million lies cannot produce collective truth nor a million indignities collective justice. Population programs seeking to promote the common welfare of society must begin by respecting the individual welfare of its members.

Appendix: Directors, authors, and original languages of the country studies

On the following page are the names and addresses of the principal participants in the country studies and the languages in which the reports were originally submitted. Persons seeking further information about these studies should contact the principal author or authors directly. In the Philippines the directors of both the major and the secondary study are no longer at the Institute of Philippine Culture; requests for information should be sent to the director of the Institute for reply or forwarding. In all cases where the language of the original report was not English, the Hastings Center arranged to have it translated into English.

The coordinating organization for the entire project was the Hastings Center, 360 Broadway, Hastings-on-Hudson, New York 10706. The project manager, Donald Warwick, can be contacted at the Harvard Institute for International Development, 1737 Cambridge Street, Cambridge, Massachusetts 02138.

Country	Project Director	Other Authors	Language of Original
Egypt	Dr. Saad Gadalla, Director Social Research Center American University of Cairo 113 Kasr El-Aini Street Cairo, Egypt	Soheir Mehanna Christine Tennant	English
Kenya	Dr. Kivuto Ndeti P.O. Box 57156 Nairobi, Kenya	Cecilia Ndeti	English
Mexico	Lic. Luis Leñero O. Instituto Mexicano de Estudios Sociales, A.C. Mexico 1, D.F., Mexico	—	Spanish[a]
Philippines – major study	Maria Elena Lopez Institute of Philippine Culture Ateneo de Manila University Manila 2801, Philippines	Ana Maria Nemenzo Lourdes Quisumbing-Baybay Nimia Lopez-Fitzpatrick	English
Philippines – anthropological study	Rosalinda Garcia-Yangas Institute of Philippine Culture Ateneo de Manila University P.O. Box 154 Manila, 2801, Philippines	June Prill-Brett	English
Dominican Republic	Lic. Frank Marino H. Instituto Dominicano de Estudios Aplicados Apartado 1005 Santo Domingo, Dominican Republic	—	Spanish
Haiti	Dr. J. B. Romain Center de Recherches en Sciences Humaines et Sociales 10, Avenue Magloire Ambroise, 10 Port-au-Prince, Haiti	—	French
India	Dr. K. Raghavendra Rao Reader in Political Science Karnataka University Dharwar, Karnataka State India	—	English
Lebanon	Prof. Samir Khalaf Department of Sociology American University Beirut, Lebanon	—	English

[a] A revised version of the report was published commercially as follows: Luis Leñero O., *Valores Ideológicos y Políticas de Población en Mexico*. Mexico City: Editorial Edicol, 1979.

Notes

1 A few countries had policies aimed at increasing population size, but the great majority of those seeking change favored a decrease in the rate of demographic growth.

2 The results of this study can be found in R. Veatch (Ed.), *Population Policy and Ethics: The American Experience*. New York: Irvington, 1977. The writer was a participant in the project, which was carried out for the U.S. Commission on Population Growth and the American Future.

3 In Latin America we were particularly interested in Colombia but could find no qualified Colombian social scientist with the time available to conduct the research. Sri Lanka was another intriguing possibility, but we were told by knowledgeable observers that the topic was too sensitive to receive the governmental approval required by UNFPA. Malaysia was also considered, but there the link between population size and ethnicity was even more delicate. In other words, the very salience of the topic created obstacles to its investigation in several countries. India was an obvious candidate for a major study, but it had so often been the subject of previous research and showed so much diversity across states that we decided against it. Another likely complication in India, according to those familiar with its clearance procedures, was a lengthy delay in obtaining the required permission. Iran was another candidate at the beginning, but preliminary discussions and a site visit by the project manager led to the conclusion that research even mildly critical of the government could not be completed. These difficulties are common in cross-national studies and make it virtually impossible to rely on conventional probability sampling in choosing countries.

4 In early meetings the Institute of Philippine Culture was represented by its then director, Mary Hollnsteiner. When the Philippine study was approved by UNFPA, Maria Elena Lopez was appointed country director and continued in that position until the work was completed.

5 Even a cursory review of the literature reveals the dominance of just a few counties, particularly India, Taiwan, Korea, and, more recently, Indonesia. One of the great drawbacks to the field of population policy studies in the early 1970s was that conclusions were often based on either one country (usually India) or a very limited range of experiences.

6 The small study in Iran was to focus on the links between population policy and nomadic populations. Unfortunately, the work could not be completed when the social scientist involved lost his eyesight. The Brazilian study was rejected on the grounds that it was too controversial, particularly for the United Nations.

7 The nature and limitations of the Knowledge–Attitude–Practice survey will be discussed in Chapter 7.

CHAPTER 2. THE COUNTRY CASES IN CAPSULE

1 A. J. Coale and E. M. Hoover, *Population Growth and Economic Development in Low Income Countries*. Princeton, N.J.: Princeton University Press, 1958.
2 Republic of Kenya, *African Socialism and Its Application to Planning in Kenya*. Sessional Paper No. 10. Nairobi: Government Printer, 1965, p. 37.
3 Commission on Population, Republic of the Philippines, "Statement on Population Policy and Program." *Impact*, April 1970, pp. 45–6. (quoted in Lopez et al.).

CHAPTER 3. THE CENTRALITY OF THEORY

1 For a clear illustration of the role of theory in implementation, see J. Pressman and A. Wildavsky, *Implementation*, 2nd ed. Berkeley: University of California Press, 1979, pp. 147–62.
2 *East African Standard*, December 8, 1972 (quoted in Ndeti and Ndeti).
3 A helpful summary of the main evidence on relationships between demographic growth and economic development can be found in R. Cassen, "Population and Development: A Survey." *World Development* 4(10–11), 1976, pp. 785–830.
4 Population Council, *Annual Report*, New York, 1966, p. 16.
5 J. Mayone Stycos, *Human Fertility in Latin America*. Ithaca, N.Y.: Cornell University Press, 1968, p. 63.
6 B. Berelson, "National Family Planning Programs: A Guide." *Studies in Family Planning*, 5 supplement, 1964, p. 11.
7 See, for example, J. W. Atkinson, *An Introduction to Motivation*. Princeton: Van Nostrand, 1964, especially chs. 4, 8, and 10.
8 Population Council, *Annual Report*, 1966, p. 17.
9 Quoted in J. Freund, *The Sociology of Max Weber*. New York: Pantheon Books, 1968, p. 60.
10 Lopez et al., p. 189.

CHAPTER 4. THE UBIQUITY OF DONORS

1 This chapter is based mainly on research conducted by the author between 1973 and 1977. This research involved interviews with key officials in AID, the Population Council, the Ford Foundation, the Pathfinder Fund, and other agencies; interviews with officials and program personnel in several of the countries covered by the study; analysis of documents by and on these agencies; and correspondence with individuals informed about the organizations in question. The main period of reference for the main-line agencies is from their respective entry into the population field until about 1977. This period corresponds to the timing of the research in the country studies. I am indebted to Michael Henry for his help and stimulation on the agency analyses.
2 P. T. Piotrow, *World Population Crisis: The United States Response*. New York: Praeger, 1973, pp. 103–42.
3 Ibid., p. 40.
4 Ibid., p. 103.
5 I base these observations not only on the sources mentioned but also on a dozen years of direct contacts with AID personnel in Washington and overseas missions, including two years as a contract employee in Peru.

6 Bureau for Population and Humanitarian Assistance, *Report on the Population Program of the Agency for International Development*. Washington, D.C.: Agency for International Development, September 5, 1973, p. v.

7 Interview with the author, 1975. Unless otherwise indicated, all quotations cited in the remainder of this chapter are taken from interviews conducted by the author in the three agencies.

8 Quoted in Lopez et al.

9 J. J. Speidel, J. T. Sprehe, and R. T. Ravenholt, *The Agency for International Development's Program for Applied Population Research*. Washington, D.C.: Bureau for Population and Humanitarian Assistance, Agency for International Development, 1972, Appendix, Table 2.

10 AID memorandum supplied to research team in the Philippines, quoted in Lopez et al.

11 A. Silayan-Go, "Towards a Filipino Population Program." In J. Hoyt (Ed.), *Development in the 70's*. Fifth Annual Seminar for Student Leaders. Manila, 1973, p. 77 (quoted in Lopez et al.).

12 *Foreign Assistance and Related Agencies Appropriations for 1976. Hearings Before a Subcommittee of the Committee on Appropriations, House of Representatives, Ninety-Fourth Congress, First Session*. Part 3, Economic Assistance. Washington: U.S. Government Printing Office, 1975, pp. 722–3.

13 Committee on Foreign Affairs, U.S. House of Representatives, *U.S. Aid to Population/Family Planning in Asia*. Report of a Staff Survey Team. Washington, D.C.: U.S. Government Printing Office, 1973, p. 7.

14 This discussion is based on a personal conversation with Ravenholt that took place in May 1980.

15 O. Harkavy, "The Rationale for International Assistance to Population Programs in the Developing World." A Ford Foundation reprint from *International Journal of Health Sciences*. New York: Ford Foundation, 1973, p. 3.

16 Ford Foundation, *Understanding Population*. New York, 1976.

17 O. Harkavy, L. Saunders, and A. L. Southam, "Ford Foundation Strategy for Population Work." A Ford Foundation reprint from *Demography*. New York: Ford Foundation, 1968, p. 7.

18 P. D. Bell, "The Ford Foundation as a Transnational Actor." In R. O. Keohane and J. S. Nye (Eds.), *Transnational Relations and World Politics*. Cambridge, Mass.: Harvard University Press, 1972, p. 121.

19 F. W. Notestein, "The Population Council and the Demographic Crisis of the Less Developed World." *Demography*, 5, 1968, p. 553.

20 *The Population Council: 1952–1964*. New York: The Population Council, 1965, p. 23.

21 One exception was the following book published under Council auspices: J. M. Stycos, *Ideology, Faith, and Family Planning in Latin America*. New York: McGraw-Hill, 1971.

22 *The Population Council, 1952–1964*, p. 29.

23 Notestein, p. 554.

24 Population Council, *Annual Report*, 1976, p. 28.

25 The following discussion of the donor underground is based on D. Warwick, "Foreign Aid for Abortion: Politics, Ethics, and Practice." In J. T. Burtchaell (Ed.), *Abortion Parley*. Kansas City: Andrews and McMeel, 1980, pp. 299–322. This discussion applies to the time period from about 1973 to 1979. The sources

used include interviews with officials at the agencies mentioned, published documents, unpublished reports, and, in the case of IPPF, the main country study on the Philippines.
26 Material drawn from Lopez et al.
27 The information summarized here was obtained from a confidential report prepared by IPPF in 1979.
28 United Nations Fund for Population Activities, *Population Programmes and Projects*, Vol. 1, Guide to Sources of International Population Assistance. New York: United Nations, 1979, p. 297.
29 Ibid., p. 297.

CHAPTER 5. THE POWER OF PROCESS

1 For a discussion of the effects of participation in business and industrial organizations, see R. Likert, *New Patterns of Management*. New York: McGraw-Hill, 1961, and *The Human Organization*. New York: McGraw-Hill, 1967. See also A. J. Marrow, D. G. Bowers, and S. E. Seashore, *Management by Participation*. New York: Harper and Row, 1967.
2 M. B. Concepción and G. E. Hendershot, "Prospect of a Fertility Decline in the Seventies." Paper presented at the Second Conference on Population, Manila, November 27–9, 1967 (cited in Lopez et al.).
3 Ibid., p. 11.
4 *Manila Chronicle*, 1969, p. 17 (quoted in Lopez et al.).
5 Lopez et al., pp. 211–12.
6 D. R. Parulan, "Family Planning Fears Allayed." *Manila Chronicle*, April 15, 1971, p. 7.

CHAPTER 6. THE PERVASIVENESS OF POLITICS

1 The title of this chapter is borrowed from Nazli Choucri, "The Pervasiveness of Politics: Political Definitions of Population Issues." Paper prepared for the Project on Cultural Values and Population Policy, Hastings Center, Hastings-on-Hudson, New York, 1976. This article, which was commissioned for the present project, provides a superb overview of the political dimensions of population policies and programs. It is particularly helpful in showing the political consequences of demographic variables such as the overall growth rate, differential growth rates, density and migration.
2 For an example of shifting contexts between formulation and implementation see Beryl Radin, *Implementation, Change, and the Federal Bureaucracy: School Desegregation Policy in H.E.W. 1964–1968*. New York: Teachers College Press, 1977.
3 Ferdinand E. Marcos, "Population and National Development." Speech delivered at the Eighth Biennial Conference, UNESCO National Commission of the Philippines, September 6–8, 1973 (quoted in Lopez et al.).
4 Incident reported to the author in an interview with an official of the Agency for International Development, Nairobi, Kenya, 1974.
5 Peter S. Cleaves, "Implementation of the Agrarian and Educational Reforms in Peru." Austin, Texas: Institute of Latin American Studies, University of Texas, 1976, mimeo.

6 Choucri, p. 23.

7 *Daily Nation*, April 1967 (quoted in Ndeti and Ndeti).

8 See R.M.A. Zwanenberg and A. King, *An Economic History of Kenya and Uganda 1800–1970*. Nairobi: East African Literature Bureau, 1975 (cited in Ndeti and Ndeti).

9 *La Frontera de la Republica Dominicana con Haiti*. Ciudad Trujillo: Editorial La Nacion, 1946, pp. 157–8 (quoted in Marino).

10 F. Marino Hernandez, *La Migración Haitiana*. Santo Domingo: Editorial Salgazo, 1973 (cited in Marino).

11 Statements made during interviews with members of the National Frontier Council; my translation.

12 Joaquin Balaguer, "Introductory Speech." *Proceedings of the Seminar on Development, Population, and the Family*, the Archbishopric of Santo Domingo and the Latin American Centers of Population and the Family, 1970, pp. 12–13 (quoted in Marino).

13 *Excelsior*, February 3, 1975, p. 14A. This discussion of the school textbook debate is based on research I did during my residence in Mexico in 1974 and 1975. Some twenty newspaper articles and editorials were published on this subject in *Excelsior* alone during February and March of 1975. The interpretations offered here are mine rather than those of the Mexican research team, although they are consistent with the latter's analysis. Translations are also mine.

14 Ibid.

15 This interpretation was offered by a well-informed respondent from Monterrey during an interview with me in 1975.

16 See W. F. Stinner and P. D. Mader, "Government Policy and Personal Family Planning Approval in Conflict Settings: The Case of the Muslim Minority in the Southern Philippines." *Population Studies*, 29(1), 1975, pp. 53–9.

17 Malasarte, in *Record of the House*, 1971a, p. 52 (quoted in Lopez et al.).

18 *Record of the House*, 1971b, p. 70 (quoted in Lopez et al.).

19 J. C. Caldwell, "Family Planning in Continental Sub-Sahara Africa." In T. E. Smith (Ed.), *The Politics of Family Planning in the Third World*. London: George Allen and Unwin, 1973, p. 61.

20 For an example of the different charge on political issues surrounding two national reforms, see Cleaves.

21 Thucydides, *The History of the Peloponnesian War*. Great Books of the Western World, Vol. 6, Chicago: Encyclopedia Britannica, 1952, p. 354.

CHAPTER 7. THE PENETRATION OF CULTURE

1 Debates over the definition of culture have raged for years, particularly in anthropology. Beyond the usual quibbles of lexicography, these discussions represent fundamental differences in theory. Writers of a Marxist or neo-Marxist persuasion are inclined to portray culture as part of the superstructure above the material conditions of life, whereas those of the Weberian tradition assign greater causal weight to attitudes, knowledge, and beliefs. In the latter tradition, Geertz speaks of culture as "a system of inherited conceptions expressed in symbolic forms by which men communicate, perpetuate, and develop their knowledge about and attitudes toward life." See Clifford Geertz, *The Interpretation of Cultures*. New York: Basic Books, 1973, p. 89.

Notes to pp. 107-15

2 *Family Planning in Kenya.* A Report Submitted to the Government of the Republic of Kenya by an Advisory Mission of the Population Council of the United States of America. Nairobi: The Ministry of Economic Planning and Development, 1965, p. 47.

3 Ndeti and Ndeti, p. 40.

4 F. Landa Jocano, "Cultural Consequences of Population Change in the Philippines." In *The Cultural Consequences of Population Change.* Washington, D.C.: The Center for the Study of Man, The Smithsonian Institution, 1975, p. 1 (each essay with separate pagination).

5 See, for example, T. H. Hull, V. J. Hull, and Masri Singarimbun, "Indonesia's Family Planning Story: Success and Challenge." *Population Bulletin*, 32(6), 1977, pp. 3–49.

6 This basic approach to social change, and its ethical implications, are discussed in D. P. Warwick, "Social Change Proposals." In W. T. Reich (Ed.), *Encyclopedia of Bioethics*, Vol. 3. New York: Free Press, 1978, pp. 1295–9.

7 This material and all the remaining examples dealing with the Philippines in this chapter are, unless otherwise noted, drawn from the anthropological study conducted for this project by Garcia-Yangas and Prill-Brett (See Appendix).

8 One notable work in this area is N. E. Williamson, *Sons or Daughters: A Cross-Cultural Survey of Parental Preferences.* Beverly Hills, Cal.: Sage, 1976.

9 Cited in Saad Gadalla, "A Summary of Some of the Results of the Sociological Survey that are Relevant to the Action Research Program in Family Planning." Social Research Center, American University in Cairo, May, 1974.

10 The most comprehensive study in this field was that coordinated by J. Fawcett at the Population Institute of the East-West Center in Honolulu. See, for example, *The Value of Children: A Cross-National Study.* Honolulu: East-West Population Institute, East-West Center, 1975.

11 Bjorn Berndtson, Donald J. Bogue, and George McVicker, *Relevant Posters for Family Planning.* Chicago: Community and Family Study Center, University of Chicago, 1975, p. 172.

12 Mahmood Mamdani, *The Myth of Population Control: Family, Caste, and Class in an Indian Village.* New York: Monthly Review Press, 1972.

13 Ibid., p. 133.

14 See F. L. Jocano, *Philippine Prehistory: An Anthropological Overview of Beginnings of Filipino Society and Culture.* Quezon City: Philippine Center for Advanced Studies, University of the Philippines, 1975, p. 57; M. Palabrica, "Attitudes and Motivations Underlying Large Families in the Philippines." *Philippine Sociological Review*, 16(3–5), 1968, pp. 202–3; and E. Brandewie, "Family Size and Kinship Pressures in the Philippines." *Philippine Quarterly of Culture and Society*, 1(1), 1973, pp. 6–18 (cited in Garcia-Yangas and Prill-Brett).

15 Jocano, pp. 13–14.

16 Population Council, *Annual Report, 1966*, New York, p. 16.

17 These items are taken from the model questionnaire suggested for KAP surveys by the International Union for the Scientific Study of Population, as reprinted in *A Manual for Surveys of Fertility and Family Planning: Knowledge, Attitude, and Practice.* New York: The Population Council, 1970.

18 John E. Laing, "The Relationship between Attitudes and Behavior: The Case of Family Planning." In Donald J. Bogue (Ed.), *Further Sociological Contributions to Family Planning Research.* Chicago: Community and Family Study Center, University of Chicago, 1970, p. 225.

19 Several of the key participants in this project had conducted KAP or similar surveys and, as a consequence, were personally critical of both the approach and its results.

20 Mamdani, p. 19.

21 Francis O. Okediji, "Changes in Individual Reproductive Behaviour and Cultural Values." Lecture delivered at the World Population Tribune, Bucharest, Romania, 1974; paper published by the International Union for the Scientific Study of Population, Bucharest, 1974, p. 43.

22 L. S. El Hamamsy, "Belief Systems and Family Planning in Peasant Societies." In H. Brown and E. Hutchings, Jr. (Eds.), *Are Our Descendants Doomed? Technological Change and Population Growth*. New York: Viking Press, 1972, p. 345.

23 H. Rizk, "Attitudes Toward Fertility in Egypt." In O. Schieffelin (Ed.), *Muslim Attitudes Toward Family Planning*. New York: The Population Council, 1972.

24 J. D. Herzog, "Fertility and Cultural Values: Kikuyu Naming Customs and the Preference for Four or More Children." *Rural Africana*, No. 14, Spring 1971, pp. 89–94.

25 Ibid., p. 93.

26 Studies that have allowed for "don't know" or similar responses include D. I. Poole, "Ghana: A Survey on Fertility and Attitudes Toward Family Limitation." *Studies in Family Planning*, 1(25), 1967, pp. 10–15; and D. Yaukey, *Fertility Difference in a Modernizing Country*. Princeton: Princeton University Press, 1961.

27 B. Berelson, "Turkey: National Survey on Population." *Studies in Family Planning*, 1(5), 1964, pp. 1–5.

28 J. Morsa, "The Tunisia Survey: A Preliminary Analysis." In B. Berelson (Ed.), *Family Planning and Population Programs*. Chicago: University of Chicago Press, 1966, p. 593.

29 See, for example, H. Blumer, "Attitudes and the Social Act," *Social Problems*, 3, 1955, pp. 59–64; D. T. Campbell, "Attitudes and Other Acquired Behavioral Dispositions." In S. Koch (Ed.), *Psychology: A Study of a Science*, Vol. 6. New York: McGraw-Hill, 1961, pp. 159–62; D. Katz and E. Stotland, "A Preliminary Statement to a Theory of Attitude Structure and Change." In S. Koch (Ed.), *Psychology*, Vol. 3, pp. 453–6; and M. Fishbein, "Attitude and the Prediction of Behavior." In M. Fishbein (Ed.), *Readings in Attitude Theory and Measurement*. New York: Wiley, 1967, pp. 477–92.

30 The basic principles of survey research, including norms about the crystallization of opinions, have changed little since the 1940s. Nearly all of the standard works on methodology in the social sciences, including those dealing specifically with opinion surveys, made specific reference to the problems noted here. See, for example, R. L. Kahn and C. F. Cannell, *The Dynamics of Interviewing*. New York: Wiley, 1957; or C. Selltiz, M. Jahoda, M. Deutsch, and S. W. Cook, *Research Methods in Social Relations*, rev. ed. New York: Holt, Rinehart and Winston, 1959.

31 R. Hill, J. M. Stycos, and K. W. Back, *The Family and Population Control: A Puerto Rican Experiment in Social Change*. Chapel Hill: University of North Carolina Press, 1959; and K. W. Back and J. Mayone Stycos, *The Survey Under Unusual Conditions: Methodological Facets of the Jamaica Human Fertility Investigation*. Ithaca, N.Y.: Society for Applied Anthropology, Monograph No. 1, 1959.

32 See D. Warwick and S. Osherson (Eds.), *Comparative Research Methods*. Englewood Cliffs, N.J.: Prentice-Hall, 1973, Chaps. 1, 5, 6, 10–12; F. Frey, P. Steven-

son, and K. A. Smith, *Survey Research on Comparative Social Change: A Bibliography*. Cambridge, Mass.: MIT Press, 1969; and F. Frey, *Cross-Cultural Survey Research in Political Science*. Cambridge, Mass.: Center for International Studies, Massachusetts Institute of Technology, 1970.

33 Laing, pp. 259–60.

34 A. Molnos, "The Sociocultural Background to Fertility and Family Planning: Analysis of 23 Studies Conducted in East Africa, 1962–1970." *Rural Africana*, No. 14, Spring 1971, p. 67.

35 A. Marino, "KAP Surveys and the Politics of Family Planning." *Concerned Demography*, 1971, 3(1), p. 47.

36 See Kahn and Cannell; and C. F. Cannell, F. J. Fowler, Jr., and K. H. Marquis, *The Influence of Interviewer and Respondent Psychological and Behavioral Variables on the Reporting in Household Surveys*. Washington, D.C.: U.S. Department of Health, Education and Welfare, National Center for Health Statistics, Series 2, No. 26, 1968.

37 Laing, p. 283.

38 J. F. Marshall, "Culture and Contraception: Response Determinants to a Family Planning Program in a North Indian Village." Unpublished doctoral dissertation, University of Hawaii, 1972.

39 Ibid., p. 264.

40 Ibid., p. 266.

41 A. I. Hermalin, R. Freedman, T. Sun, and M. Chang, "Do Intentions Predict Fertility? The Experience in Taiwan, 1967–74." *Studies in Family Planning*, 10, 1979, pp. 75–95.

42 S. B. Kar and J. M. Talbot, "Attitudinal and Non-Attitudinal Determinants of Contraception: A Cross-Cultural Study." *Studies in Family Planning*, 11, 1980, pp. 51–64.

43 See Laing, p. 277.

44 S. B. Kar and S.A.K. Bhatia, "Motivational Correlates of Family Planning among Government Employees." *Journal of Family Welfare*, 16, 1969, pp. 3–17.

45 *Family Planning in Kenya*, p. 16.

46 J. W. Ratcliffe, "Analyst Biases in KAP Surveys: A Cross-Cultural Comparison." *Studies in Family Planning*, 7, 1976, pp. 322–30.

CHAPTER 8. ORGANIZATIONAL SETTINGS: THE AMBIVALENCE OF BUREAUCRACY

1 One example of a policy left vague for political reasons was the agrarian reform law enacted in Peru in 1969. Because of the conflicts within the military leadership about the content of agrarian reform and about the most suitable mechanisms for carrying it out, the law itself was phrased fairly broadly. More importantly, its operational meaning was subject to continual discussion and negotiation between 1969 and 1975. See Cynthia McClintock, "Reform Governments and Policy Implementation: Lessons from Peru." In M. S. Grindle (Ed.), *Politics and Policy Implementation in the Third World*. Princeton: Princeton University Press, 1980, pp. 64–97.

2 D. Snodgrass, "The Family Planning Program as Model for Administrative Improvement in Indonesia." Development Discussion Paper No. 58, Harvard Institute for International Development, 1979.

3 N. Caiden and A. Wildavsky, *Planning and Budgeting in Poor Countries*. New York: Wiley, 1974, p. 277.

4 J. Pressman and A. Wildavsky, *Implementation,* 2nd ed. Berkeley: University of California Press, 1979, pp. 134–5.
5 R. M. Galang, "To the Barrios: The New Course Charted by the National Population Program." *Initiatives in Population,* 1(1), 1975, p. 9 (quoted in Lopez et al.).
6 R. Esmundo, Comments at the Seventh Anniversary of the Family Planning Organization of the Philippines, August 4, 1976 (quoted on Lopez et al.).
7 Lopez et al.
8 Snodgrass, p. 11.
9 These comments are based on my work in the development program implementation study in Indonesia, a joint effort between the Harvard Institute for International Development and the government of Indonesia. One of the programs covered by the research is the national family planning program. Interviews with senior officials as well as local implementers bring out the importance of commitment by President Suharto, the provincial governors, and other key officials.
10 Lopez et al.
11 Garcia-Yangas and Prill-Brett.
12 Lopez et al.
13 Similar patterns have been observed in the U.S. Department of State. See D. Warwick, *A Theory of Public Bureaucracy: Politics, Personalty and Organization in the State Department.* Cambridge, Mass.: Harvard University Press, 1975.
14 Lopez et al.
15 See M. R. Hollnsteiner, "Philippine Bureaucracy: The Interplay of Two Legitimate Value Systems." Paper read at the third session of the Philippine Executive Academy, Baguio City, the Philippines, February 9, 1966.
16 J. V. Abueva, "Administrative Culture and Behavior and Middle Civil Servants in the Philippines." In E. W. Weidner (Ed.), *Development Administration in Asia.* Durham, North Carolina: Duke University Press, 1970, p. 181.
17 This gap was noted in an internal memorandum prepared by a USAID population official in the Philippines (cited in Lopez et al.).
18 W. F. Arce and N. S. Poblador, "Formal Organization in the Philippines: Motivation, Structure, and Change." *Philippine Studies,* 25, 1977, p. 24. (quoted in Lopez et al.).
19 Lopez et al.

CHAPTER 9. THE COMMITMENT OF IMPLEMENTERS

1 This approach is presented most systematically in M. Lipsky, *Street Level Bureaucracy: Dilemmas of the Individual in Public Service.* New York: Russell Sage Foundation, 1980. In the same tradition are R. Weatherley, *Reforming Special Education: Policy Implementation from State Level to Street Level.* Cambridge, Mass.: MIT Press, 1979; and J. Prottas, *People-Processing: The Street-Level Bureaucrat in Public Service Bureaucracies.* Lexington, Mass.: Lexington Books, 1979. The major limitation of this material for a broad theory of implementation is its exclusive focus on the United States and its inattention to culture.
2 Quoted in Lopez et al.
3 Interview with Karan Singh, *People,* 5(3), 1978, p. 10.
4 The literature on consistency theory is now vast and covers several different research traditions. This discussion draws on the notion of balance theory developed by Fritz Heider and Theodore Newcomb. See, for example, F. Heider, *The*

Psychology of Interpersonal Relations. New York: Wiley, 1958; and T. M. Newcomb, "Varieties of Interpersonal Attraction." In D. Cartwright and A. Zander (Eds.), *Group Dynanics*. Evanston, Ill.: Row, Peterson, 1960, pp. 104–19. A concise summary of balance theory can be found in T. Newcomb, R. Turner, and P. Converse, *Social Psychology: The Study of Human Interaction*. New York: Holt, Rinehart and Winston, 1965, esp. pp. 129–36.

5 Although different in focus, an article that comes close to the concerns of this discussion is H. C. Kelman and R. M. Baron, "Determinants of Modes of Resolving Inconsistency Dilemmas: A Functional Analysis." In R. P. Abelson et al. (Eds.), *Theories of Cognitive Consistency: A Sourcebook*. Chicago: Rand McNally, 1968, pp. 670–83.

6 J. Waterbury, *Manpower and Population Planning in the Arab Republic of Egypt. Part IV: Egypt's Governmental Program for Family Planning*. American Universities Field Staff, Fieldstaff Reports, Northeast Africa Series, Vol. 17, No. 5, 1972, p. 7 (quoted in Gadalla et al.).

CHAPTER 10. THE SWAY OF OPINION LEADERS

1 For an overview of the literature on communication issues see E. M. Rogers, *Communication Strategies for Family Planning*. New York: Free Press, 1973, Chap. 7. Studies showing the power of interpersonal channels include W. T. Liu and R. W. Duff, "The Structural Effect on Communication Flows in a Pre-Industrial City." Unpublished paper, South Bend, Ind.: University of Notre Dame, 1971; and T. R. Balakrishnan and R. J. Matthai, *Evaluation of a Family Planning Publicity Program in India*. Calcutta: Indian Institute of Management, 1966.

2 Gadalla et al.

3 Laila El Hamamsy, *The Daya of Egypt: Survival in a Modernizing Society*. Cairo: The American University of Cairo, Social Research Center, Reprint Series, No. 22, p. 19 (quoted in Gadalla et al.).

4 Ibid., p. 17.

5 Ibid.

6 El Hamamsy, "Belief Systems and Family Planning in Peasant Societies." Cairo: The American University in Cairo, Social Research Center, Reprint Series No. 16, p. 350 (quoted in Gadalla et al.).

7 Articles reporting opposition to family planning from local Islamic leaders include "The Muslim World." *People*, 6, 1979, p. 14; M. Jusuf, "Islam, Society, and Development: Focus on Indonesia." *Birthright*, 7, 1972, p. 41; L. S. Sodhy, G. A. Metcalf, and J. S. Wallach, "Islam and Family Planning: Indonesia's Mohammadiyal." *Pathpapers*, 6 March 1980, p. 8; "Islamic Africa Endorses Family Planning," *People*, 7, 1980, p. 26; and I.A.B. Balogun, "Islam, Polygamy, and Family Planning in Nigeria." *Birthright*, 7, 1972, p. 41.

8 J. B. Romain, country report on Haiti.

9 These rumors started to spread shortly after I took up residence in Mexico in September 1974 and continued for several weeks. The summary presented here is extracted from newspaper clippings gathered at that time, mainly from the daily *Excelsior*.

CHAPTER 11. THE SIGNIFICANCE OF CLIENTS

1 M. Mamdani, *The Myth of Population Control: Family, Caste, and Class in an Indian Village*. New York: Monthly Review Press, 1972, p. 23.

2 For a general discussion of interactions between clients and implementers see M. Lipsky, *Street Level Bureaucracy: Dilemmas of the Individual in Public Services.* New York: Russell Sage Foundation, 1980, especially chaps. 5 and 9.

3 In an essay on the agrarian reform in Peru, McClintock writes: "Because field personnel were meagerly reimbursed, they could often be bribed and manipulated by the peasants." C. McClintock, "Reform Governments and Policy Implementation: Lessons from Peru." In M. Grindle (Ed.), *Politics and Policy Implementation in the Third World.* Princeton: Princteon University Press, 1980, p. 84.

4 I. F. Rothenberg, "Administrative Decentralization and the Implementation of Housing Policy in Colombia." In Grindle, pp. 170–9.

5 For a discussion of freedom, coercion, and other modes of social intervention see G. Bermant, H. Kelman, and D. Warwick (Eds.), *The Ethics of Social Intervention.* Washington, D.C.: Hemisphere Publishing, 1978, Chap. 1.

6 Estimate based on statistics compiled and reported by the Population Council, especially D. Nortman and E. Hofstatter, *Reports on Population/Family Planning,* No. 2, October 1976; and D. Nortman and E. Hofstatter, *Population and Family Planning Programs: A Compendium through 1978.* New York: Population Council, 1980. The figures reported here are an estimate for 1976. Data were not available for Kenya, but there is no reason to believe that contraceptive prevalence there was above the estimate. Such data are notoriously unreliable, but the bias is generally toward overestimation of contraceptive usage rather than underestimation.

7 Garcia-Yangas and Prill-Brett.

8 D. J. Bogue, *Twenty-Five Communication Obstacles to the Success of Family Planning Programs.* Media Monograph No. 2. Chicago: Communication Laboratory, Community and Family Study Center, University of Chicago, 1975, p. 8.

CHAPTER 12. IMPLEMENTATION AS TRANSACTION

1 E. Bardach, *The Implementation Game.* Cambridge, Mass.: MIT Press, 1977.

2 Ibid., pp. 57–8.

3 I am indebted to Wendy Griswold for pointing out these limitations of the game metaphor in Bardach.

4 G. Majone and A. Wildavsky, "Implementation as Evolution." In J. Pressman and A. Wildavsky, *Implementation,* 2nd ed. Berkeley: University of California Press, 1979, pp. 177–94.

5 Ibid., p. 191.

6 *The Compact Edition of the Oxford English Dictionary,* Vol. 2. Glasgow: Oxford University Press, 1971, p. 251.

7 For an elegant case study of the impact of decision points on implementation, see Pressman and Wildavsky, pp. 1–162.

8 The use of bureaucracy to prevent or stall action is discussed further in D. Warwick, in collaboration with M. Mead and T. Reed, *A Theory of Public Bureaucracy: Politics, Personality and Organization in the State Department.* Cambridge, Mass.: Harvard University Press, 1975.

9 The effects of boredom on implementation are well illustrated in the case of the Peruvian education reform of 1972. See P. S. Cleaves, "Implementation of the Agrarian and Educational Reforms in Peru." Austin, Tex.: Institute of Latin American Studies, 1976.

10 For a case in point see S. A. Quick, "The Paradox of Popularity: 'Ideological' Program Implementation in Zambia." In M. Grindle (Ed.), *Politics and Policy*

Implementation in the Third World. Princeton: Princeton University Press, 1980, pp. 40–63.

11 This point is again brought out by the education reform in Peru, as discussed by Cleaves.

12 G. Chase, "Implementing a Human Service Program: How Hard Will It Be?" *Public Policy*, 27(Fall), 1979, pp. 385–435.

13 The pervasive effect of routines on organizational behavior is emphasized in J. March and H. Simon, *Organizations.* New York: Wiley, 1958.

CHAPTER 13. PROGRAMS VERSUS PEOPLE: TOWARD AN ETHICS OF RESPECT

1 A helpful summary of UN statements on human rights can be found in United Nations, "Report of the Symposium on Population and Human Rights." New York: World Population Conference E/CONF. 60/CBP/4. 19 March 1974.

2 Ibid.

3 United Nations, *Report of the United Nations World Population Conference, 1974.* E/CONF. 60/19. New York: United Nations, 1975, p. 7.

4 *Treaties and Alliances of the World.* "The Universal Declaration of Human Rights and the Covenants on Human Rights." New York: Scribner's, 1974, p. 16.

5 United Nations, *Report of the United Nations World Population Conference*, p. 7.

6 Ibid., p. 10.

7 The most complete work now available on justice is J. Rawls, *A Theory of Justice.* Cambridge, Mass.: Harvard University Press, 1971. For a perspective closer to that adopted here, see R. M. Veatch, "Justice." In R. M. Veatch (Ed.), *Population Policy and Ethics: The American Experience.* New York: Irvington, 1977, pp. 31–9.

8 United Nations, *Report of the United Nations World Population Conference*, p. 12.

9 Ibid., p. 12.

10 Ibid., p. 6.

11 Rawls.

12 Veatch.

13 Newspaper articles too numerous to list here chronicled the unevenness with which sterilization was implemented during the Emergency. Some of the better accounts appeared in *The New York Times* from 1975–7. Other useful reports were carried by the Toronto *Globe and Mail* during the same period.

14 The following discussion draws on D. Warwick, "Compulsory Sterilization in India." *Commonweal*, September 10, 1976, pp. 582–5. The framework of analysis used here follows the logic of the "just war" theory. For a more explicit application of that theory to compulsory sterilization, see P. G. Clark, "Selected Moral Dilemmas in Population Program Implementation: Kenya and the Philippines." Unpublished doctoral dissertation, Harvard School of Public Health, 1979, pp. 238–55. Clark's study, which made use of empirical materials collected for this project, contains a thorough analysis of the ethics of implementation in population programs.

15 Detailed information on India's use of compulsion during the Emergency was compiled by D. R. Gwatkin in memoranda from India to the New York office of the Ford Foundation, May 10 and November 2, 1976. Both Gwatkin and newspaper articles from that period document how policemen, railroad conductors, teachers, and other officials were asked to recruit accepters for sterilization. It is obvious

from the context that the power of these officials was much greater with the poor than with the rich.

16 R. E. Elder, Jr., *Development Administration in a North Indian State: The Family Planning Program in Uttar Pradesh*. Chapel Hill: Carolina Population Center, University of North Carolina, 1972, Chap. 6.

17 These examples were cited in the memoranda prepared by Gwatkin.

18 The claim that strictly enforced targets and similar devices are necessary for high productivity is not supported by a great deal of research on modern management. See, for example, R. Likert, *The Human Organization*. New York: McGraw-Hill, 1967. The argument of this and similar works in the "human relations" tradition is that employees will do better work with positive incentives, such as those created by participation in management decisions or identification with the organization.

19 This example, which has the ring of the apocryphal, was recounted to the author by an American doctor who had worked in India and claimed familiarity with the case. Other examples, including those cited below, make it plausible.

20 Elder, p. 122.

21 Ibid., p. 124.

22 United Nations, *Report of the United Nations World Population Conference*, p. 11.

23 Ibid.

24 This section is based on D. Warwick, "Foreign Aid for Abortion: Politics, Ethics and Practice." *Hastings Center Report*, April 1980, pp. 30–7.

25 Immanuel Kant, "Fundamental Principles of the Metaphysic of Morals." In R. M. Hutchins (Ed.), *Great Books of the Western World*, Vol. 42. Chicago: Encyclopedia Britannica, 1952, p. 272. In the same section Kant set down the following as a practical imperative: "So act as to treat humanity, whether in thine own person or in that of any other, in every case as an end withal, never as means only."

Index

223

population policy formulation (*cont.*)
 and language of presentation, 73–4,
  76, 81–2, 84, 89
 in Mexico, 79–82
 and national circumstances, 73, 77–8,
  81, 84, 88
 and opinion leaders, 73, 77, 80, 83–4,
  87–8
 in Philippines, 84–8
 and senior executives, 72, 78, 80, 87
population policy and political context,
  91–2
 actors influencing, 92–6
 conditions affecting, 102–5
 issues affecting, 97–102
Population Problem in Egypt, 10
PRI (Institutional Revolutionary Party)
  (Mexico), 80, 96, 104, 161
Program on Maternal and Child Health
  (Mexico), 129
Project on Cultural Values and
  Population Policies
 country directors, 4
 country sites, 4–5, 23, 209n3
 research strategy and topics, 5–6
 time period, 8
Project Office of Maternal and Child
  Health (Philippines), 85
pronatalism, 108–14
Provincial Population Office (PPO)
  (Philippines), 127

quotas, 33, 137, 145, 197–8

Ratcliffe, John, 122
Ravenholt, Reimert T., 46, 47, 48, 49,
  50, 51, 60
Rawls, John, 194
Revised Population Act of 1972 (P.D.
  79) (Philippines), 18
Rizk, Hanna, 116
Rockefeller, John D., III, 46, 57, 58
Rockefeller Brothers Fund, 58
Rockefeller Foundation, 54, 57, 58, 60,
  63
Rockefeller University, 59
Roman Catholic church
 in Mexico, 21, 73, 80, 101, 160–1
 in the Philippines, 16, 18, 33, 87–8,
  89
rumor, 37, 84, 142, 151, 155, 160–1
Rural Health Unit (Philippines), 89

Sadat, Anwar, 93
Salas, Rafael, 16, 87
Saunders, Lyle, 75
Scaife/May family, 58
sex preferences, 110–11
Shari'a law, 110
Singh, Karan, 140
Snodgrass, Donald, 130
Social Service of Dominican Churches,
  26
Statement on Population (Philippines),
  16–17
sterilization, 60, 61, 63, 173
 in Dominican Republic, 25, 151
 in Egypt, 11
 in India, 28–9, 140, 198
 in Kenya, 13
 in Lebanon, 24
 in Mexico, 137
 in the Philippines, 17, 18, 33, 137,
  139, 141, 146, 150
Studies in Family Planning, 37
Stycos, J. Mayone, 117
Sullivan, John, 51
Supreme Council for Family Planning
  (Egypt), 9, 10, 11, 82, 83, 103,
  126, 134
Supreme Council for Population and
  Family Planning (Egypt), 11, 83

Taiwan, 66, 121
Talbot, J. M., 121
Taylor, Howard, 75
Taylor-Berelson program, 60
Technical Assistance Division, 57, 60
Theory of Justice, 194
Title X, 46, 49
Total Integrated Development Approach
  (TIDA), 48, 127–8, 133
Toussaint L'Ouverture, Pierre, 99
transactional model of implementation
 assumptions, 181–4
 summary hypotheses, 184–90
Trujillo, Rafael, 99

United Nations Fund for Population
  Activities (UNFPA), 3, 5, 45, 47,
  50, 58, 64
 in Mexico, 22
Universal Declaration of Human Rights,
 as a source of ethical principles,
  192–3